KIM HAINES-EITZEN

The Gendered Palimpsest

Women, Writing, and Representation in Early Christianity

OXFORD
UNIVERSITY PRESS

OXFORD
UNIVERSITY PRESS

Oxford University Press, Inc., publishes works that further
Oxford University's objective of excellence
in research, scholarship, and education.

Oxford   New York
Auckland   Cape Town   Dar es Salaam   Hong Kong   Karachi
Kuala Lumpur   Madrid   Melbourne   Mexico City   Nairobi
New Delhi   Shanghai   Taipei   Toronto

With offices in
Argentina   Austria   Brazil   Chile   Czech Republic   France   Greece
Guatemala   Hungary   Italy   Japan   Poland   Portugal   Singapore
South Korea   Switzerland   Thailand   Turkey   Ukraine   Vietnam

Published by Oxford University Press, Inc.
198 Madison Avenue, New York, NY 10016

www.oup.com

Oxford is a registered trademark of Oxford University Press

Library of Congress Cataloging-in-Publication Data
Haines-Eitzen, Kim.
The gendered palimpsest : women, writing, and representation in
early Christianity / Kim Haines-Eitzen.
      p.   cm.
Includes bibliographical references and index.
ISBN 978-0-19-517129-7 (hardcover : alk. paper)
1. Christian literature, Early—History and criticism. 2. Women and literature.
3. Women in literature. I. Title. II. Title: Women, writing, and representation
in early Christianity.
BR67.H255   2011
270.1082—dc 22   2011003542

What welcomes, and ignores, and doesn't question?
Sheer emptiness. It's like a husk
for her alone. It's like a shell for absence.

Without an audience, she makes a noise
swallowed by waves and wind, just as
the waves themselves—or no, just like the drops

lost in the waves, which neither care nor keep
distinctions—sweep out a place
inside an amphitheatre she imagines

rising around her, with columns that crash
instantly, like the white foam that collides
and shreds its layered castles. Her words drift,

dissolve, and disappear. A crest
of words has surged and poured into the sea.
It doesn't matter now what the lines say.

From "Woman Reading to the Sea" after a painting
by Franco Mondini-Ruiz, by Lisa Williams

Contents

Illustrations

Preface

Years ago, the plan for this book was quite simple: to tell the story of how scribes modified early Christian texts in order to circumscribe and control the roles of women and to reinscribe women's proper character and place. It was not for lack of evidence that this project never quite materialized, for a full half of this book is now devoted to the subject. But over time, I found myself resisting a rather one-sided reflection on women and books—namely, how books, almost entirely written and copied by men, rewrote the stories about women; instead, I began to press our evidence for glimpses of women's roles in the production, reproduction, and dissemination of early Christian literature, something I had begun to do in my first book. In some sense, my struggle was with representation and reality, and a stubborn refusal to allow one or the other to dominate the project. What follows, therefore, could be read as my attempt to trace several points of contact between women and books in early Christianity: the extent to which women actively participated in early Christian book culture, how they came to be represented as readers, and why and how stories about women were changed by copyists.

The truth is, however, that books are like life—always partial, fragmentary, and refracted by experience. I am more aware of this now than ever. Life is punctuated by loss and fragmentation, and it has no doubt shaped my desire for wholeness. But a finished book is hardly the whole story. Perhaps it is best to think of books and life as endlessly palimpsestuous—layers upon layers of writing, interpretation, memory, and experience. Consider, then, *The Gendered Palimpsest* as but one layer among many.

Books and life also remind us continually that we are not alone (to extend Lewis's phrase). Friends and colleagues have been enormously helpful and generous to me by reading chapters and offering critique, listening to me go on about women and books and asking excellent questions, allowing me to use some of their images, or generally supporting me with encouragement (and sometimes a helpful impatience!).

In this regard, I would especially like to thank Ross Brann, Stephen Davis, Bart Ehrman, Georgia Frank, Ross Kraemer, Thomas Kraus, AnneMarie Luijendijk, and Claude Vibert-Guigue. In addition, my two anonymous readers gave me much to consider, and I have done my best (despite an innate stubbornness) to incorporate their excellent suggestions. I have given many papers related to this book at conferences or invited lectures in various institutions, and the hosts of these visits have been wonderful at reenergizing my interest: thanks especially to Claire Clivaz, Kate Cooper, Malcolm Choat, Alanna Nobbs, and Philip Rousseau. Georgia Frank, Derek Krueger, and Eugene Rogers helped me find "women with books" during our inspiring trip to Greece. The poetry of Lisa Williams— above all, her beautiful poem "Woman Reading to the Sea"—was my daily muse. I am very grateful for her poetic eye and ear, and for her allowing me to include an excerpt here.

Grants from the Society for the Humanities at Cornell as well as a Fellowship from the National Endowment from the Humanities gave me funding for travel and writing. The staff at Olin Library, especially Kornelia Tancheva (who protected my library study), and the staff in my own department were extraordinary in all sorts of ways. Two excellent graduate students, Adam Bursi and Zachary Yuzwa, were very helpful and I am grateful to both of them. At Oxford University Press, Lisbeth Redfield answered countless questions and my editor Cynthia Read was patient beyond all measure, flexible, and encouraging. Thank you.

I am grateful for the permission to reproduce material from two essays previously published: "The Apocryphal Acts of the Apostles on Papyrus" from *New Testament Manuscripts* (ed. Thomas Kraus and Tobias Nicklas) appears here in revised form in chapter 3; "Engendering Palimpsests: Reading the Textual Tradition of the Acts of Paul and Thecla" from *The Early Christian Book* (ed. William Klingshirn and Linda Safran) has been reworked and portions have been drawn into several chapters.

I am sure I could locate some kernel of this book in my own childhood: my sister was, and is, a voracious reader and I hardly recall a childhood memory that does not include her with a book in her hand; I found my mother reading every morning when I woke early; and my father used to read and memorize (with book in hand!) Greek, Hebrew, and Arabic texts as he drove around Nazareth, Jerusalem, or Tel-Aviv, no doubt inspiring my love of languages and travel. In more recent years, the women in my women's group—you know who you are—have taught me about the life of community and a life of wholeness, and they have reminded me of what matters.

But my work simply would not be possible without those who show me each day what it means to live a whole life: John, Eli, and Ben—you have my heart. I dedicate this book to you (inverting the ancient model) and I thank you for asking me so frequently, "Mom (or Kim), did you finish your book today?" I felt acutely the tug between the love of writing and solitude and a life shared with those I love, but I would not have had it any other way.

tradition about the virtues of women's silence, from Sophocles, who declared women's ornament to be silence (*Ajax* 1.293), to Sirach ("a silent wife is a gift from the Lord," 26:14), to the Pauline writings (1 Cor. 14:34–35; 1 Tim. 2:11–12), to Clement of Alexandria ("silence is the excellence of women, and the safe prize of the young," *Paedagogus* 2.7), and to Ambrose of Milan ("to the virgin it must be said, 'Be silent lest you sin,'" *De Virginibus* 3.3.11). Thus, the reading found in Codex Alexandrinus—our earliest complete Greek manuscript of 1 Clement—is all the more striking and apparently unique, a singular reading if you will.[3] We might, then, press its history further.

Fifth-century Alexandrinus is "one of the three earliest and most important manuscripts of the whole Christian Bible."[4] And the placement of 1 Clement within Alexandrinus suggests that this is a text to be considered scriptural right alongside, say, the epistles of Paul or the Gospels. Appearing immediately after the book of Revelation, 1 and 2 Clement conclude with the words ομου βιβλια—suggesting that this was the conclusion of the biblical materials. B. H. Cowper noted long ago that it was not "unusual to append to the New Testament writings bearing the name of Clement . . . it is well known that at a very early period the writings of this Father were publicly read at least in some churches, and were by some regarded as part of the canon."[5] Thus, our earliest Greek manuscript of 1 Clement accords it scriptural status and at 1 Clement 21:7 offers wives voice. Is there any way to account for this reading? Particularly tantalizing is the history of Alexandrinus, whose provenance has been the subject of long and wide debate. Was it produced in Alexandria (as its name suggests), Constantinople, or Ephesus? Its origin remains a mystery.[6]

What we do know is that it was given by Cyril Lucar, patriarch of Constantinople, to Charles I in 1627 and Cyril's note affixed to the beginning contains a striking claim:[7]

> This book of the sacred scriptures, New and Old Testaments, according to the tradition we have, has been written by the hand of Thecla, the noble Egyptian woman (est scriptus manu Theclae, nobilis foeminae Aegyptiae), approximately 1,300 years ago, shortly after the council of Nicea. The name of Thecla had been written at the end of the book, but because of the annihilation of the Christians in Egypt by the Muslims, other books of the Christians are similarly in disrepair.

And so the name of Thecla was torn off and destroyed, but the memory and the tradition are observed recently."[8]

In addition to Cyril's note, a thirteenth- or fourteenth-century Arabic marginal note on the second page of the codex reads, "They say that this book was written by the hand of Thecla, the martyr."[9] Sir Thomas Roe, who delivered the manuscript from Cyril to Charles I, appears to have received two different stories from Cyril: in the first story, he claims that the codex was written by Thecla, "protomartyr of the Greeks, that lived in the time of St. Paul"; in the second story, from several years later, he says the book was written by Thecla, "daughter of a famous Greek, called Abgierienos, who founded the monastery in Egypt upon Pharaos tower, a devout and learned maid, who was persecuted in Asia, and to whom Gregory Nazianzen hath written many epistles. . . . She died not long after the council of Nicea."[10]

A tradition about a female scribe named Thecla for a codex that contains a singular reading giving women voice—the conclusions we might draw are tempting. Was it an attempt by some kind of "proto-feminist" at rewriting the silencing of women? The weight of the diverse witnesses to the reading of "silence" makes Alexandrinus's reading stand out all the more. We might add yet a further layer to the puzzle, the early modern and modern assessment (representation) of Alexandrinus. In his *Prolegomena* of 1730, J. J. Wettstein dismissed the notion of Thecla herself as scribe, arguing it was anachronism in the extreme; at the same time, however, he thought a female scribe might well have written Alexandrinus because it was so full of mistakes, especially in orthography.[11] Cowper, on the other hand, criticized Wettstein for reading the prefixed note too literally and by contrast suggests in 1860, "For aught we know that Codex A may have been written by a Thecla, and it was very likely the production of feminine hands."[12] More recently, Scot McKendrick has argued that we should "give little credence to the whole story about Thecla."[13]

What interests me in this piece of the 1 Clement 21:7 story is the historical problem of scribal work it raises, the role that textual variants might play in our understanding of early Christianity, and the gendered representation of writing. Indeed, the layered history of the Codex Alexandrinus can be read as a metaphor of a palimpsest— literally, a manuscript whose underwriting has been rubbed out and replaced with a new text: a reading (possibly "silence") replaced by another (possibly "voice"), manuscripts with added colophons naming scribes, and contemporary assessments of readings and colophons. Such layered histories are at the heart of this study.

How might the malleability of ancient texts, through the very processes of production, copying, and dissemination, be in turn interwoven with the malleability of the bodies they construct? In this case, of bodies silenced or voiced? To what extent can variant readings shed light on disputes about women in early Christianity? And if the naming of Thecla has little claim to historicity, might we find other evidence that shows women's involvement with the production of early Christian literature? To what extent is the representation—ancient or contemporary—of women and books in early Christianity filtered by male authors? What might the physical form of ancient books—their very material form—suggest about their owners, readers, and users?

In what follows, I propose some answers to these questions, all of which are related to the multiple connections among women, writing, and representation in early Christianity. The first half approaches the ties between women and writing—or, more precisely, between women and books—sociohistorically by attending to the roles that women played in the production, transmission, and consumption (i.e., reading) of early Christian literature. Here I begin with the evidence for women as producers and transmitters of early Christian literature in their roles as authors, scribes, readers, owners of libraries, and patrons of literature (chapter 1). I then turn to the representation of women readers, which is almost exclusively found within Christian asceticism (chapter 2); here, the examples of the ideal woman reader come to the fore, particularly those readers who have replaced husbands and food with reading. Fasting and (silent) reading go well together; we might parallel our case, for example, to Tova Rosen's argument about medieval Hebrew poetry that "anticipates" Chaucer's Wife of Bath: "garrulousness (the wife's verbose monologues) and gluttony (her desire for bread and meat) are two female sins performed by the mouth."[14] Finally, I explore the particular example of the *Apocryphal Acts of the Apostles* in their physical form on papyrus and parchment; because these texts, insofar as they have prominent female characters who defy social norms to live celibate lives, have been thought of as "women's literature," they deserve particular attention (chapter 3).

The second half of the book turns to the "sexual/textual politics" evident in the rewriting (and rereading) of texts—the engendering of palimpsests—that feature prominent women or discuss women's various roles. In a world in which all literature was copied and recopied by the hands of human scribes, texts were malleable and subject to manipulation not just through interpretation but rather through the very process of copying and inscribing new words. As we shall see here, the case of 1 Clement 21:7 is not alone, for there are multiple textual variants—in the transmission of New Testament texts, apocryphal literature, and martyrologies—that betray controversy about women, about the body and its nakedness, and about appropriate behavior among men and women in early Christianity. Thus the transformation of biblical characters such as Eve, Mary the mother of Jesus, Mary Magdalene, and other female biblical characters can be viewed through the lens of textual transmission alongside the interpretive traditions (chapter 4). The case of Thecla from the *Acts of Paul and Thecla* and her subsequent tradition occupies its own chapter because its textual and iconographic remains are so rich and instructive (chapter 5). In the final chapter, I highlight glimpses of ascetic paradoxes—and, indeed, what appear to be controversies about such paradoxes—in textual variants of the *Apocryphal Acts*: eroticism and celibacy, the naked yet chaste body, the manly woman, the gaze of a pure eye—each of these tensions, productive as they may be in early Christian ascetic literature, become contested in the process of copying (chapter 6). In all of these chapters, I am mindful of a theme larger than women and writing—namely, the relationship between books and bodies in early Christianity.

Books and Bodies

> . . . *a book, like its writer, is made of body and soul.*
>
> —Borges, 1962

> *Words were indeed more enduring than the body.*
>
> —John Fuller, *Flying to Nowhere*

Books and bodies, corpus and corporeal, word and flesh—inextricable ties bound such materialities together in the world of late ancient Christianity. The "word became flesh and dwelt among us" (John 1:14) opens up a wide world of embodiment and textuality. But these bonds were not simply etymological in nature nor those solely of theology and heady debate, for the layered and multiple points of contact adhered likewise in the lives of men and women. Just as Christ's body might be debated and interrogated, the bodies of men and women—think martyrs and ascetics—were charged with flesh and fashioned in word. Indeed, it is precisely in the world of early Christian martyrs, ascetics, and their hagiographers that the intertwining of book and body was so productive.[15] The qualitative similarities between books and bodies lent themselves well: just as bodies were considered malleable, porous, corruptible, and susceptible to invasion, pollution, and disease as well as to shaping and formation, so also books and the texts they contained were vulnerable to modifications, misinterpretations, and misuse as well as correction and reformation. Like bodies, books were anything but fixed. Hence the need for comments such as those inserted by the author of Revelation ("I warn everyone who hears the words of the prophecy of this book: if anyone adds to them, God will add to him the plagues described in this book, and if anyone takes away from the words . . . God will take away his share of the tree of life . . .," Rev. 22:18–19). Clement of Alexandria, Irenaeus of Lyon, and Rufinus of Aquileia—these church fathers, as well as others, attest to an awareness that texts were prey to scribal tampering, and thus they inscribe curse formulas to ward off corruption:

> I adjure you, who will copy out this book, by our Lord Jesus Christ, by his glorious advent when he comes to judge the living and the dead, that you shall compare what you transcribe and correct it with this copy that you are transcribing, with all care, and you shall likewise transcribe this oath and put it in the copy.
> —Irenaeus, according to Eusebius, *Historia Ecclesiastica* 5.20

Books and bodies were vulnerable and the fact that pains were taken to protect both books and bodies alludes to their power.

Take, for example, the disputes with Donatist–Catholic debates in fourth-century North Africa, which have their roots in a controversy about books. Indeed, the Donatist martyr stories use books to condemn Catholics and legitimize Donatist separation.[16] In the *Acts of the Abitinian Martyrs*, for example, the author describes the faithfulness of the martyrs while they were in prison and claims that they warned all those who might be tempted to communicate with the "traitors" (i.e., Catholics) that such persons "will have no part with us in the heavenly kingdom," quoting directly from Revelation:

> It is written in the Apocalypse, "Whoever adds to this book one part of a letter or one letter, to him will the Lord add innumerable affliction. And whoever blots them out, so will the Lord blot out his share from the Book of Life" (Rev. 22:18–19). If, therefore, a part of a letter added or a letter omitted cuts off a person at the roots from the Book of Life and if such constitutes a sacrilege, it is necessary that all those who handed over the divine testaments and the honored laws of the omnipotent God and of the Lord Jesus Christ to be burned in profane fires should be tormented in the eternal flames of Gehenna and inextinguishable fire."
>
> —*AAM* 21

A text—that from Revelation—that implies a rather different kind of concern with tampering—changing of the very words of the texts—now comes to mean quite literally the destruction of texts by handing them over to be burned. And those that handed the books over for burning should likewise be burned; books and bodies aflame and destroyed.

But we might also locate a more direct link between books and bodies in the rise of early Christian asceticism as the narratives of Augustine, Anthony, and Amoun show—three very different paradigmatic stories that are unified on the role of scripture as a guide, reformer, and shaper of the body. In short, the book tells you what to do with the body—just as a book can be "perfected" through the process of "correction," so also the body can achieve some measure of "perfection" by its re-formation. For Augustine, this meant taking seriously the words of Paul and vowing chastity (*Confessions* 8.12); for Anthony, it meant enacting the literal reading of the gospel, which he heard read at church, and selling all that he had and leaving for the desert (*Life of Anthony* 2). And the cases of Augustine and Anthony are further linked by Augustine's own recall of the Anthony narrative. The differences in the two cases notwithstanding—for Brian Stock, Anthony's hearing of the gospel is a decisive event, whereas Augustine's private reading "confirms what he already knows"—the stories are a remarkable testament to the role that scripture comes to play in "conversion" and, more specifically, a conversion to the ascetic life.[17] Indeed, each of these examples focuses the broader ideal that develops in early Christianity regarding books—namely, the privilege given to oral teachings gradually gives way to the role that books and reading play in conversion and education: Epiphanius, writing about a certain Joseph, claims that "he was being prodded by two events, the reading of the books and the sacred initiation of the patriarch . . . " (*Panarion* 30.6.9).

The case of Amoun of Nitria offers an additional paradigm, especially for the married. Palladius reports that he, being unable to withstand familial pressures, finally agreed to marry at the age of twenty-two. On his wedding night, he called his bride to his side and said, "Come, my lady, and I will explain this matter to you finally. The marriage that we have just entered is not necessary. We will do well if from now on each of us sleeps alone so that we may please God by keeping our virginity sacred." Then he took a small book from his cloak and read to her "from the apostle and the saviour himself as it were, for she lacked knowledge of scriptures. And adding to most of what he read ideas from his own mind, and he explained the word about virginity and purity, so that she was convinced by the grace of God" (*Historia Lausiaca* 8).[18] What did they do? They proceeded to live together, but sleep "in separate beds"; they lived this way until they "had reached a state of insensibility to lust" and then Amoun, at his wife's encouragement—for she wanted him to display his virtue—departed into the mountains of Nitria to take up the life of a hermit. This story, paradigmatic of many narratives about the emergence of monasticism in Egypt, offers a causal link between books and bodies. It is the book, and the texts therein, that effects a bodily response of protected and preserved virginity and lifelong celibacy. Thus the act of reading becomes, as John Dagenais suggests, "an ethical activity": "Texts were acts of demonstrative rhetoric that reached out and grabbed the reader [or hearer, we might add], involved him or her in praise and blame, in judgments about effective and ineffective human behavior. They engaged the reader, not so much in the unraveling of meaning as in a series of ethical mediations and of personal ethical choices. They required the reader to take a stand about what he or she read."[19]

The interrelationship between books and bodies in early Christianity can also be located in the very genesis of early Christian literature, for human bodies were, of course, the producers and (re)producers of early Christian books. That copying was a task for the body, and a continual reminder of embodiment, is clear from marginal notes and colophons found in ancient and medieval manuscripts: "He who does not know how to write supposes it to be no labor, but though only three fingers write, the whole body labors"; "Writing bows one's back, thrusts the ribs into one's stomach and fosters a general debility of the body"; "As travelers rejoice to see their home country, so also is the end of a book to those who toil in writing"; "The end of the book; thanks be to God."[20] Marginal notes attest, too, to the physical annoyances of copying: take, for example, the Syrian manuscript whose scribe complains, "Lord, help me to fight against these accursed flies!" and, later, "May God smite these flies, which war with me these days."[21] So write the scribes who labored in copying books.[22] And yet, although we know that it was human bodies that copied, or (re)produced, written texts throughout antiquity, we still know so little about the persons responsible—their location, their work environment, their socioeconomic standing, their gender.

Of course, the lines between book production and book consumption were not always clearly delineated—writers were also readers. As we shall see, reading became a way to discipline, control, and protect the body. And material books had an even more direct apotropaic function:

> Trophime entered the brothel and prayed incessantly. Whenever men came to touch her, she would place the Gospel which she had with her on her breast, and all the men would fail to approach her, and when she resisted, he tore off her clothes, and the Gospel fell to the ground. Trophime wept, stretched her hands toward heaven, and said "Do not let me be defiled, O Lord, for whose name I value chastity!"
>
> —Gregory of Tours, *Liber de miraculis* 23[23]

Here in a dramatic narrative, Trophime uses a physical book to protect her vulnerable body. But such a story, though helpful for the book/body connection, highlights an attendant problem throughout this study: Can the textual image, as well as the visual, take us beyond the realm of representation?

Word, Image, and Representation

Women and books—the literary associations and figurative imagery are fraught with the problem of representation: "Language and imagery," W. J. T. Mitchell reminds us, "are no longer what they promised to be for critics and philosophers of the Enlightenment—perfect, transparent media through which reality may be represented to the understanding."[24] Consider the many textual images with long histories: the figure of the gullible illiterate woman, the learned woman who is likened to a deadly snake, the woman caught reading inappropriate material—the images are full of paradox and ambivalence. If the textual images bear the problem of representation, so also do the visual iconographic remains. Because the visual appears in the pages that follow, I want briefly to highlight the challenges that attend any interpretation of images, which are, of course, no fewer than the challenges of interpreting language. Nowhere is this more apparent than in the image of the woman as muse. Textually, the female muse is located at the

FIGURE I.1. Detail from a sarcophagus. Ephesus. Courtesy of author.

very genesis of Greek literature: "Tell me, O Muse, of the man . . ." begins the Odyssean bard. And the frequent representation of the Muses in Greek and Roman iconography—carved on stone and marble, painted on vases and walls—point both to the appeal of such images and also our challenge in moving beyond "dominant traditions of representation."[25]

But the image of the woman as a muse illustrates well the problem of representation and, in particular, the representation of the ideal. Part of my project is unapologetically interested in the real and the extent to which we can reconstruct something of women's engagement with books in antiquity. Thus, the projected fantasy of "woman as muse"—echoed so frequently throughout history—will not suffice for my project.

Consider another example, which harkens back again to the muse—that of the funerary reliefs of a married couple with the husband holding an open scroll and the wife standing next to him, sometimes with a closed scroll in hand. The interpretations of such images are laden with problematic overtones: Hemelrijk's reading—indeed, her label for the image on this third-century sarcophagus of Pullius Peregrinus and his wife—is that "the seated husband is reading to his wife, who is standing before him and listening attentively. They are

FIGURE I.2. Sarcophagus of L. Pullius Peregrinus and his wife. Third century. Courtesy of the German Archaeological Institute in Rome.

surrounded by six philosophers and eight Muses, which suggests that they are to be regarded as the seventh Wise Man and the ninth Muse."[26] The Wise Man and his Muse, the wife who listens attentively—how often we find such images in literature. Even if Christians come to replace the muse with the Holy Spirit as source of inspiration,[27] the figure of the muse continues to resurface.

Another example I take from an entirely anachronistic, but still illustrative, source: David Roberts, the nineteenth-century lithographer. Roberts's lithographs and engravings are a wonderful window onto the problem of "representation," and, even more, onto the problematic relationship we have between words and images. Take, for example, the following well-known image from Roberts's collection of scenes from life in Cairo and published in 1849. There are many observations one might make by viewing the lithograph: a woman wearing blue and white; a man with a beard, wearing a red cloak, who is apparently writing; a building edifice and pipe in the background. In the publication of this piece, Roberts's journal entry is printed just below with the heading "The Letter-Writer"; his entry reads as follows: "The letter-writer is usually found in the market-place, or in known stations, where those who are unable to write can with his aid communicate their joys or their sorrows to those far distant from them. The woman in this group, a Copt or Christian, is pouring into the ear of the old man the news to be conveyed to those whom the imagination can supply,—a husband, a son, or a brother, torn perhaps from her by the hatred and cruel conscription . . ."[28] What is instructive here is the stylized portrait alongside a represented (indeed, entirely imagined) "story" of what is taking place—a Christian woman pouring her sorrows into the ear of a male letter-writer, who writes of these sorrows that are directed toward male relatives. As Mark Twain would say, "A good legible label is usually worth, for information, a ton of significant attitude and expression in a historical picture."[29] But we might press the image and the words a bit: to what extent is the entire image one of the imagination—a construction of some imagined reality that comes to be constrained by a particular interpretation? Indeed, is the picture not an illustration of W. J. T. Mitchell's claims, namely that "language and imagery have become enigmas";[30] "the relationship between words and images reflects," as he puts it, "within the realm of representation, signification, and communication,

FIGURE I.3. Lithograph. "The Letter Writer," by David Roberts, from his *Egypt and Nubia* (1846). Lithograph and photograph courtesy of author.

the relations we posit between symbols and the world, signs and their meaning."[31]

The Muse, the wife listening to her husband, the woman "pouring into the ear" of a letter-writer—in differing ways each of these visual representations offers a parallel to what we find in our literary sources. Attending to the power of images—both textual and visual—as well as their very constructedness does not signal, however, the end of social history, for I return to Joan Scott's notion of the "fantasy echo," which can be applied as helpfully to textual variants as it can to the textual and visual representations of women with books:

> Fantasy echo is not a label that, once applied, explains identity. It is rather the designation of a set of psychic operations by which certain categories of identity are made to elide historical differences and create apparent continuities. Fantasy echo is a tool for analysts of political and social movements as they read historical materials in their specificity and particularity. It does not presume to know the

substance of identity, the resonance of its appeal, or the transformations it has undergone. It presumes only that where there is evidence of what seems enduring and unchanging identity, there is a history that needs to be explored.[32]

The Gendered Palimpsest

For those who study ancient or medieval manuscripts, a palimpsest is simply "a parchment or other writing surface on which the original text has been effaced or partially erased, and then overwritten by another."[33] But I hope it is by now clear that the title of my project—*The Gendered Palimpsest*—is not restricted to palimpsests in this strict sense, although such palimpsests will appear in what follows. Rather, I employ the term *palimpsest* metaphorically to highlight the "process . . . of layering" inherent in the term.[34] Textual variants, multiple interpretations of female literary characters, representations of ideal women readers and writers, labels for visual imagery—in each of these cases, the notion of palimpsest illuminates well the process of layering, difference, erasure, and reinscription. The book and body, women and books—both pairs point us toward a gendered, and layered, history.

Part I
Women and Books

Naturally, any exploration of women and books in antiquity must begin with the larger problem of women's literacy and education. Although scholarship on the subject has presented two very different and conflicting pictures—that women were largely illiterate and uneducated, or that women had the same access to education as men—the most compelling conclusion is less simplistic. Our literary sources written by men are divided on whether women should be educated. Menander, for example, claims that anyone who teaches a woman to write is giving poison to a deadly snake (*Synkrisis* 1.209–10). A statement attributed to the philosopher Diogenes is translated in Coptic as follows: "Diogenes the philosopher saw a girl being taught to write. He said, 'Behold a knife being sharpened.'"[1] Similarly, we can recall Juvenal's well-known caustic remarks about the woman who presumes to know anything about philosophy and grammar (*Satire* 6.434–456). The framers of the Mishnah claimed that if anyone should teach a woman torah, she will become promiscuous (*mSotah* 3:4).[2]

Musonius Rufus, on the other hand, insisted that women were given the same ability to reason as men; moreover, the study of philosophy will aid in a woman's household duties (*Ep.* 3.4.13a) (but presumably not much else?). Quintilian likewise claims that both parents should be involved in the education of their children, thereby implicitly suggesting that women should be educated (*Institutiones* 1.1.6). These literary sources provide insight into the varied male attitudes toward the education of women. If we want to know something about the actual levels of literacy among women, however, we are better served by turning to material evidence.

Most secondary work on women's education has focused on ancient Greece and the vases portraying women with scrolls, who are engaged in "intellectual" activities.[3] For the Hellenistic period and, in particular, for Egypt, our most helpful evidence comes from the papyri that illuminate the following aspects of women's literacy in antiquity: women tended to be less educated than men on the whole;[4] they occasionally appear as "slow writers";[5] and women were more often the recipients of letters than the senders.[6] According to Cribiore, "Preserved letters by women are roughly one-fourteenth as numerous as the letters sent by men."[7] To the evidence of the papyri, we can add (admittedly problematic) visual images that depict women with books—take, for example, the terracotta figurines of women holding books. Although we surely cannot take such evidence as support for some notion of widespread literacy among women, as William Harris and Raffaella Cribiore have shown so persuasively, such images do suggest that the association of women with books was not entirely extraordinary. Likewise, for a slightly later time period, Terry Wilfong has shown in his study of the women at the Egyptian town of Jeme that "it is certain that at least some women learned to read and write somewhere: a large number of letters and documents were written to and by women from Jeme, and, although it is possible that most were, in fact, written and/or read for the women by scribes, for practical reasons this is unlikely to be true for all."[8]

On the whole, our material evidence corroborates the picture provided by our literary sources: women were less educated and literate than men throughout antiquity, and the women who were able to read and/or write were typically women of the upper classes. These upper-class women gradually came to have higher levels of education, so that it became unusual for upper-class women to be illiterate. Indeed, according to William Harris, "There is not even a known instance of female illiteracy in high-ranking Roman society in the fourth century."[9]

A necessary corollary to an assessment of education in antiquity is the question of the difference that it made in the lives of those who were privileged enough to acquire it. In other words, did being literate and/or educated make any real difference in women's lives? A few examples from our sources will suffice to show that, in fact, literacy was useful to ancient women. In 263 CE, a certain Aurelia Thaisus from Oxyrhynchus petitioned the prefect in her district:

> (Laws have been made), most eminent prefect, which enable women who are honored with the right of three children to be independent and act without a *kyrios* in all business they transact, especially those women who know how to write. Accordingly I too, fortunately possessing the honor of being blessed with children, and a writer who is able to write with the greatest ease, in full confidence I petition your eminence with this application for the right to transact business without hindrance in all household affairs.
>
> —*P.Oxy.* 1467, trans. modified

Unfortunately, we have no record in the law digests of antiquity of women being accorded such privileges because they were literate. The importance of this letter, however, is that it provides a glimpse into the benefits of literacy for women in the Roman world. We could add to this example the occupations that were open to women who were literate. Soranus, for example, suggests that a midwife should be literate: She should study the medical texts and retain them in her memory (*Gynaecology* 1.3–4). The sum of the documentary evidence suggests to Jane Rowlandson that "while literacy was never an official prerequisite for women to undertake business independently, it seems to have been widely perceived as necessary."[10]

In chapters 1 and 2, I argue that the emergence of the figure of the ideal woman reader appears in late ancient Christian asceticism. For a number of reasons, I will propose that this is not likely to be a coincidence, or simply a matter of our extant evidence, but rather may instruct us about women and education in antiquity. In chapter 3, I take the particular case of the *Apocryphal Acts of the Apostles*, about which much has been written since the 1980s that has claimed them as "women's literature." I argue against this notion on several grounds, among them their physical form.

Women Writers, Writing for Women

Authors, Scribes, Book-Lenders, and Patrons

A writing tablet signifies a woman, since it receives the imprints of all kinds of letters.

—Artemidorus, *Interpretation of Dreams* 2.45

Woman's weaving, her text, is thus a signal instance of the inebriated oscillation of truth and imitation, stability and mobility, sound and silence, speech and writing, and writing and drawing that constitutes for Greek the γραφή "drawing, writing."

—Ann Bergren, *Weaving Truth*, 250

THE BODY WRITES, REPRODUCES, AND DISSEMINATES THE BOOK. The point hardly needs making. Furthermore, one could argue that women are implicated in the process of text production from the earliest stages, from the Muse to the close association of women with weaving, which indeed is a form of text-writing. Not too different is the association of narrative and weaving in Euripides, in whose writings "women are often paired with a specific reference to the recitation of myths as opposed to other types of conversation."[1] The association of women and books even extends to the world of dreams, as Artemidorus suggests. But my goal in this chapter is to shift our attention from the metaphorical to the sociohistorical and, in particular, to the roles that women played in the production, reproduction, and dissemination of early Christian literature.

We have in our sources some (admittedly limited) hints of the roles of women in four capacities related to the production and transmission of early Christian literature: as authors, as scribes, as owners of libraries who lent books to others, and as literary patrons. This chapter aims to catalog the evidence for women in the production, transmission, and dissemination of early Christianity. The goal is not to present a glorified portrait or to overread our evidence, but rather to think through the roles women played in the material production of early Christian literature and what implications these have for our understanding of representation, rhetoric, and reality.

The larger context into which the arguments of this chapter must be set is that of the ancient book trade. Unlike book publishing in our own day, the publication of ancient books entailed an ever-widening circle of acquaintances, friends, and professionals. Frequently, an author would hold a public reading of a new work to which friends would be invited. These friends might have brought along their personal scribes who copied the text as they heard it read. Other means of circulating and disseminating books included booksellers and libraries. But one of the most important and widely used mechanisms for disseminating texts was the private book trade alongside the services provided by booksellers, as a much-cited papyrus letter illustrates:

> "Make and send me copies of books 6 and 7 of Hypsicrates' *Characters in Comedy*. For Harpocration says that they are among Polion's books. But it is likely that others, too, have them. He also has prose epitomes of Thersagora's work on the myths of tragedy." [Then in a new hand, the letter continues,] "According to Harpocration, Demetrious the bookseller has them. I have instructed Apollinideas to send me certain of my own books which you will hear of in good time from Seleucus himself. Should you find any, apart from those which I possess, make copies and send them to me. Diodorus and his friends also have some which I do not have."
>
> —*P.Oxy.* 2192

The letter illustrates a conversation about how and where to obtain copies of books; in doing so, it offers us a glimpse into the ancient book trade.[2] The author did not reign supreme in the transmission of ancient literature; rather, the process required multiple participants and depended on scribes, booksellers, book-lenders, owners of libraries, and, for the very support of the author, patrons. What is striking for my purposes is that we have good evidence for women occupying all of these roles: as authors, as scribes, as book-lenders, and as patrons.

Authors

Nearly every ancient book that goes by the name of a woman has generated speculation on women's authorship—Esther, Judith, Ruth, Susanna, Aseneth. The underlying assumption is that only women would write books about prominent female characters—a point to which we shall return in chapter 3. But speculation has not simply relied on book titles, for arguments about women's authorship of ancient books have ranged from the literary (e.g., Harold Bloom on the *Book of J*) to philological and papyrological (Bagnall and Cribiore on handwriting). Nowhere has speculation run more wild than in treatments of the ancient novel and, in particular, the *Apocryphal Acts*—a point to which we will return in greater detail in the following chapter. Two kinds of evidence predominate: the content of ancient anonymous books and the physical features of ancient books. In both cases, arguments depend on assumptions—about women's voice or women's concern or women's handwriting. All of these assumptions can be unraveled rather quickly: "Content," Mary Lefkowitz rightly teaches us, "is not always a sure or reliable means to determining authorship"; and Bagnall and Cribiore's collection of women's letters from Egypt demonstrates that there is no "solid basis for identifying such a link between gender ideology and handwriting styles in the papyri."[3] It is worth noting that the same applies to determining female hands of medieval manuscripts.[4]

On the other hand, we do know of women writers in the ancient world: the most famous of these is Sappho. Jane McIntosh Snyder's collection of Greek and Roman women writers includes some twenty different individuals, but in many of the cases, the precise nature of women's authorship depends on modern interpretations.[5] The best survey of the evidence for Jewish and Christian women writers continues to be that of Ross Kraemer, who begins with an exploration of the Pseudo-Ignatian epistle from Mary to Ignatius and treats the more problematic case of Perpetua.[6] For our purposes, it will suffice to consider the examples of Perpetua, Proba, and Egeria, each of which provides a different set of challenges and opportunities.

The case of Vibia Perpetua is particularly enigmatic and problematic. The *Passion of Perpetua and Felicitas*, written in the early third century, contains a "diary" account set within a third-person narrative. The framing narrative identifies Vibia Perpetua as a "newly married woman of good family and upbringing" and claims that "from this point on the entire account of her ordeal is her own, according to her own ideas and in the way that she herself wrote it down (conscriptum manu sua)" (*Pass. Perp.* 2). But it is surely an overstatement of the evidence to suggest, "We can still today hear Perpetua's voice, and envisage precisely her experience."[7] In fact, we continue to ask whether Perpetua is indeed the author of her so-called diary—the "memoir" of persecution and imprisonment set within a framework that concludes with her martyrdom. Can we detect in the first-person "voice" of the text clues that would verify or dispute the attribution of the text to her? Is there such a thing as a "female voice"? And what is the relationship between the framing text and the first-person narrative? Does it mediate between or control the voice of the embedded narrative?

It is probably not a coincidence that the *Passion of Perpetua and Felicitas* and its framing narrative that speaks of "new prophecies" have come to be associated with the "heretical" movement Montanism. Heresiologists fueled the notion that one of the problems of Montanism was the authority it gave to women, as exemplified in its founder figures Priscilla and Maximilla. A curious text, conventionally entitled *The Debate between a Montanist and an Orthodox*, anonymously written and possibly dated to the fourth century, claims that although the "holy Mary," Maximilla, and Priscilla all prophesied, Mary (unlike Maximilla and Priscilla) did not write books under her own name "so that she might not bring shame on her head by exercising authority over men."[8] While we are here in the realm of polemic and cannot press the evidence for women authors too far, it remains instructive that women's authorship is a point of contention.

The fourth-century Latin *Cento* of Proba provides more reliable evidence for women's authorship. As has often been noted, Proba's *Cento* is composed almost entirely of quotations from Virgil's *Aeneid* woven—the metaphor is particularly apt here—into a poem about the creation of the world and the life of Jesus:

> Now, O all-powerful God, accept, I pray, my sacred song, and unloose the voices of your sevenfold, eternal spirit. Unlock the innermost regions of my heart, so that I, Proba the seer (*vatis*), may tell of everything that is hidden. . . . For my task is not to extend my fame through words nor to cultivate meager praise through the pursuits of men. . . . Be present, O God, and direct my mind. I shall tell how Virgil sang of the sacred offices of Christ. I shall proceed from the beginning as I recall a matter obscure to no one, if there be any faith within my heart, if a true mind, pouring through my limbs stirs up my strength and the spirit mingles itself throughout my whole body (*corpora*). . . .
>
> *Cento* 9-27[9]

The afterlife of Proba's *Cento* demonstrates its popularity and influence. There are numerous medieval copies of the work, and it was praised by Isidore of Seville and others.[10]

With the example of the late fourth- or early fifth-century nun Egeria, we have a different genre—the travel narrative known as the *Itinerarium Egeriae* or *Peregrinatio Aetheriae*.[11] Although the sole surviving (eleventh-century) manuscript containing the travel narrative is broken at the beginning and the end, leaving the precise identity of the name of the writer somewhat ambiguous, there is a consensus now among scholars that the Latin writer was a woman, likely a nun, from Spain named Egeria. For our purposes, there are several important features: (1) The author is clearly a woman, as embedded self-referents show (e.g., bishops and monks she visits address her as "daughter" in 19.5, 11; 20.9, 10, 12). (2) It is written to her "loving sisters" at home (see "reverend ladies my sisters" at 3.8 and throughout the narrative). (3) The rituals of reading that appear in the diary highlight the intersection of women and books. Each time Egeria arrives at a pilgrimage site, she either hears read or reads herself the texts appropriate to the location: "It was always our practice," she writes, "when we managed to reach one of the places we wanted to see to have first a prayer, then a reading from the book, then to say an appropriate psalm and another prayer. By God's grace we always followed this practice whenever we were able to reach a place we wanted to see" (10.7).[12] Much attention has been spent on assessing the historical value of Egeria's account. Is it an "idealized account of an ideal pilgrimage" and, thus, tells us little about "real" pilgrimages and even less about its author?[13] Or do we find here an autobiographical account that depends upon "the implicit close relationship between author and audience"?[14] Such questions depend in part on assumptions about literary genre and voice that go beyond our concern here.

In addition to such examples of literary texts, we can now—with the collection of women's letters from Upper Egypt by Roger Bagnall and Raffaella Cribiore—reflect on the role of women writers of letters. These letters permit us also to consider women's handwriting as well as the insight into women's daily life as manifested in these letters. Take, for example, the first-century letter from Diodora to Valerius Maximus that reads, "Diodora to Valerius Maximus greetings and be in all good health. I want you to know that it is ten days that we came first to the metropolis and I went straightaway to your sister and right away I wrote to you that I am free from harm and we were saved with the gods' will. Salute the mother and Paulina and Poplis (Publius) and Diodoros and Grania and Tyche. And please write to me. . . . Farewell" (*P.Köln* I.56).[15] In contrast to many of our ancient letters, which were produced by professional scribes, the writer of this letter has a "slow" hand, which "might well be Diodora's own hand"—according to Bagnall and Cribiore.

Beyond the extant writings of Proba and Egeria, and the letters of women from Upper Egypt, we know about other women writers whose texts have not survived. We know, for example, that elite Roman women wrote letters with some frequency. The best evidence for this comes from the letters of Jerome, who claims that women such as Marcella, Paula, and Eustochium wrote to him daily. Occasionally, we catch glimpses of the contents of their letters when Jerome claims he is writing in direct to some question of interpretation, for example, that they have asked. In fact, we would do well to think of Jerome's circle of women friends, correspondents, and interlocutors as a veritable textual community, emerging in Rome in 382 CE and enduring well into the fifth century. Central to the birth of the community were two events: first, Jerome arrived in Rome in

382 CE with bishops Paulinus and Epiphanius;[16] and second, the educated aristocrat Marcella—owner of a house of ascetic women on the Aventine—initiated contact with Jerome concerning the interpretation of scriptures.[17] In the months that followed, Jerome met and formed friendships with other aristocratic women in Rome, most closely with the family of Paula.[18] Although what remains is only one side of a conversation—in this case Jerome's side—his letters suggest that he must have received letters from them with some frequency: Marcella, for example, sent him a written request for interpretation (*Ep.* 42); in his later letter to Furia, Jerome begins, "In your letter you beg and beseech me to write—or rather to write by return—and tell you how you ought to live . . ." (*Ep.* 54);[19] and after leaving for Rome, Marcella and Jerome had "continuous correspondence" in writing (*Ep.* 127).

We can conclude by simply cataloging a number of other possible, but problematic, pieces of evidence for women writers. One possible exception to the loss of all the letters written by Jerome's women friends exists in *Epistle* 46, which H. W. Freemantle claimed—with no compelling evidence—is a letter in which "Jerome writes to Marcella in the name of Paula and Eustochium."[20] But here the problem of authorship remains unresolved. Pelagia appears as a writer in the Syriac and Latin versions of the *Life of Pelagia* as writing on "dyptiches" a letter to the bishop Nonnus;[21] the story of Febronia purports to be written by a woman;[22] and the example of Euphrasia, who writes to the emperor in her own hand.[23] Melania the Younger, to whom we shall return momentarily, writes assiduously and frequently in her notebooks, according to her biographer Gerontius. It is not altogether clear what the contents of her writing are—beyond the copies she makes of scripture—but Gerontius clearly presents her as a writer: "She wrote," he claims, "with great talent and without mistakes in small notebooks (σωματίοις). She decided herself how much she ought to write each day . . ." (*Life* 23) and he repeats this later, "She wrote in small notebooks" (*Life* 36).[24] Gerontius here returns us to the book and the body: it is not just that Melania writes in the book, the book itself is a *soma*, a body.

Somewhat earlier and from a different region, we find this image of a woman writing in a codex. This particular image comes from the tomb of Lucian at Abila, Jordan.[25] Here we are forced to attach our own label to the depiction, but the label we choose will certainly be informed by our imagination: For example, is this woman an author? A letter-writer? A scribe? A teacher? A priestess? A muse? Does the depiction represent what was out of the ordinary to ancient inhabitants of Abila? Or what was commonplace? There is much we cannot know for certain about this figure, but even the briefest survey of literary sources for women writers suggests that we should attend seriously to the possibility that such visual images may offer a useful parallel to literary representations of women writing.

Scribes

Women do occasionally appear in our ancient evidence as scribes. In early Christian sources, the most well-known examples are those of the "girls trained in calligraphy" and working in the service of Origen, Melania, and Caesarea.[26] According to Eusebius, for example, Origen had at his disposal "seven shorthand writers, who relieved

FIGURE 1.1. Woman writing on a tablet. Loukianos Tomb, Abila, Jordan. Third century. Courtesy of Claude Vibert-Guigue.

each other at fixed times, and as many copyists, as well as girls trained in calligraphy [literally, for the purpose of beautiful writing]; for all of these Ambrose supplied without stint the necessary means" (*HE* 6.23). Although we cannot rely on Eusebius's claims uncritically, what is instructive is that Eusebius nowhere suggests that women calligraphers were unusual. Unfortunately, within the space of just decades, the record of Origen's female calligraphers is lost: Jerome depends heavily upon Eusebius for his comments about Origen and includes the "seven or more short-hand writers . . . and an equal number of copyists," but the female calligraphers are strangely missing from his account (*De Viris Illustribus* 61). Better known is the example of Melania the Younger, whose biographer Gerontius calls attention to her assiduous and extensive practice of copying: "The blessed woman read the Old and New Testaments three or four times a year. She copied them herself and furnished copies to the saints by her own hands" (*Life* 26). In a similar vein and somewhat later, the companions of Caesarea of Arles, along with Caesarea as their teacher, "beautifully copy out the holy books" (*Life of Caesarius* 1.58). More obscure is the example of Litia of Thessalonica, found in the Coptic version of Palladius's *Lausiac History*—she is said to be "a scribe writing books and living in great asceticism in the manner of men."[27] In each of these cases, we have literary references to women copying biblical texts or the works of Origen and a telling failure to indicate anything unusual in the appearance of women in such roles.

When set against the backdrop of Latin inscriptions that identify various women as *libraria* or amanuenses, the evidence seems to suggest all the more that at least occasionally women could serve as scribes, clerks, and/or copyists. Take, for example, the cases of Hapate, identified in an inscription as a shorthand writer (*CIL* 6.33892 = *ILS* 7760); Corinna, who is called a storeroom clerk or scribe (*CIL* 6.3979); Tyche, Herma, and Plaetoriae, all identified as amanuenses (*CIL* 6.9541; *CIL* 6.7373; *CIL* 6.9542); and Sciathis Magia, Pyrrhe, and Vergilia Euphrosyne, identified by the label *libraria*, the Latin term used most often for *scribe* (*CIL* 6.9301; *CIL* 6.9525 = *ILS* 7400; *CIL* 6.37802). Such examples do not exhaust the evidence, but offer a representative sample to demonstrate the existence of women who are identified in a variety of scribal roles.[28]

Material examples can sometimes be brought to bear on the existence of female scribes. Two are highly problematic, but worth noting.

Recall, for example, the claims about Codex Alexandrinus with which we began; although errors in a text do not provide good evidence for female scribes, notable in that example is a similar lack of surprise at any point in the tradition. Interestingly enough, the scribe of the Freer manuscript of the Gospels appears to have "characterized himself as the servant of a monastery, or a church, or a female saint" as the use of a feminine article suggests.[29] Nearly as problematic are the cases of women's letters among the documentary papyri. Although the norm was to have a scribe pen one's letters, Bagnall and Cribiore argue for some cases in which it appears the hand of the woman sender is extant.[30]

The well-known relief of a butcher shop provides a visual representation. Here we have a butcher on the right, with cleaver in hand, a weight measure behind him, and hanging strips of meat (along with what appears to be a pig's head) in front of him. On the left, we have a woman—with a high-style hairdo—writing in some kind of a book. What should we make of this image? Indeed, interpretations of this relief have varied widely: some have argued that she is an accountant, keeping the records of the shop; others have suggested that she might be a patron of the shop, providing some funds to back it; still others have suggested that she is simply the butcher's wife; and, finally, some interpreters have removed her altogether from the scene by suggesting that she has no relation to the image on the right.[31] I would

FIGURE 1.2. Funerary relief. Woman in a butcher shop. Second century. Photo: Elke Estel. Courtesy of Staatliche Kunstsammlungen Dresden.

argue that the image can be "read" quite well alongside literary references to women as scribes and clerks.

Owners of Libraries/Book-Lenders

In a world in which obtaining books by means of formal booksellers was far from the norm, and all the less so for Christian literature, we should not underestimate the role that owners of libraries who lent out books for copying and/or reading played in the dissemination of literature. And not unlike the cases of authors and scribes, we find here again that women played a role. The anonymous Christian letter-writer in Upper Egypt who requested that his "dearest lady sister in the Lord" loan him a copy of the book of Ezra (*P.Oxy.* 4365) offers us one window into the roles women played as owners of books that could be put out for lending. Although we cannot know for certain the precise role the women were playing, letters from the monastery of Epiphanius are suggestive in this regard. Epiphanius's mother seems to be playing some sort of role with regard to his access to books (see *P.Mon.Epiph.* 374) and a very fragmentary letter on a potsherd refers to the brothers who appear to have ordered a book from a certain Tmanna (*P.Mon.Epiph.* 388).[32]

Our best literary evidence comes from patristic writers: Jerome's friend Marcella appears throughout his letters as an important book owner and lender. On several occasions, Jerome tells his male addressees (such as Desiderius and Pamachius) to obtain copies of certain books from her (*Ep.* 47 and 49): "Several of my little pieces have flown away out of their nest, and have rashly sought for themselves the honor of publication. I have not sent you any lest I should send works which you already have. But if you care to borrow copies of them, you can do so either from our holy sister, Marcella, who has her abode upon the Aventine, or from that holy man, Domnio . . ." (*Ep.* 47); or "I have lately translated Job into our mother tongue: you will be able to borrow a copy of it from your cousin, the saintly Marcella. Read it both in Greek and in Latin, and compare the old version with my rendering" (*Ep.* 49).

In *Epistle* 126 to Marcellinus and his wife Anapsychia (written in 412), Jerome laments how the "sack of Rome" and the barbarian incursions on the east have prevented him from writing as much as he would have liked. He only has two books prepared, both of which he sent to Fabiola (not to be confused with the other Fabiola in Jerome's letters), "from whom you can if you like borrow them" (*Ep.* 126.2). Thus, she also serves as a book-lender.

In a somewhat different vein, but still conveying the importance of women's libraries, is the mention of Juliana in both Eusebius and Palladius. According to Palladius, Juliana was a "most learned and trustworthy woman," who "took in Origen the writer when he fled from the insurrection of the pagans, and she kept him at her own expense for two years and looked after him. This is what I found written in a very old book of verses, and it is written there in Origen's own hand: 'I found this book among the things of Juliana the virgin in Caesarea when I was hidden by her. She used to say that she had it from Symmachus himself, the translator of the Jews'" (*Lausiac History* 64). A similar story appears in Eusebius (*HE* 6.17).

As repositories of books for lending, women such as Marcella were (in part) acting as literary patrons, a role to which I now turn.

Literary Patrons: "They Demand Complete Books"

Literary patronage is an extension of other forms of patronage—for example, civic and imperial—that are better studied in our secondary literature.[33] We know from the earliest stages of the Christian movement that women served in a variety of roles that can be considered broadly as patronage. For example, early Christians met sometimes in the homes of women, and in later periods women served as bene-factors of churches and monasteries. In addition to these roles, we have evidence already in the third century of women serving as literary patrons—that is, supporting male writers by offering them lodging, possibly pay—and in the fourth century, women are becoming consumers of the literature itself.

In his "biography" of Origen, the church historian Eusebius tells us that upon his father's death, Origen found himself destitute. Yet, "he was deemed worthy of divine aid, and met with both welcome and refreshment from a certain lady, very rich in this world's goods, and otherwise distinguished, who nevertheless was treating with honor a well-known person, one of the heretics at Alexandria at that time. . . ." The implication of this passage suggests that the unnamed woman—a "certain lady"—provided Origen with the financial support he otherwise lacked so that he could "apply himself with renewed zeal to a literary training . . . [and] a proficiency in letters" (*HE* 6.2). Interestingly, Palladius also mentions a woman—named Juliana— who took in Origen and supported him "at her own expense for two years and looked after him" (*Lausiac History* 64.1). Moreover, it is clear that Juliana was, according to Palladius, a source of books for Origen: "This is what I found," Palladius writes, "written in a very old book of verses, and it was written there in Origen's own hand: 'I found this book among the things of Juliana the virgin in Caesarea when I was hidden by her. She used to say that she had it from Symmachus himself, the translator of the Jews'" (*Lausiac History* 64.2). Although this brief glimpse, almost an aside from Eusebius, offers only evidence of inference, we are on much surer footing when we come to the figure of Jerome and his circle of female friends.

At the close of the preface to his commentary on Zephaniah, written in 392 and addressed to his friends Paula and Eustochium, Jerome sums up his defense: he is writing this book for women because throughout Greek and Latin history there have been "virtuous women" and "they demand complete books." This statement is instructive as a testimony to the role of patrons who commission ("demand") writings, support the writer while he composes, and become the dedicatees of the works. But the preface to his Zephaniah commentary is simply one of the more interesting prefaces—including as it does a long justification for his writing for women and a "genealogy" for these women that includes pagan as well as biblical women. A simple survey of his prefaces reveals just how significant they were to Jerome: his Vulgate translations of the books of Joshua, Judges, Ruth, Samuel, Kings, Esther, Isaiah, Jeremiah, Ezekiel, Daniel, the Twelve Minor Prophets; translations from the Septuagint of Job, Psalms, Books of Solomon; and commentaries on Galatians, Ephesians, Philemon, Titus, Isaiah, Ezekiel, Daniel, Micah, Nahum, Habakkuk, Haggai—all of these works (along with others) are addressed to Paula, Eustochium, and/or Marcella.[34] Given what Jerome tells us about the nature of his relationship with these women, I do not think we can simply dismiss these dedications as honorific or self-serving.

In a letter to Principia—a member of Marcella's ascetic group of women—Jerome provides a memoir to Marcella who had died two years previously. In doing so, he recounts how he first met Marcella when he came to Rome in 382:

> And, as in those days my name was held in some renown as that of a student of the scriptures, she never came to see me that she did not ask me some question concerning them, nor would she at once acquiesce in my explanations but on the contrary would dispute them; not, however, for argument's sake but to learn the answers to those objections which might, as she says, be made to my statements.
>
> —*Ep.* 127. 7

Here we see quite clearly how Marcella visited Jerome to discuss the interpretation of scriptures. Jerome's letters also convey the predominating concern with text interpretation in his correspondence with Marcella. And he emphasizes her tenacity: in his preface to his *Commentary on Galatians*—written in 387 and addressed to Paula and Eustochium—Jerome writes concerning Marcella:

> Certainly, when I was at Rome, she never saw me for ever so short a time without putting some question to me respecting the Scriptures, and she did not, like the Pythagoreans, accept the "Ipse dixit" of her teacher, nor did authority, unsupported by the verdict of reason, influence her; but she tested all things, and weighed the whole matter so sagaciously that I perceived I had not a disciple so much as a judge.
>
> —*Comm. Gal.*, Preface

As with the women in Marcella's family and ascetic group, Jerome's initial contact with Paula's family in the early 380s involved the study of texts. Jerome teaches Paula and Eustochium Hebrew; he reads biblical texts to and with Blaesilla, and he reads both Testaments with Paula and Eustochium. Once Jerome, and soon thereafter Paula and Eustochium, had established themselves in Bethlehem, it appears that Jerome had daily contact—both oral and written—with his close female friends. Elsewhere, Jerome suggests that he met with other female virgins, a fact that may well have led to his departure from Rome. In a letter to Asella, Marcella's sister, in 385, Jerome writes to defend himself against the claim that he spent too much time with women. He admits that he did often find himself surrounded by female virgins, and in such situations, he "expounded the divine books" as well as he was able (*Ep.* 45). To be sure, we must read this in part as rhetoric *par excellence*—how better to defend himself against charges of impropriety than to claim that he was teaching scripture. Though we may not be able to completely escape the constructed nature of his writings, the frequency with which he notes the focus on textual interpretation as a foundation of these relationships, surely suggests something more than mere rhetoric.

In every case, the pretext for oral and written contact between Jerome and his women friends is textual in orientation. We could add to these examples the numerous letters that Jerome writes to women located on the periphery of this textual community concerning exegetical issues, as well as his instructions to women concerning some of the necessary features of an ascetic life: reading, memorization, and the study of texts. What provides sustenance to Jerome's relationships is not merely his instruction of women in biblical languages, his reading of texts with them, or his written response to specific exegetical questions, but the ongoing commentary on the sacred text that he provides in order to validate the existence of the textual community itself.

The evidence suggests that this circle of women—who seem to prod, question, and encourage Jerome in his literary work—should be seen within the broad realm of patronage. It was common for ancient writers to dedicate their work to those of higher rank, wealth, and power; indeed, this might earn them a measure of publicity and approval. But it also might more simply enable them to continue writing. What we have in Jerome's situation is not entirely dissimilar. He surrounded himself—perhaps opportunistically, perhaps pragmatically, and perhaps genuinely—with women of significant status and wealth who could serve as patrons of his work in the dual sense of support and consume. This leads us naturally into the topic of women readers, the subject of the following chapter.

Conclusion

Before shifting to women readers, however, it is worth summarizing the evidence of this chapter. The goal here has been simple: to demonstrate that women were (occasionally? rarely? sometimes?) involved in the many and various stages of the production, reproduction, and dissemination of early Christian literature. We cannot know the precise extent of their involvement, but our male writers fail to remark on anything unusual in the appearance of women as authors, scribes, book-lenders, and patrons. And the combined documentary, epigraphic, and literary evidence surely suggests we must rethink the ancient book world as being entirely male. The significance of such an argument is admittedly modest: rather than concede that we have nothing more than male representations of "reality"—a claim that relegates any attempts at historical reconstruction to an outdated positivism and simultaneously reifies an assumed essentializing difference between men and women—I have attempted to present a more diverse and variegated picture of ancient book culture, particularly as found among Christians in late antiquity.

Reading, Not Eating
Women Readers in Late Ancient Christian Asceticism

So I went to the angel and told him to give me the little scroll; and he said to me, "Take it, and eat (λάβε καὶ κατάφαγε αὐτό); it will be bitter to your stomach, but sweet as honey in your mouth." So I took the little scroll from the hand of the angel and ate it; it was sweet as honey in my mouth, but when I had eaten it, my stomach was made bitter.

—*Revelation* 10:9–10

And after she was satisfied with [reading in the canonical books and homilies], she would go through the Lives *of the fathers as if she were eating dessert (καθάπερ πλακοῦντα ἐσθίουσα).*

—Gerontius, *Life of Melania* 23

Reading is eating on the sly.

—Hélène Cixous, *Three Steps on the Ladder of Writing*, 21

THE BODY CONSUMES THE BOOK. IN A MOST DRAMATIC AND VIVID image, the author of the Apocalypse of John echoes (and at times even quotes) the words of Ezekiel: "'O mortal, eat what is offered to you; eat this scroll, and go, speak to the house of Israel.' So I opened my mouth, and he gave me the scroll to eat. He said to me, 'Mortal, eat this scroll that I give you and fill your stomach with it.' Then I ate it; and in my mouth it was as sweet as honey" (Ezek. 3:1–3). For the early Christians, of course, the body also consumes the incarnated word—the bodily book—in language that is strikingly similar to that of Revelation and Ezekiel: "Take, eat, this is my body" (λάβετε φάγετε, τοῦτό ἐστιν τὸ σῶμά μου) (Matt. 26:26). The image of the body consuming the book extends, once again, to the world of dreams: "Eating books signifies benefits for teachers, sophists, and for all those who earn a living from words or books. But for other men, it portends sudden death" (Artemidorus, *Interpretation of Dreams* 2.45).[1]

Eating books; consuming the word. The image is multiply allusive and particularly rich for our purposes, for if the body can ingest the book in a gastronomic sense, then books can be devoured metaphorically and etched on the heart. Such notions have a long history by the time Christianity emerges. Recall, for example, the language of Jeremiah: "'This is the covenant that I will make with the house of Israel after those days,' says the Lord: 'I will put my law within them, and I will write it on their hearts; and I will be their God, and they shall be my people'" (Jer. 31:33).[2] The idea of the heart being a tablet inscribed—with sins or with the covenant—is closely associated with the larger Deuteronomic themes of tradition, memory, and covenant. Again, the connection between books and body comes to the fore, here in the usage of texts in the well-known words of Deuteronomy: "Hear, O Israel. . . . Keep these words I am commanding you today in your heart. Recite them to your children and talk about them when you are at home and when you are away, when you lie down and when you rise. Bind them as a sign on your hand, fix them as an emblem on your forehead, and write them on the doorposts of your house and on your gates" (Deut. 6:4–9). That words consumed by the body can also be inscribed or worn on the body will bring us, as we shall see in this chapter and the next, directly into the world of late ancient Christian asceticism and bring into focus a central argument. The association of women as readers and users of books in late ancient Christianity appears not coincidentally, I will argue, in ascetic contexts. Melania, according to Gerontius, reads "as if she were eating dessert"; the substitution of reading for eating was just one of the replacements alongside fasting, prayer, and silence. Indeed, we might even go so far as to claim that if women's reading is implicitly silent (a subject that has been debated recently), we are returned again to the debate about women and silence—reading becomes, then, a way to ensure silence.[3] Or perhaps with Cixous we might ask whether ascetic women's reading is really "eating on the sly."

Two points are worth highlighting at the outset. First, the role of patrons discussed in the last chapter serves as both a bridge and an entry to the subject of reading literature. Though we cannot assume that literary patrons in the classical world were always the primary readers of this literature, we have already seen that Jerome's patrons, for example, were simultaneously among his most avid readers. And prominent among them were women, a point to which we will return. Second, the world of early Christian asceticism was a decidedly ambivalent world, and the same ambivalences and paradoxes attached to the body (e.g., the body as both powerful and yet vulnerable; the body as a necessary evil) adhered also to books. On the one hand, books were a luxury to be discarded: Theodore, we read in the *Sayings of the Desert Fathers* (6.6),

> had three good books. He went to Macarius, and said, "I have three good books, and I am helped by reading them. Other monks also want to read them, and they are helped by them. Tell me what to do." Macarius replied, "Reading books is good, but possessing nothing is more than anything." When he heard this, he went and sold the books, and gave the money to the poor.[4]

Simultaneously, books are a benefit, "for the mere sight of these books renders us less inclined to sin, and incites us to believe more firmly in righteousness" (*Sayings, Alphabetical Collection on Epiphanius* 8–9).[5] Although "reading and writing were part of the life fabric" for at least some ascetics,[6] the ambivalence toward books is significant and may well be an extension of the ambivalence toward writing found at the earliest stages of Christianity.[7]

The best way to begin to think through the appearance and function of women readers in early Christianity is to study three examples that derive from very different sources—an apocalypse or visionary text, a papyrus letter, and a late ancient literary letter.

Where they find common ground is in their shared assumption that women are indeed readers of texts.

Women Readers: Three Diverse Cases

Hermas and the Elderly Lady

The earliest mention of a woman reader in Christian literature is found in the story of Hermas and the "elderly lady."[8] Written sometime in the second century, the *Shepherd*'s opening narrative (1.1) sets the scene for the reading to come:

> The one who raised me sold me to a certain woman named Rhoda, in Rome. After many years, I regained her acquaintance and began to love (ἀγαπᾶν) her as a sister. After some time, I saw her bathing in the Tiber river and I gave her my hand and helped her out of the river. Seeing her beauty, I reasoned (διελογιζόμην) in my heart saying, "I would be fortunate if I found a wife of such beauty and character." I wished only this and nothing else.[9]

Hermas's defense notwithstanding, the narrative that follows contains a series of visions that condemn him for his thoughts; the woman herself comes to him in a vision and accuses him: "Upon your heart rose up the desire of evil (ἡ ἐπιθυμία τῆς πονηρίας). Or do you not consider it an evil thing for a righteous man if an evil desire rises up in his heart?" (*Shep.* 1.1.8). The connection here between desire and evil is explicit. And the linguistic and ideological proximity between evil and sex—πονηρίας and πορνείας—was not lost on scribes who copied the passage, at least one of whom wrote the latter term in the first appearance of the word *evil*.[10]

We shall return to such scribal corruptions in the following chapters. For now, the story leads us from desire to reading, for in the following vision, an "elderly woman" comes to Hermas with a book in hand. She questions him about why he is so sad, he briefly recounts the earlier vision, and the elderly woman encourages him to "take courage" and keep his household in order. Then, in a curious segue, she asks him if he wants like to hear her read from the book she is holding. "Yes, lady, I do," Hermas replies. She then reads to him "amazing matters" and words that were "terrifying" (*Shep.* 1.3.3–4).

When she is finished she asks Hermas, "Did my reading please you?" to which he admits he only understood some of her words. She then departs by saying, "Be courageous [or, more literally, be manly ἀνδρίζου] Hermas" (*Shep.* 1.4.3).

A year later, Hermas has another vision of the elderly lady, who is again "walking and reading a little book"; this time, she asks him to relay the words to the "ones chosen by God" and he responds, "Lady, I cannot remember so many things. Give me the book to make a copy" (*Shep.* 2.5.3). Sometime later, the elderly lady comes to him yet again and, after adding more words to the book, she instructs Hermas to "write two little books, sending one to Clement and the other to Grapte. Clement will send his to the foreign cities . . . but Grapte will admonish the widows and orphans. And you will read yours in this city, with the presbyters who lead the church" (*Shep.* 2.9.3).

The language of visions, one of the critical elements of apocalypses and apocalyptic literature, is used here to embed a story about books, likewise a feature common to ancient apocalypses. What is most instructive for us is the role of the female reader—first, the elderly woman who reads to and instructs Hermas in a role that echoes that of the Muses. Indeed, at one point in the narrative, Hermas mistakes her for the Sibyl. But a female reader also appears in the character of Grapte who presumably is to use the little book she is given to instruct the widow and orphans. The representation of women readers is both part and parcel of positioning of Hermas as a recipient of visions and prophetic words and in its setting here serves to tie reading and desire to one another: reading follows after lustful thoughts.

A Virgin Book Thief

In an altogether different genre and context, a letter from fourth-century Egypt reveals a curious story about a certain Thaesis:

> Pharmouthi 18, in the entrance of the catholic church (καθιλικῆς ἐκκλησίας), under Plousianos the most respected bishop. At the arbitration held between Thaesis the ever-virgin (ἀειπαρθένου) and the heirs of Besarion, the arbitration judgment delivered by the same bishop Plousianos as arbitrator in the presence of Dioskorides son of Hymnion, town-councillor, and E . . . alias Herakleios son of Eith . . ., and . . . deacon, was that: either the heirs of Besarion are to produce

witnesses who will identify Thaesis, as regards the theft of Christian books (βιβλίων χρειστιακῶν), as the one who did it, and she is to bring them back, or she is to swear an oath that she has committed no theft, and then everything which is left in the house [is to be divided] into two halves, and Thaesis is to receive one half and the heirs the other half, and this is to happen by the thirtieth of the same Pharmouthi."

—*P.Lips.* 43

The letter raises a number of questions: Who is Thaesis? What are the books? Why would Thaesis have stolen them? And what might the term *aeiparthenos* mean in this context? Although we cannot answer any of these with a great deal of certainty, it is likely that the books are either scriptures or some kind of religious writings and that the term used to identify Thaesis, who notably acts here without a guardian, suggests she has some "recognizable status."[11] Has she stolen books to read them, possibly "on the sly"? To sell them? To protect them? Speculation will not take us very far in the specifics of this case. Even if we assume that the letter leaves us only with an accusation, what is instructive for us is that the accused—a woman whom, we must assume, was seen as a reader or user of books—is simultaneously one who is identified as a virgin, an ascetic.

Sidonius Apollinaris on the Women's Section of a Library

A third example of female readers, from still a different kind of source, appears very briefly in Sidonius Apollinaris.[12] In his letter to his friend Donidius, written sometime between 461 and 467 CE, Sidonius describes his visits to the villas of Tonantius Ferreolus and Apollinaris, the comforts of which rival each other. While describing the books located in one of them, Sidonius marvels at their abundance and arrangement. In particular, he notes that "the devotional works were near the ladies' seats . . ." (qui inter matronarum cathedras codices errant, stilus his religiosus inueniebatur) (*Letters* II.9.4).[13] Although this example does not suggest that the women who may have occupied these seats would have been ascetic, what is striking here is that certain types of reading are considered appropriate reading for women (and the passage continues by contrasting these works with the works of "Roman eloquence" placed near the master's seat). Religious or devotional books for women; eloquent books for the master. This comment, nearly an aside, offers just a hint of a cultural ideology that differentiates—here in terms of gender—its readers. As we shall see, just as certain kinds of works were considered appropriate for different categories of readers more broadly (think of the heresiologists who complain about heretical books or Origen's system of tiered readership and interpretation), so too there is a kind of literature that appears especially appropriate for women.

Each of these three examples offers a different piece to an ethnography of women readers in late antiquity—female characters who read in an apocalyptic text; a virgin who is charged with stealing books in a papyrus fragment; and the description of a gendered library in a late ancient letter. At the very least, they provide a basis for moving toward the more prescriptive and rhetorically constructed references to the figure of the ideal women reader in late ancient Christian literature.

Exemplary Women Readers

> *We seem to be special women here, we have liked to think of ourselves as special, as long as our words and actions didn't threaten their privilege of tolerating or rejecting us and our work according to their ideas of what a special woman ought to be.*
>
> —Adrienne Rich, "When We Dead Awaken," 38

In some sense, our most exemplary women readers are those named as recipients of letters, treatises, translations, and commentaries. Here the line between patron and reader becomes quite blurred. Consider, for example, the dozens of letters written to women by Jerome and the numerous commentaries and translations he prepared and addressed to them: to Eustochium, he addressed one of his lengthiest letters and surely one he expected to have a treatise-like status (*Eps.* 22, 31); to Marcella (*Eps.* 23–29, 32, 34, 37–38, 40–44); to Paula (*Eps.* 30, 33, 39); and to other women (*Eps.* 45, 52, 54, 64, 65, 75, 78, 79, 97, 106, 107, 117, 120, 121, 123, 127, 128, 130); and we have already seen, in the previous chapter, the numerous translations and commentaries Jerome addressed to Paula, Eustochium, or Marcella. But did these women actually read all these texts? In these spectacular cases of exemplary women readers, we can be fairly certain that they did.

Jerome's letters are filled with references to questions Marcella, Paula, and Eustochium (as well as other women readers) put to him. And he urges his women readers, "Read often and learn all you can. Let sleep steal upon you with a book in your hand, and let the sacred page catch your drooping head" (*Ep.* 22.17); and he immediately follows this with injunctions for daily fasts.[14]

In his instructions to Laeta on how to raise her daughter, also named Paula, in 403 CE, Jerome outlines how little Paula should learn to read, to learn by heart verses in Greek and Latin, and to "let reading follow prayer with her, and prayer again succeed to reading" (*Ep.* 107). At the conclusion, he outlines a quasi program of reading appropriate for Paula, and it is worth quoting in full:

> Let her treasures be not silks or gems but manuscripts of the holy scriptures (pro gemmis aut serico divinos codices amet); and in these let her think less of gilding, and Babylonian parchment, and arabesque patterns, than of correctness and accurate punctuation. Let her begin by learning the psalter (discat primum psalterium), and then let her gather rules of life out of the proverbs of Solomon. From the Preacher let her gain the habit of despising the world and its vanities. Let her follow the example set in Job of virtue and of patience. Then let her pass on to the gospels never to be laid aside when once they have been taken in hand (Ad Evangelia transeat, numquam ea positura de manibus). Let her also drink in with a willing heart the Acts of the Apostles and the Epistles. As soon as she has enriched the storehouse of her mind with these treasures, let her commit to memory the prophets, the heptateuch, the books of Kings and of Chronicles, the rolls also of Ezra and Esther. When she has done all these she may safely read the Song of Songs but not before (ut ultimum sine periculo discat Canticum Canticorum): for, were she to read it at the beginning, she would fail to perceive that, though it is written in fleshly words (carnalibus verbis), it is a marriage song of a spiritual bridal. And not understanding this she would suffer hurt from it. Let her avoid all apocryphal writings (caveat omnia apocrypha); if she is led to read such not by the truth of the doctrines which they contain but out of respect for the miracles contained in them, let her understand that they are not really written by those to whom they are ascribed, that many faulty elements have been introduced into them, and that it requires infinite discretion to look for gold in the midst of

dirt. Cyprian's writings let her have always in her hands. The letters of Athanasius and the treatises of Hilary she may go through without fear of stumbling. Let her take pleasure in the works and wits of all in whose books a due regard for the faith is not neglected. But if she reads the works of others let it be rather to judge them than to follow them (ceteros sic legat, ut magis iudicet quam sequatur).

—*Ep.* 107.12

Here we have an "order of books" for a young ascetic girl: a sequence and program of reading along with injunctions about what readings to avoid. We cannot assume, of course, that the program was followed in detail. As Roger Chartier reminds us, the book—and the orders of books produced by bibliographers, librarians, and scribes— aims at order, but "the dialectic between imposition and appropriation, between constraints transgressed and freedoms bridled" suggests that no attempt at order will be entirely successful.[15] But Jerome's letter is instructive: first, note the language of embodiment—drinking in the books of Acts, holding books in her hand, a concern about the fleshly words of the Song of Solomon. The book reminds the reader of the body; in turn, the body (both metaphorically and physically) apprehends the book. Second, the program outlines a sequence that accords well with what we know of other ascetic "programs" of reading and, in particular, the privileging of the book of Psalms.

Jerome is not alone in late antiquity in writing to and for women readers: for just a few examples, we can look at writers such as John Chrysostom, among whose letters are letters to a deaconess named Amproukla (*Eps.* 96, 101, 103); Severus of Antioch's letters 69, 70, 71, 72 (all addressed to Anastasia the deaconess); letter 110 to Eugenia, deaconess and monastic superior; letter 7.2 to Jannia; Theodoret of Cyrrhus, letter Patmos 48 (44) to Axia, deacon; Sirm. letter 17 to Casiana, deacon; Sirm. letter 101 to Celerina deacon. Nor is Jerome alone in writing at the behest of women, as we already saw in chapter 1. We can add, too, the comment Rufinus makes in his Latin translation of the Clementine *Recognitions*: "This work is nothing but the payment of a debt due to the command laid upon me by the virgin Sylvia whose memory I revere. She it was who demanded of me, as you have now done by the right of heirship, to translate Clement into our language" (preface).[16] Nor is Jerome alone in calling for literacy education for ascetic women. In the *Life of Eupraxia*, Eupraxia says to

Theodula, "If you want to remain here, you have to learn to read and to pray the Psalter and to fast like all the sisters."[17] Regarding reading and praying the Psalter: the Psalms were the reading material appropriate for ascetics as well as new initiates to Christianity.

Gregory of Nyssa's *Life of Macrina* emphasizes Macrina's childhood reading practices of the Psalms:

> Whatever of inspired Scripture was adaptable to the early years, this was the child's subject matter, especially the Wisdom of Solomon and beyond this whatever leads us to a moral life. She was especially well versed in the Psalms, going through each part of the Psalter at the proper time; when she got up or did her daily tasks or rested, when she sat down to eat or rose from the table, when she went to bed or rose from it for prayer, she had the Psalter with her at all times (παντανχοῦ τὴν ψαλμῳδίαν εἶχεν), like a good and faithful traveling companion.
>
> —Gregory, *Life* 3[18]

Like Jerome, Gregory emphasizes the Psalms. His treatise *Inscriptions on the Psalms* begins by discussing how the "Psalter has made living in accordance with virtue . . . so pleasant and easy to accept" (*Ins.Psalms* 1.3.17).[19] Furthermore, one of the benefits of the Psalms is that they are helpful not only to "perfect men" (τελείοις ἀνδράσι): "it also belongs to the women's quarters (γυναικωνίτιδος ἴδιον γενέσθαι κτῆμα); children find it as pleasing as a toy, and among the elderly, it replaces the cane and the nap" (*Ins.Psalms* 1.3.17).

Palladius has surprisingly few references to women and books, and thus his account of Melania the Elder, which draws attention to her reading, stands out as unusual: he calls Melania

> erudite and fond of literature, and she turned night into day going through every writing of the ancient commentators (αὕτη λογιωτάτη γενομένη ἡ καὶ φιλήσασα τὸν λόγον τὰς νύκτας εἰς ἡμέρας μετέβαλε πᾶν σύγγραμμα τῶν ἀρχαίων ὑπομνηματιστῶν διελθοῦσα)—three million lines of Origen and two and a half million lines of Gregory, Stephen, Pierius, Basil, and other worthy men. And she did not read them once only and in an offhand way, but she worked on them, dredging through each work seven or eight times. Thus it was possible for her to be liberated from knowledge falsely so called and to mount on wings,

thanks to those books—by good hopes she transformed herself into a spiritual bird and so made the journey to Christ.

—*Lausiac History* 55.3[20]

In just one other instance, Palladius refers to a learned woman—that of Juliana in Cappadocian Caesarea, "said to be a most learned and trustworthy woman," who took in Origen "at her expense for two years" (*Lausiac History* 64.1), as we saw in the previous chapter.

Ambrose's treatise on virginity, written to Marcellina in 377 CE, confirms what we have already seen in what we might call the construction of the ideal woman reader. He praises her fasting and reading:

> "For we are bidden to practice fasting, but only for single days; but you, multiplying nights and days, pass untold periods without food, and if ever requested to partake of some, and to lay aside your book a little while, you at once answer, 'Man does not live by bread alone, but by every word of God.' Your very meals consisted but of what food came to hand, so that fasting is to be preferred to eating what was repugnant; your drink is from the spring, your weeping and prayer combine, your sleep is on your book"
>
> —(*De Virginibus* 3.4.15).

A Woman Reader Par Excellence

Among the lives of ascetic women and reports of reading practices among them, one stands out for its extensive reference to the image of the ideal woman reader—that of Gerontius's *Life of Melania the Younger*. This text is full of references to Melania's assiduous and extensive reading, going well beyond the claim that "she reads as if she eats dessert." Indeed, in this text she reads, she does not eat. After Melania and Pinion settled in Thagaste, near the home of Alypius: "The blessed ones chose this as their place to live, especially because this aforesaid holy man Alypius was present, for he was most skilled in the interpretation of the Holy Scriptures. Our blessed mother held him dear, for she was a friend of learning. Indeed, she herself was so trained in Scriptural interpretation that the Bible never left her holy hands (μηδέποτε τὴν βίβλον ἀφίστασθαι ἐκ τῶν ἁγίων αὐτῆς χειρῶν)" (*Life* 21). But the text continues with repeated references to her reading:

The blessed woman read (ἀνεγίνωσκεν) the Old and New Testaments three or four times a year. She copied them herself and furnished copies to the saints by her own hands. She performed the divine office in company with the virgins with her, reciting by heart on her own the remaining Psalms. So eagerly did she read the treatises of the saints that whatever book she could locate did not escape her (οὕτως δὲ συντόνος τὰ τῶν ἁγίων συντάγματα ἀνεγίνωσκεν ὥστε μὴ λαθεῖν αὐτὴν βιβλίον ὅπερ εὑρεῖν ἠδυνήθη). To the contrary, she read through the books that were bought, as well as those she chanced upon, with such diligence that no word or thought remained unknown to her. So overwhelming was her love of learning that when she read in Latin, it seemed to everyone that she did not know Greek, and, on the other hand, when she read in Greek, it was thought that she did not know Latin.

—*Life 26*

And sometimes when her mother, full of compassion for her daughter, went to enter Melania's little cell when she was writing or reading (γράφουσα ἢ ἀναγινώσκουσα), Melania would not even recognize her or speak to her until she finished her usual office.

—*Life 33*

It happened that Melania was sick when we were first in Jerusalem and had nowhere to lie down except in her sackcloth. A certain well-born virgin presented her with a pillow as a gift. When she became healthy again, she spent her time in reading and prayer (τῇ ἀναγνώσει καὶ τῇ προσευχῇ), sincerely serving the Lord.

—*Life 35*

In Gerontius's prolonged narrative about Melania's death and her farewell to the virgins around her, Melania reads the Acts of the martyr Stephen to the sisters near to her own death and says that "you will no longer hear me read (ἐμοῦ γὰρ οὐκέτι ἀναγινωσκούσης ἀκούσετε)" (*Life 64*). The cumulative effect of all these references to Melania illustrates, I would argue, a new ideal and a new way in which to construct the female ascetic body—here absorbed in reading, free from distraction, celibate, and fasting. That this is a rhetorically constructed image does not require that we dismiss any historical kernel to such stories; rather, there is a helpful confluence between the hagiographical representation of women readers and, for example, evidence of women readers—and women's literacy more broadly—in the papyrological, epigraphic, and material remains.

In all of these examples, the construction of the ideal woman reader depends on the combination of fasting and reading; in other words, reading has become yet another means by which the body can be disciplined.[21] Reading, not eating; having and holding a book (and not a husband); and a constructed reading list—these features of the construction of women readers come to the fore. As the genre of hagiography develops and flourishes, so also the references to ascetic women who read increase: Febronia, for example, reads to Hieria, and Platonia reads to the sisters of her convent;[22] Eugenia and Basilia in the *Life of Eugenia* both appear as readers, as do Euphrosyne/Esmeraldus, Onesima, and Irene.[23] We should also recall the example of Egeria, whose reading practices at pilgrimage sites offer the only example of a woman writer in late antiquity who talks about her own reading practices. It is noteworthy that her descriptions of reading practices, and of obtaining the books she needs, offer what appear to be her own "order of books."[24] But, like the other women here, she is clearly an ascetic.

The examples of women readers surveyed in this chapter must be set in a broader historical context, the *longue durée* that extends from well back into the classical period's negative attitudes toward women and education and forward into the medieval contemplative female monastic life. But I think there may well be more to the story than the simple transformation of gendered constructions of education as well as a gendered experience of reading.

We are caught here by the problems of our evidence, which is almost entirely mediated through the lens of male representations. On the one hand, we might be tempted to argue that women's reading here becomes yet one more strategy for men to control the female body, to keep women silent, and to circumscribe their activities. Jerome's instructions to Laeta on the education of her daughter would fit well here; the benefits that accrue from reading must here go in tandem with the restrictions about the reading material. Such tensions are still current some 1,500 years after Jerome, as Kate Flint highlights the visual representation of women readers in the nineteenth century: "Either the woman is improved and educated through access to approved knowledge, which builds on the innately valuable characteristics which she was presumed to retain within her body; or reading of the forbidden leads to her downfall."[25] Yet, on the other hand, we might read against the grain of our literary remains and argue—compellingly, to my mind—that one of the reasons that our patristic writers take such pains to construct a program of reading is because women (at least elite women within ascetic circles) were not reading what they should read (recall that Jerome needs to forbid the apocryphal texts). Asceticism may well have been the replacement of one set of restrictions with another—and the debate about whether asceticism provided women with any advantages continues to circulate—but it did come to provide women with a new option, the life of anchoritic or cenobitic monasticism instead of the life of marriage and children (although we do not know how freely they chose).

Whatever we make of the rise of asceticism and its effect on women's lives, I do not think we can dismiss the appearance of women readers—whether historical or rhetorical, real or imagined—within late ancient asceticism as mere coincidence. Rather, we might draw a rather commonsensical (and decidedly still-current) conclusion. After all, there is a plausibility to the claims of Paul and Jerome: Those who are distracted by the things of this world (e.g., marriage, children) are not free to pursue spiritual and heavenly things (e.g., celibacy, fasting, reading, praying). I am struck by the similarities to sentiments among women writers such as Adrienne Rich, Alice Walker, and many others. Rich put the tension starkly in 1971: "To be a female human being trying to fulfill traditional female functions in a traditional way *is* in direct conflict with the subversive function of the imagination."[26] And Katha Pollitt's poem "Martha," which we might think of as yet another palimpsest, encapsulates beautifully the tension.[27]

Finally, the appearance of women readers in late antiquity should be set alongside the paradigmatic stories of "ethical" reading—namely, those stories of Anthony, Augustine, and Amoun. If we detect anything in their stories of reading (or hearing) a text for practice—and especially for an ascetical praxis—surely the same adheres in the stories of women readers.

Women's Literature?
The Case of the Apocryphal Acts of the Apostles

Novels constitute a principal part of the reading of women, who are always impressionable, in whom at all times the emotional element is more awake and more powerful than the critical, whose feelings are more easily aroused and whose estimates are more easily influenced than ours, while at the same time the correctness of their feelings and the justice of their estimates are matters of the most special and preeminent concern.

—W. R. Greg, "False Morality," 1859

The religious romance known as the Acts of Paul and Thecla *has of late become the object of peculiar interest.... Its purpose was clearly threefold: first, to defend the apostle against his Ebionite traducers, with their hints of personal attachment to his women converts; second, to inculcate the practice of virginity and celibacy; and, third, to assert the right of women to preach and to baptize.... The popularity of this singular romance is well attested and easily understood.*

—Edgar J. Goodspeed, 1901

Romance fiction is smart, fresh and diverse. Whether you enjoy contemporary dialogue, historical settings, mystery, thrillers or any number of other themes, there's a romance novel waiting for you!

—Romance Writers of America, 2009

IMPRESSIONABLE AND EMOTIONAL WOMEN WHO READ (EVEN, consume) novels, religious romances associated with women, romance fiction as smart—undergirding each of these claims are a set of assumptions about fiction, the novel, and women.[1] Particularly noteworthy is that all three writers emphasize the popularity of the romance novel. According to the Romance Writers of America website, romance novels generate "$1.375 billion in sales each year, more than a quarter of all books sold are romance, and they are read by 51 million people each year."[2] But can the notion of *popular* and the contemporary demographics of romance readers—some 90% female, 10% male—be applied to the ancient context? In the last chapter, my aim was to describe and account for the emergence of the ideal female reader in late antiquity; here, my aim is more specific: Can the claims of Goodspeed (and others, as we shall see) be substantiated? Was the *Acts of Paul and Thecla*, and by extension the other Apocryphal Acts, women's literature? When we look closely at the evidence to support such claims, what emerges is a fantasy that relies heavily on nineteenth-century assessments of the novel, and particularly the romance, and an altogether anachronistic imposition of the notion *popular*.

The *Apocryphal Acts* on Papyrus and Parchment

The core of the *Apocryphal Acts* literature—consisting of the *Acts* of Paul, Peter, John, Andrew, and Thomas—betrays a fascination with travel, miracles stories, erotic language in the service of an ascetic message, and prominent female characters.[3] These features—and, in particular, the female characters Thecla, Candida, Rufina, Eubula, Mygdonia, Drusiana, Maximilla—have been precisely the elements drawn on in modern arguments, especially in the past twenty years, about the authors and audiences for these works. Moreover, the claim that these texts are novels—romance novels to be precise—has become commonplace: the Greek romance form has been transformed into a romance that culminates not in marriage but in celibacy. The use of prominent and even subversive women in the *Apocryphal Acts* led Stevan Davies in 1980 to claim "that many of the *Apocryphal Acts* were written by women" and had "an audience which was predominantly female";[4] Virginia Burrus took up this issue in her master's thesis, published in 1987, writing that "the stories [probably] reflect the experience of some second-century women who were converted to Christianity and chastity";[5] more recently, Jan Bremmer has argued that women were both the intended and the actual readers of the AAA;[6] and most recently, Stephen Davis has continued in the tradition of the *Apocryphal Acts*—here specifically the *Acts of Paul and Thecla*—as literature about and for women.[7] The claim that the *Apocryphal Acts* are "women's literature"—or that they are "literature by, about, and for women"—is often elided with the idea that they were "popular literature," a notion that derives at least in part from a scholarly denigration of this literature and one that shares much in common with proposals made about the ancient (classical) "novels" more generally. These texts were written—so this position goes—to entertain the popular masses; they were certainly not written for ancient elite intellectuals (one sees here the imposition of modern "scholarly" ideals upon the ancient world).

But the argument that the *Apocryphal Acts* and the classical novels were written for a "popular audience" can be challenged on a number of fronts: first, the extent to which we should plausibly imagine popular reading at all, given limited literacy in antiquity. Since William Harris's influential book *Ancient Literacy,*[8] there has been a virtual explosion of literature on levels of literacy in antiquity, the intersections of orality and literacy, and the uses of texts.[9] Although there is little consensus on the issue of levels of literacy, at the very least we have become more cautious and more nuanced in our estimates of how many people could read, how many people could write, and how these skills intersected with economic status. Second, some scholars have pointed out that the tropes, allusions, and rhetoric of the novels suggest a rather educated elite (implied) audience for whom, through the novels, aristocratic men negotiated relationships among themselves and vied for status. The most compelling proponents of such views are Simon Goldhill and Kate Cooper, who approach the novels and the *Apocryphal Acts*, respectively, in differing ways; Goldhill sees in the language of *eros* in the Greek novels how "representations of women" served constructions of male desire; Cooper claims that the "Christian rhetoric of virginity," written by and for men, transformed religious identity in late antiquity.[10] In his recent edition of the *Acts of Paul and Thecla*, Jeremy Barrier offers a balanced assessment on the issue of readership/audience: "Women are given special attention in the text, but the alignment of this text with other ancient novels suggests a mixed audience, primarily coming from a wealthy and elite status, but also possibly including listeners and readers from the poor and with a lower status."[11]

But if we can plausibly argue that our ancient novels were written by male authors, can we go any further on the issue of the consumers or readers of these texts? In the case of the classical novels, several authors—Susan Stephens and Ewen Bowie most prominently—have taken the approach of studying the material (papyrological) remains of these novels to see what they might yield about audience or readership. Susan Stephens, for example, has collected the fragments of ancient Greek novels on papyrus; she counts some 42 papyrus fragments of ancient "novels" in comparison with the more than 1,000 fragments of Homer, 120 of Demosthenes, 77 of Thucydides.[12] Although what numbers of remaining papyri can really tell us about readership is debatable, this comparison is quite striking and suggests at least some reevaluation of the notion of popular (i.e., widespread) readership for ancient Greek novels. But Stephens goes further in her analysis of the papyri of Greek novels to argue that the features they exhibit are "indistinguishable" from those that appear in "rolls and codices of Sappho, Thucydides, Demosthenes, and Plato."[13] Moreover, in her study of the papyrological fragments of the Greek novels, Stephens notes that the "novel fragments are written in practiced hands ranging from workmanlike to elegant; books contain wide margins and employ the formats in vogue for the prose writing of oratory, philosophy, or history."[14] Stephens claims that the form of the papyrus remains of ancient novels "tends to undermine a common misconception about them, namely, that they were targeted for a clientele qualitatively different from that for other ancient books."[15] In other words, the very "indistinguishability" of these papyri suggests perhaps that the readership may well have also been indistinguishable—in other words, the same—from that for philosophical, historical, and poetic works more generally.

This brings me to the question at the center of this chapter: Can the earliest papyri of the *Apocryphal Acts of the Apostles* shed light on who read them? And is there any basis for the continued label *women's literature*? Such questions depend first on the notion that the physical form of a book can tell us something about the readers of the book—an idea that has found some of its most compelling treatment in the work of Roger Chartier.[16] For the ancient world, we might recall (in addition to Stephens's work) Eric Turner's typology of "scholars' texts"—papyri whose features suggested that they were made for use by scholars. Turner stressed the following features: (1) "the presence or absence in the texts as we have them of indications of informed revision, especially of revision involving collation with a second, perhaps named, exemplary; (2) the addition of critical signs, additions which . . . show that the text was revised in connection with a scholarly commentary."[17] Working with the earliest Christian papyri, Colin H. Roberts (and others) tried to determine which papyri might have been used for public liturgical readings. He pointed, for example, to the size of a codex, large handwriting, breathing marks, "reading aids," and critical markings as indicators of public reading.[18]

What can we learn about the producers and consumers of the *Apocryphal Acts* by attending to their physical form? My argument in what follows is a negative one. Based on the extant papyri and parchment remains of the *Apocryphal Acts*, there is nothing to suggest a gendered readership. We currently have approximately twelve Greek fragments of the *Apocryphal Acts of the Apostles*: for the *Acts of Peter*, 1; for the *Acts of Andrew*, 1; for the *Acts of John*, 1; for the *Acts of Paul*, 9.[19] The *Acts of Thomas* was probably originally written in Syriac, so for my limited purposes here, it will not be included.[20] We should not limit ourselves to Greek papyri for a comprehensive discussion of the popularity of these texts, since we know that they were translated into Latin, Syriac, Coptic, Armenian, Georgian, Ethiopic, and Arabic. Moreover, we know—particularly since Stephen Davis's recent book *The Cult of St. Thecla*[21]—that material remains and literary allusions can shed light on the popularity of the stories, the pilgrimages and cult centers they inspired, and their use by patristic writers. But here I am particularly interested in what papyrological remains can tell us about ancient readers and readers of the Christian "novels" in particular.

The estimate of twelve papyrus (and parchment) fragments, all of which derive from pre-sixth-century codices, stands in marked contrast to the canonical New Testament more generally for which we have upward of one hundred papyri dated from the second through sixth or seventh centuries (the comparison is somewhat misleading because I am considering here four apocryphal acts in comparison to the twenty-seven books that eventually become canonized). The *Acts of Paul* is indeed attested most widely, leading Colin H. Roberts to claim, in 1950, that the *Acts of Paul* "together with the *Shepherd* [of Hermas] must rank as the most popular work of Christian literature outside the canon."[22] However, it is worth noting that the *Acts of Paul* is perhaps the lengthiest of the *Apocryphal Acts* and originally circulated, it appears, in various parts: the *Acts of Paul and Thecla*, the *Acts of Paul*, the *Correspondence of Paul and the Corinthians*, and the *Martyrdom of Paul*.[23] Furthermore, extant numbers of papyri—especially when we do not have a big pool to begin with—are not particularly compelling evidence for the popularity of a text, much less for the gender of the readership.

A survey of some illustrative examples from the thirteen papyri, beginning with the earliest fragment, yields the following.

P. Bodmer X: The *Apocryphal Correspondence of Paul and the Corinthians*

The *Apocryphal Correspondence of Paul and the Corinthians*[24] (also called III Corinthians) is part of the larger Acts of Paul, but appears to have circulated on its own in antiquity and may well have had an independent origin.[25] The third-century dating makes it the earliest of the *Acts of Paul* fragments and at 14.2 cm × 15.5 cm it is one of the largest fragments. The handwriting here is clearly legible and careful, but not particularly elegant or calligraphic. The margins are only approximately even and there is some variation in the lines themselves. Of all the papyri of the *Apocryphal Acts*, this one is the least elegant, and yet the scribe does appear to be practiced and professional. This particular fragment derives from a composite third–fourth-century codex, which appears to contain the work of multiple scribes who copied different texts (and possibly placed into different codices originally) that were later bound into a single codex.[26]

P.Oxy. 849: Acts of Peter Fragment

This fragment has been dated to the early fourth century; it is written on vellum not papyrus; and the size of the fragment is 9.8 cm × 9 cm—a small, nearly square codex. The handwriting does not look unusual in any way for a fourth-century book-hand; it is medium-sized, carefully and professionally written, and regular.[27] The scribe has used the familiar *nomina sacra* and though there are some rather glaring grammatical errors, overall it is a good copy. Although this is not a lavish deluxe codex, there is nothing to suggest that this was poorly made—or made with limited means.

P.Oxy. 850: Acts of John

This fragment is also dated to the fourth century; it is a papyrus codex, the fragment of which measures somewhat larger than the first fragment: 12.1 cm × 10.7 cm. Any words we use to describe handwriting are necessarily subjective, but overall the handwriting here is less calligraphic and less regular than that for *P.Oxy.* 849. The editors describe the hand as "a good-sized, irregular and rather inelegant uncial of the fourth century."[28] The lines are not as even, there is more of a tendency toward ligatures, but it certainly remains within the range of professional book-hands for the fourth century. This scribe also employs punctuation marks—middle and low points—and occasional breathings. And again we find the use of the *nomina sacra* we would expect.

P.Fackelmann 3: Acts of Paul and Thecla

Published and edited by M. Gronewald in 1978, dated to the early fourth century, this fragment of a papyrus codex measures approximately 4 cm × 6 cm.[29] The editor suggested that originally there would have been thirty lines to a page and each line would have had twenty to twenty-five letters, so that it would have been larger than the others fragments we have seen, possibly 9 cm × 18 cm. It is hard to glean much of anything from such a tiny fragment, but at the very least we can make out a fairly regular book-hand, a type quite familiar to us from other late third- and early fourth-century Christian papyri. There is nothing here to suggest a hand that is distinguishable from other papyri of Christian literature from this period.

P.Antinoopolis I.13: Acts of Paul and Thecla

This parchment fragment was first published and edited by Colin H. Roberts in 1950; it can also be dated to the fourth century; and its dimensions (7.2 cm × 8.7 cm) put it well within the category of a miniature codex. Each column of writing measures 4 cm × 4.8 cm and the outer margin is 2.4 cm. Given its small size, the codex probably only contained the *Acts of Paul and Thecla*. It is also a deluxe codex; Roberts's description is as follows: "Both the material, which is thin and translucent to an unusual degree, and the script, in its regularity and delicacy reminiscent of the great Biblical codices, are of exceptional quality."[30] The handwriting is for the most part bilinear in Turner's terms;[31] certainly, it is the work of a highly trained and professional book scribe. Such a copy could only have been produced with a certain kind of infrastructure—either in a monastic setting with highly trained scribes or by a wealthy individual who could afford such a copy. Even Roberts argued that this particular fragment suggested that the *Acts of Paul* must not have been popular "only among the poorer strata of the population."[32]

What can we say from this sampling? As we should expect, they are all codices; the codex form does not really tell us about readership. Not one of these papyrus (and vellum) fragments shows evidence that it was poorly or unprofessionally made. If the quality of the papyrus or the quality of its script is an indicator of cost and hence suggestive of the economic and educational level of its funders, readers, and/or users, these copies appear to be prepared by and/or for those who had sufficient economic means and education. At the very least, the physical form of these books suggests nothing of a qualitatively different kind of audience (or scribes, producers, users) for this literature. If anything, the features of this admittedly small sampling show fewer signs of unprofessional productions: we can think, for example, of the papyrus copy of 1 and 2 Peter and Jude (P^{72}) contained in the same codex as the *Correspondence of Paul and the Corinthians* but produced by a very different—and, as I have argued elsewhere, less professional or perhaps unprofessional—scribe.[33]

There is, however, another feature that we see only in two of the examples, but it is one that has played a significant role in the argument that the *Apocryphal Acts* are women's literature—the size. In the examples, just two copies are in miniature format (under 10 cm in height and width); and among all twelve extant *Apocryphal Acts* codices just three are in miniature form. What does size matter? For modern scholars, the miniature format of the extant remains has been put alongside several other pieces of evidence—namely, Tertullian's claim that the story of Thecla is being used to legitimate women teaching and baptizing (*De Baptismo* 17); Egeria's reading of the story of Thecla on her pilgrimage; and, above all, claims made by John Chrysostom about women wearing small books.

Excursus: Women and Miniature Books?

Around the year 390 CE, John Chrysostom delivered his homilies on Matthew in Antioch. In his homily on Matthew 23:5, which reads, "They do all their works to attract the attention of human beings, for they make their phylacteries broad and their fringes long," Chrysostom comments on this passage as follows:

> And what are these phylacteries, and these fringes? Since they were continually forgetting God's benefits, He commanded His marvelous works to be inscribed on little tables, and that these should be suspended from their hands . . ., which they called phylacteries; as many of our women now wear Gospels hung from their necks (ὡς πολλαὶ νῦν τῶν γυναικῶν εὐαγγέλια τῶν τραχήλων ἐξαρτῶσαι ἔχουσι).
> —*Homily on Matthew 72*

Just a few years earlier, in his homilies on the Statues (of Theodosius and the Imperial family), Chrysostom had impressed upon his audience the prohibition against swearing:

> You have heard the sentence of Christ declaring, that not only to commit perjury, but to swear in any way, is a diabolical thing, and the whole a device of the evil one. You have heard that everywhere

perjuries follow oaths. Putting all these things then together, write them upon your understanding. Do you not see how women and little children suspend Gospels from their necks as a powerful amulet, and carry them about in all places wherever they go? (Οὐχ ὁρᾷς πῶς αἱ γυναῖκες καὶ τὰ μικρὰ παιδία ἀντὶ φυλακῆς μεγάλης εὐαγγέλια ἐξαρτῶσι τοῦ τραχήλου καὶ πανταχοῦ περιφέρουσιν ὅπουπερ ἂν ἀπίωσιν;)

—*Homily on the Statues* 19

Such references have suggested to some that women had a particular affinity for miniature books. But can we give any credence to Chrysostom's claims? More to the point, however we interpret Chrysostom's claims about women wearing books, does this have anything to do with the *Apocryphal Acts*? The more one pursues such questions, the more problematic the evidence becomes. Women wearing codices as amulets fits perfectly well within the ancient rhetoric that connects women, superstition, and magic. Should we not be particularly cautious, then, in using claims like those of Chrysostom to substantiate assumptions about women and miniature books, or women and the *Apocryphal Acts* in miniature format? Moreover, it is worth emphasizing that the fact that Chrysostom identifies the codices as "Gospels" suggests entirely different texts from the *Apocryphal Acts*. To be sure, there exist numerous Christian amulets—often a passage from one of the Gospels, an incipit, the Lord's Prayer, or one of the Psalms—but there is nothing to suggest a gendered clientele for such devices.[34]

Conclusions

With so few fragments of the *Apocryphal Acts*, and still fewer for the sections of the acts that feature women (which leads to the arguments about popular/female audiences), it is hard to come to any more of a conclusion than a negative one. It is highly problematic to continue to argue for the popular readership—or the popular/female readership—of the *Apocryphal Acts of the Apostles*. These fragments do not testify to a qualitatively different kind of audience and, if anything, can be used to bolster the claim that reading in antiquity remained predominantly a activity of the elite few. If, indeed, the form of ancient books can tell us something about their readers—a subject we still have much to learn about—then these apocryphal acts were read not by the "popular" masses or necessarily by "women" but rather by those members of the upper echelons who likewise enjoyed poetry, history, and perhaps philosophy.

By way of conclusion, it is worth reflecting on the larger issue of the constructions of "popular culture" that are so often elided with "women's culture." Roger Chartier has outlined some of the assumptions behind "the dominant and classical understanding of popular culture in Europe and perhaps in America": "First, that popular culture can be defined in contrast to what it is not; second, that it is possible to characterize as popular the public of particular cultural productions; and third, that cultural artifacts can be considered socially pure, as popular in and of themselves."[35] This serves as a useful reminder that any construal of an ancient popular culture—or

FIGURE 3.1. Auguste Toulmouche, "Forbidden Fruit," Gravure, 1865. Courtesy of author.

popular readership—in some sense assumes a comparative model. For the ancient world, the term *popular culture* or the construction of a *popular readership* carries with it an implicit assumption about what constitutes sophisticated, elite, educated, and dominant. And that such assumptions rely heavily on modern denigration of the novel, especially the romance, fits well with what we see in nineteenth-century visual representations of women readers: women as secretive readers, reading on the sly, and reading the forbidden.

Part II
Sexual/Textual Politics

In the first half of this book, my goal was to illustrate women's participation in the transmission of and engagement with early Christian literature; my interests and approach were mostly sociohistorical. We now shift from women and books to women *in* books—in other words, the way that female characters come to be transformed through the process of copying and recopying their stories. To explore the malleability and fluidity of early Christian texts about women, we need to shift to the world of textual criticism, which seeks to identify textual variants in manuscripts and, at least traditionally, to determine the "original" reading on the basis of a number of criteria: the assessment of external witnesses to the different readings (e.g., What are the dates and distribution of the manuscripts that contain the variants? How are these manuscripts related to one another? What is the quality and character of each representative witness?) and an evaluation of key internal considerations (e.g., Which reading is most likely to be earlier on the basis of scribal tendencies? Which reading fits better with what we know about an author's language and style?).[1]

Because my approach in the following chapters departs from traditional textual criticism in several respects, a brief theoretical and methodological introduction is important. My goal is not to arrive at "original readings"; in most of the cases of textual variation that I treat, our evidence simply does not permit conclusive arguments in this regard. I cannot show that there was a deliberate and systematic rewriting of the stories about women that derives from specific intentions on the part of scribes. This point is worth emphasizing: demonstrating scribal intentionality is just as problematic as identifying an author's intentions, an extension of "the intentional fallacy" that Wimsatt and Beardsley described so well.[2] Let me illustrate this by unpacking briefly the world of text copying.

First, copying texts in antiquity—while seemingly a conservative practice—was not simply mechanical. This hardly needs to be stated: "The enormous changes which printing, the mechanical reproduction of writing, has brought about in literature are a familiar story."[3] Second, one of the aspects of text copying that is critical for understanding the role of scribes is the notion that by copying a text, one memorizes and internalizes that text. To some extent this extends the ascetic "writing as devotion" ideal so well illuminated by Derek Krueger.[4] But it is more; recall, for example, the display of piety, memorization, and recitation in the portrayal of Melania: reading, copying, reciting by heart—these are the activities that demonstrate her piety. Jerome instructs Rusticus to keep his hands and eyes on his books (the scriptures) at all times, to devote himself to reading and memorizing, and to copy books (*Ep.* 125.11). Even more explicit is the example, offered by Claudia Rapp, of three young monks who come to visit an old monk in Scete: "The first one says that he has learned the Old and the New Testament by heart, whereupon the second one joins in: 'Me, too, I have copied the Old and New Testament for myself.'"[5] If copying aided memorization and internalization, it was also intimately connected to interpretation, for the texts that scribes copied were in some sense "living texts," which "did not have an existence independent of scribal activity, and their use in the churches."[6]

One of the best illustrations of the power of copying comes from an entirely different context, but the relevance to our period is striking. In his autobiography, Richard Wagner—with no little arrogance—talks of his childhood dissatisfaction with schoolwork. In addition, he writes, "As my musical instruction also did me no good, I continued in my willful process of self-education by copying out the scores of my beloved masters, and in so doing acquired a neat handwriting."[7] His pride in his handwriting aside, Wagner goes on in what follows to describe his act of copying further:

> Beethoven's Ninth Symphony became the mystical goal of all my strange thoughts and desires about music. . . . It was considered the *non plus ultra* of all that was fantastic and incomprehensible, and this was quite enough to rouse in me a passionate desire to study this mysterious work. . . . I felt irresistibly attracted by the long-sustained pure fifths with which the first phrase opens: these chords, which . . . had played such a supernatural part in my childish impressions of music, seemed in this case to form the spiritual keynote of my own life. This, I thought, must surely contain the secret of all secrets, and accordingly the first thing to be done was *to make the score my own by a process of laborious copying.*[8]

The process of making a text one's own through copying is one of the goals of copying texts. And what scribes produce is not an identical replica of their exemplar, but rather a similitude, an echo, or, metaphorically, a palimpsest. The manuscript evidence for the textual traditions of the *Apocryphal Acts*, as we shall see, is so often in such a woeful state of disarray that we cannot tell whether a scribe has produced—to use Foucault's language—a "resemblance" to an exemplar or whether we should think of our textual witnesses as "similitudes," "propagating themselves from small differences among small differences."[9] Given such limits and constraints on the conclusions we can draw from variant readings, perhaps the best we can do is to think in terms of the performative function of scribes—the act of copying that does not render the text fixed but rather open and malleable.

In the three chapters that follow, my goal is to bring hermeneutical and textual traditions of early Christian texts to bear on the transformation of female characters. In doing so, I am cognizant of recent work—both my own and others'—that has attended to textual variants and the history of women in the early church, and, more broadly, to similar work in related fields.[10] The bulk of chapter 4 is devoted to three main biblical female characters who have long and complex afterlives—Eve, Mary the mother of Jesus, and Mary Magdalene; at the end, I consider the variety of text transmissional issues that attend more minor female characters (e.g., Junia, women in the book of Acts).

Chapter 5 is devoted expressly and solely to Thecla, because her textual and iconographic tradition is so exceptionally rich and provocative. And, finally, in chapter 6, I propose that we rethink the fixity of ancient texts and ancient bodies by examining textual variants that can be read most instructively within the debates about asceticism, about erotic language used in the service of asceticism, and about manly women.

Sinners and Saints, Silent and Submissive?

The Textual/Sexual Transformation of Female Characters in the New Testament and Beyond

Each community creates its culture, subjectively perceiving and objectively constructing new texts. These texts are new worlds, which, once invented, can then be represented, recreating eternal patterns of thought and action.

—Brian Stock, *Listening for the Text*, 112

Surely there is no human culture, however "primitive," without its stories and habits of storytelling, its myths of the origin of the world, its legends of the tribe or groups of stories about folk-heroes.

—J. Hillis Miller, "Narrative," 66

THE SIGNIFICANCE OF STORYTELLING IN EARLY CHRISTIANITY CAN hardly be overestimated. Indeed, from the very beginning, Christians told and retold stories that would come to shape the development of the movement as well as individual lives.[1] The power of stories and images in miniature is apparent in the use of metaphor and symbol in early Christian literature. Christians did not invent the use of metaphor and symbol nor were they alone in using such rhetoric to convey religious meaning, for they inherited storytelling from both the classical and the Jewish world. When we explore, however, the way in which Christians employed the power of the written and said word, the language of paradox, and the dramatic transformation of symbols and characters, the result is rather striking: Christians indeed created community through the creation of new texts and, simultaneously, the rewriting of the old texts. In this chapter and the chapters that follow, we shift our attention from the sociohistorical questions of the production and consumption of texts to the transformation of these texts and the stories they contain. More precisely, and in keeping with the large theme of books and bodies, we turn to how the process of reproducing the book comes to reshape, fashion, and mold the early Christian body.

Symbols with the greatest multivalence and paradox might, it seems, be the ones that have the longest lasting and most widespread use. Take, for example, the symbol of the serpent: One can scarcely imagine a symbol with more divergent meanings or more lasting use. In the ancient world, the serpent—or snake—symbolized Asklepios, the god of healing. Reliefs depict Asklepios and his daughter opposite the snake, and Asklepios most commonly appears with a snake entwined around his staff. The first-century Roman poet Statius writes of the Asklepios shrine of Pergamum: "Where the great helper of the sick is present to aid . . ., a kindly deity, over his health-bringing snake" (Statius, *Silvae*, 3.4.23). Divine demigods and emperors were sometimes said to be the children of snakes. And in Egypt, the snake was the image associated with the goddess Renenutet, as well as the protector of kings and shipwrecked sailors. But simultaneously, the snake symbolized death, and the ancient world was replete with images and stories of snakebites and portrayals of fearsome and loathsome snakes. It is this image that comes to predominate in the world of early Christian biblical interpretation, although even here we might recall that the literature from Nag Hammadi, with its glorification of knowledge, sometimes regards the snake in the Garden of Eden as a life-giver. How is it that a symbol comes to be full of such paradoxes? How might such paradoxes reveal visceral ambivalences?

To what extent can we see the associations of a particular symbol change over time? Such questions go well beyond the focus of the present study, but in its starkest form, the paradox attached to the image of the serpent serves as a helpful entry into how the stories of women in early Christian literature came to be changed over time.

In each of the following examples, the problems of story transmission—or, the retelling of the story of a woman—involve a different set of issues and betray different methods by which Christians fashioned an identity for women through the medium of story. A central point here is that stories are not closed; they do not close down interpretation, but rather invite it; and the manifold tensions presented by stories require, even demand, different resolutions. We can see these points illustrated well on both the macro- and microlevels by tracing the transformation of female characters in stories, by attending to the interpretation of individual biblical verses, and by looking closely at the transmission history of a single passage. Female

FIGURE 4.1. Relief of snake. Asklepion, Bergama (Pergamum), Turkey. Courtesy of author.

characters are remarkably, perhaps even uniquely or particularly, elastic when it comes to thinking with a story or constructing a community through a story.

Sinners and Saints: Transforming Eve, Mary the Mother, and Mary Magdalene

Eve: "Mother of the Living" or "Bringer of Death"?

Consider the character most closely associated with the snake—Eve. Can there be a more wildly ambivalent, paradoxical, and multivalent character in ancient (and modern) Judaism and Christianity? The biblical story of Adam and Eve is full of problems that later commentators addressed: Why would Adam and Eve be forbidden knowledge of good and evil? How does one explain a talking serpent? Why is it that the character given to Adam as a partner then deceives him? And how does someone named "mother of the living" lead to expulsion from the garden? Such questions, along with many others, were pressing in a world that depended on the authority of texts and, in particular, the medium of story. The narrative of Eve truly epitomizes what is meant by paradox, and the history of interpretation bears this out, for this is a story that abounds with possibilities for subsequent interpreters.

The history of the interpretation of the story of Adam and Eve is enormous and complex; here it suffices to illustrate how a character—in this case Eve—comes to be so multivalent and elastic. At the hands of Jewish and Christian writers and interpreters, Eve variously becomes the "mother of all living" (as she is called in Genesis), an allegory of the church who bears children; the "bringer of death"; and a "gateway to the devil." To follow just one interpretive issue, we can take the etymological derivation of her name alongside the interpretations of her character and her error. According to Genesis 3:20, "The man [i.e., Adam] called his wife's name Eve (חוה) because she was the mother of all living (חי)." The Greek translation reads rather literally: "And Adam called the name of his wife Life (ζωή) for she is the mother of all living things (ζωντῶν)." We can note, however, that the Septuagint is faced with a difficulty, for the name *Eve* etymologically is similar to the word for life in Hebrew, but phonetically *Eve* in Greek hardly has the same etymological connections. Even the most ascetic of the patristic writers faces these verses and attempts to explain them. Tertullian suggests that Eve is given a personal name at this point to differentiate her from her former state (in which she was not the mother of all living) and to indicate her roles in the future (to bear children) (*On the Veiling of Virgins* 5); Jerome allegorizes Eve as the church: "As there is one Eve who is 'the mother of all living,' so there is one church which is the parent of all Christians" (*Ep.* 123). In a striking inversion of the naming of Eve, two texts from the Nag Hammadi corpus offer a different reading—namely, that Eve is called the mother of all living because she gives birth to Adam:

> After the day of rest Sophia sent her daughter Zoe, being called Eve, as an instructor in order that she might make Adam, who had no soul, arise so that those whom he should engender might become containers of light. When Eve saw her male counterpart prostrate she had pity upon him, and she said, "Adam! Become alive! Arise upon the earth!" Immediately her word became accomplished fact. For Adam, having arisen, suddenly opened his eyes. When he saw her he said, "You shall be called 'Mother of the Living.' For it is you who have given me life."
>
> *—On the Origin of the World* 115–116

Likewise, in another text from the same codex, we find the following: "And the spirit-endowed woman, came to him and spoke with him, saying, 'Arise, Adam.' And when he saw her, he said, 'It is you who have given me life; you will be called "Mother of the living." For it is she who is my mother. It is she who is the physician, and the woman, and she who has given birth'" (*Hypostasis of the Archons* 89).[2] That these two texts interpret Eve as Adam's mother, the one who gives him life, accords well with the privileging of knowledge; indeed, Eve comes to play a positive role in these texts because she gives knowledge to Adam.

But there are other ancient interpreters who take a different approach altogether with the name of Eve. In some Rabbinic and early Christian texts, the derivation of Eve's name links her with the serpent. Consider, for example, the following passages from *Genesis Rabbah*:

> And the man called his wife's name Eve—Hawwah (חוה), i.e., Life (3.20). She was given to him for an adviser (חיותו), but she played the

eavesdropper like the serpent (חויא). [Another interpretation]: He showed (חוה) her how many generations she had destroyed. R. Aha interpreted it: The serpent (חויא) was thy [Eve's] serpent (חוייך), and thou art Adam's serpent (חויא)" (GR 20:11).

—*GR* 20:11

The notion that Eve becomes the serpent of Adam (rather than his mother!) appears a second time in *Genesis Rabbah*, repeating again the saying of R. Aha: "The serpent was your serpent, and you were Adam's serpent" (*GR* 22:2). But Eve as a serpent is not restricted to rabbinic literature. Clement of Alexandria, in a likely conflation of the name Eve with the call the Baccants make in ceremony (Eua) suggests a knowledge of the Aramaic term used for *snake*—חויא:

> The raving Dionysus is worshipped by Bacchants with orgies, in which they celebrate their sacred frenzy by a feast of raw flesh. Wreathed with snakes, they perform the distribution of portions of their victims, shouting the name of Eva, that Eva through whom error entered into the world; and a consecrated snake is the emblem of the Bacchic orgies. At any rate, according to the correct Hebrew speech, the word "hevia" with an aspirate means the female snake.
>
> —*Exhortation to the Greeks* 2.11

Although it is difficult to understand how Clement can see the practices of the worshipers of Dionysus as connected to the biblical character of Eve, what is instructive is his knowledge of an etymological connection between Eve and the serpent. In a wide range of texts, we find indeed a very specific (nonetymological) connection between Eve and the serpent—namely, those texts that understand Eve's sin as sexual in nature and, even more specifically, as her copulation with the serpent (hence Cain comes to be called the "child of the Serpent"). Rabbinic texts are quite explicit on this: "For R. Johanan stated, 'When the serpent copulated with Eve, he infused her with lust. The lust of the Israelites who stood at Mount Sinai came to an end, the lust of the idolaters who did not stand at Mount Sinai did not end," (*bYebamoth* 103b).[3] The Gospel of Philip claims that Cain is the child of the serpent (61:4–12); Epiphanius accuses the Archontics of a legend that the devil came to Eve and they had Cain and Abel (*Panarion* 40.5.1–4); and such an idea is even implied by the infamous accusation Jesus makes in the Gospel of John: "You are of your father the devil, and your wish is to do the desire of your father. He was a people-killer from the beginning . . ." (8:44).

In a telling passage from the second-century *Protevangelium of James*, a story that seeks to demonstrate Mary's virginity, Joseph returns from "his residences" to find Mary pregnant. Throwing himself on the ground, he "weeps bitterly," saying:

> With what sort of countenance shall I look to the Lord God? What shall I pray concerning this maiden? For I received her a virgin (παρθένον) from the Temple of the Lord God, and I did not guard her. Who is he who has deceived me? Who did this evil thing in my house and defiled her (Τίς τὸ πονηρὸν τοῦτο ἐποίησεν τῷ οἴκῳ μου καὶ ἐμίανεν αὐτήν)? Is not the story of Adam summed up in me? For just as Adam was in the hour of his giving glory to God and the serpent came and found Eve alone and deceived her (καὶ ἦλθεν ὁ ὄφις καὶ εὗρεν αὐτὴν καὶ ἐμίανεν αὐτήν), thus it has also come about for me.
>
> —*Prot. James* 13

The implication here is difficult to miss: When Joseph sees Mary pregnant, he fears that he has been deceived just like Adam; Eve's sin, it is implied, was sexual in nature. Although several Greek witnesses add in a brief clause prior to the first "and he defiled her" so that they have Joseph asking, "Who is this that has taken captive the virgin from me and defiled her" the sexual connotation of μιαίνω is difficult to miss. What is more instructive for our purposes is that the primary witness—indeed sometimes the sole witness—for this language of defilement is the fourth-century copy of the *Prot. James* embedded within a codex containing a seemingly disparate collection of texts. In addition to the *Protevangelium*, here called the *Gospel of Mary*, we find the *Apocryphal Correspondence of Paul and the Corinthians*, the 11th *Ode of Solomon*, Jude, Melito's *Passover Homily*, a hymn fragment, the *Apology of Phileas*, Psalms 33 and 34, and 1 and 2 Peter.[4]

As I have argued previously, one of the striking features of this particular third–fourth-century codex is its concern with the body.[5] Just as the scribe of the story of Mary works to show the contrast between Mary and Eve and to demonstrate Mary's body inviolate, so also scribes of the *Apocryphal Correspondence between Paul and the Corinthians* respond to those who deny the resurrection of the flesh, the epistles of Jude and 1 and 2 Peter affirm Christ's suffering in the flesh, and so forth. As we shall see, the concerns over the virginal body and the body of Christ are so interwoven in the second to fourth centuries that one can scarcely separate them. What may seem a doctrinal issue finds its way into an ideology of praxis.

The retelling of the story of Eve within a story about Mary in the second century takes us directly to that most famous of female characters in early Christianity—Mary the mother of Jesus.

Mary: From "A Virgin Betrothed" to the "Mother of God"

If Eve is the bringer of death, Mary is her polar opposite—the epitome of purity, virginity, and life. Mary becomes both the "deliverer of the tears of Eve" and she who "gives birth to the Word" (in yet another striking image connecting women and books).[6] And in every context throughout history, Mary becomes a representation of the identity of different communities: one of the best visual tours of such identifications is in the present-day Church of the Annunciation in Nazareth, a cathedral that is lined with panels representing the Madonna—in dramatically different forms—given by nations around the world. But the texts that come to be included in the New Testament are remarkably minimal when it comes to Mary the mother of Jesus. Herein lies one of the central problems faced by biblical interpreters and patristic writers at the forefront of Christological controversies and apologetic wars in the second century. How is it that an apparently young unmarried Jewish girl comes to be the mother of the Messiah, the Christ? Why do the gospels say so little about her? Who was she and where did she come from and, even more pressing, how do we know she was a virgin? And, as time went on, they asked, Was she a virgin only before Jesus's birth or also during and after? And what evidence might be brought to bear to answer these questions? Central to the development of stories and traditions about Mary is the lack of information in the earliest biographies of Jesus and the need to expand on her identity. But the figure of Mary also came to be implicated in the Christological debates of the second centuries and beyond; by the fifth century, the role of Mary and her titles became sufficiently acute as to require an ecumenical council.

Because so much has been written on the cult of the Virgin Mary, I will simply illustrate here three points: (1) the starting point for the problems we see in interpretation are an inherent dissatisfaction about the lack of detail in the Gospels; (2) a desire (early on) to demonstrate Jesus's divinity by appropriate attention to his divine birth; and (3) above all, the need to represent Mary as the undefiled virgin par excellence.[7] Christian apologists and interpreters followed in classical footsteps well, for how better to show an individual's divinity than to show his divine birth? Caesar Augustus, Plato, Alexander the Great, even Apollonius of Tyana—stories circulated widely of the divine birth of these men and others. What is striking in the Christian case is that a cult develops around the figure of Jesus's mother—and a cult that has elaborate rituals, iconography, and texts. And the tradition quickly begins to emphasize Mary's virginity far more than is noted in the New Testament.

In the New Testament, Mary receives just brief mention by name in the birth narratives of Matthew and Luke (Matt. 1–2 and Luke 1–2); the pericope of Jesus's family coming to see him (Matt. 12:46–50; Mark 3:31–35; and Luke 4:16–40); the pericope in which the residents of Nazareth identify him by association with his family (Matt. 13:53–58; Mark 6:3–4; Luke 8:19–21); the narratives of the wedding in Cana and the scene at the cross from John (2:1–12 and 19:25–27). With the exception of the birth narratives, throughout the Gospels, Mary is simply called "the mother" ($\dot{\eta}\ \mu\dot{\eta}\tau\eta\rho$). And she speaks only rarely: briefly during the story of the wedding in Cana in John and at a couple of points in the birth narratives. Given the subsequent history of Marion devotion, however, what is surprising is how little the earliest stories of Mary emphasize her virginity—precisely the quality that comes to define her from the second century onward.

Matthew and Luke identify Mary as a "virgin" ($\pi\alpha\rho\theta\acute{\epsilon}\nu\sigma$), but in different ways. The key passages in Matthew concern two passages: "When his mother Mary had been betrothed to Joseph, before they had come together, she was found to be pregnant from the Holy Spirit ($\mu\nu\eta\sigma\tau\epsilon\upsilon\theta\epsilon\acute{\iota}\sigma\eta\varsigma\ \tau\hat{\eta}\varsigma\ \mu\eta\tau\rho\grave{o}\varsigma\ \alpha\grave{\upsilon}\tau o\hat{\upsilon}\ M\alpha\rho\acute{\iota}\alpha\varsigma\ \tau\hat{\wp}\ {}'I\omega\sigma\acute{\eta}\varphi,\ \pi\rho\grave{\iota}\nu\ \mathring{\eta}\ \sigma\upsilon\nu\epsilon\lambda\theta\epsilon\hat{\iota}\nu\ \alpha\grave{\upsilon}\tau o\grave{\upsilon}\varsigma\ \grave{\epsilon}\nu\ \gamma\alpha\sigma\tau\rho\grave{\iota}\ \acute{\epsilon}\chi o\upsilon\sigma\alpha\ \grave{\epsilon}\kappa\ \pi\nu\epsilon\acute{\upsilon}\mu\alpha\tau o\varsigma\ \grave{\alpha}\gamma\acute{\iota}o\upsilon$)" (Matt. 1:18); and the quotation from Isaiah 7:14 just a few verses later, "All this took place to fulfill what the Lord had spoken by the prophet, 'Behold, a virgin shall conceive ($\grave{\iota}\delta o\grave{\upsilon}\ \dot{\eta}\ \pi\alpha\rho\theta\acute{\epsilon}\nu o\varsigma\ \grave{\epsilon}\nu\ \gamma\alpha\sigma\tau\rho\grave{\iota}\ \acute{\epsilon}\xi\epsilon\iota$) and will bring forth a son, and they will call his name Emmanuel'" (Matt. 1:22–23). Much attention has been given to Matthew's use of *parthenos* here, especially in his quotation of Isaiah; what is significant for our purposes is what is not here in Matthew's depiction of Mary—an emphasis on her virginity.

In fact, Mary's earliest appearance in the Gospel of Matthew is in the problematic verse at the end of the genealogy: "And Jacob the father of Joseph the husband of Mary, of whom Jesus was born, who is called Christ" (Ἰακὼβ δὲ ἐγέννησεν τὸν Ἰωσὴφ τὸν ἄνδρα Μαρίας, ἐξ ἧς ἐγεννήθη Ἰησοῦς ὁ λεγόμενος χριστός) (Matt. 1:16). Attested by a wide array of diverse and early witnesses to the passage (e.g., the earliest papyrus fragment from the third century, Codex Sinaiticus, Codex Vaticanus, other Greek witnesses as well as Latin, Syriac, Coptic, and Georgian versions), this verse comes into tension with the Christological controversies of the second century and the rise of Marian devotion. Are Joseph and Mary both the biological parents of Jesus as the verse implies? What precisely is the nature of the relationship between Joseph and Mary? Why was Mary chosen? What is special about her? Multiple variant readings for this verse demonstrate how the very words of scriptural texts become contested within the context of doctrinal debates.[8] One scribe, the scribe of the fifth-century Sinaitic Syriac manuscript of the gospels (to which we shall return), probably through simple oversight, writes, "Jacob begot Joseph; Joseph, to whom was betrothed Mary *the virgin*, begot Jesus who is called the Christ"—Joseph as the father of Jesus! And, simultaneously, the description of Mary as "the virgin." More widely attested is a different reading: "And Jacob begot Joseph, to whom was engaged *the virgin* Mary who begot Jesus who is called the Christ"; a similar reading is found in another Syriac witness (the Curetonian manuscript): "Jacob begot Joseph, him to whom was betrothed/engaged Mary *the virgin*, she who bore Jesus the Christ"; and the Armenian version: "Jacob begot Joseph the husband of Mary, to whom was betrothed Mary *the virgin*, from whom was born Jesus who was called Christ." Although these variants convey essentially the same meaning, what is instructive is that all of them—the problematic Sinaitic manuscript included— identify Mary by the epithet "the virgin" (*parthenos*) and they all seem to wrestle with the relationship between Joseph and Mary. This is a telling clue, for the variants come into existence at precisely the same time as Mary's virginity comes to be increasingly emphasized and her status elevated; although they might also be read as an attempt to harmonize the Gospel of Matthew to the Gospel of

Luke, such variant readings should remind us that books, and copies of books, were not produced in a vacuum, but rather within specific contexts and these contexts shaped the process—and very words—of the copies.

Now let us turn briefly to the depiction of Mary in the birth narrative of Luke, the most important narrative for the development of subsequent Marian devotion. Luke's account offers much more emphasis on Mary's virginity, especially in these key passages: "In the sixth month the angel Gabriel was sent from God to a city of Galilee named Nazareth, to a virgin betrothed (παρθένον ἐμνηστευμένην) to a man whose name was Joseph, of the house of David; and the virgin's name (τὸ ὄνομα τῆς παρθένου) was Mary" (Luke 1:26–27); after Gabriel tells Mary she will conceive and bear a son, she replies: "How will this be, since I have not known a man?" (πῶς ἔσται τοῦτο, ἐπεὶ ἄνδρα οὐ γινώσκω) (Luke 1:34); and in response to the census, Joseph goes from Galilee to Bethlehem "to be enrolled with Mary, his betrothed, who was with child" (ἀπογράψασθαι σὺν Μαριὰμ τῇ ἐμνηστευμένῃ αὐτῷ οὔσῃ ἐγκύῳ) (Luke 2:5). In each of these cases where Mary is called "a virgin betrothed," "a virgin," or "the betrothed," the readings are attested by wide support from diverse and early witnesses, so the "originality" of the readings is not in question.

But note the following, arguably minor, variants: in the first and third passages, the word *betrothed* appears in a different verbal form in some manuscripts. Instead of the aorist middle ἐμνηστευμένην, a diverse and strong set of manuscripts have the perfect passive form μεμνηστευμενη, suggesting that Mary's betrothal to Joseph had already taken place sometime in the past. Furthermore, a small group of witnesses strengthen the idea that Mary is now Joseph's wife by substituting γυναίκι αὐτοῦ ("his wife") for his betrothed in Luke 2:6 (e.g., the equivalent in old Latin witnesses and the Sinaitic Syriac codex) and others simply add the word "wife" γυναίκι after the perfect form to indicate that she had been betrothed to him and now was his wife.

The question of whether Mary is Joseph's wife by the time of Jesus's birth is a subject of real concern for later rewriters of the story and is certainly interwoven with the question of her virginity before, during, and after Jesus's birth. In the *Protevangelium of James*, the scribe reports to the priest having seen Mary pregnant and accuses

Joseph: "The virgin, whom Joseph received out of the temple of the Lord, he has defiled her (ἐμίανεν) and has stolen her in marriage and did not bring it out into the open to the sons of Israel" (15:2).[9] Joseph and Mary are subjected to a test of their purity and honesty, which they pass fully, and then the narrative proceeds to the census and Joseph taking Mary to Bethlehem. Joseph wonders how to register Mary. As his daughter? As his wife? In part, his quandary has to do with the emphasis in this text on Joseph's great age in comparison to Mary's youth, and these details are present in the text precisely to demonstrate both Joseph's and Mary's purity; but the issue here also has to do with whether they are married and the implication that if they are married then surely people will doubt Mary's virginity all the more. Just a few chapters later, the matter becomes even clearer when Joseph seeks a midwife to assist Mary, here written from the perspective of Joseph:

> And behold, a woman came down from the hill-country and said to me, "Man, where are you going?" And I said, "I seek a Hebrew midwife." And she answered me, "Are you from Israel?" And I said to her, "Yes." And she said, "And who is she who brings forth in the cave?" And I said, "My betrothed" (μεμνηστευμένη). And she said to me, "Is she not your wife?" And I said to her, "She is Mary, who was brought up in the Temple of the Lord, and I received her by lot as my wife, and she is not my wife, but she has conceived by the Holy Spirit."
>
> —*Prot. James* 19

The text variants in this passage are too numerous to detail here, but the passage as a whole, as well as the multiple variants, center on a particular problem: proof of Mary's virginity. In contrast to the accretions and modifications to the story of Eve, which sought to sexualize Eve's error, the textual developments of the story of Mary seek precisely the opposite—the demonstration of her purity (as well as the purity of Joseph, which helps confirm Mary's purity). Note that the same term—μιαίνω, "defiled"—is used both for Eve and for Mary in these passages. Later retellings of this piece of the story of Mary (dependent on the *Prot. James*) further distance Joseph from Mary by identifying her as "the virgin" or "a woman."[10] Such stark contrasts between Eve and Mary develop further in the hermeneutical traditions of late antiquity and the Middle Ages.

Already in the second century, however, we are on the way to the image that appears in the *Akathistos*: "Hail, deliverance of the tears of Eve."[11]

The passage that became so significant for the doctrinal issues of Perpetual Virginity is the well-known story of Salome the midwife who comes to test Mary's virginity in the *Prot. James*: "And Salome inserted her finger to test her condition. And she cried out, saying 'Woe for my wickedness and my unbelief; for I have tempted the living God; and behold, my hand falls away from me, consumed by fire!'" (20:1). In the parallel retelling of this passage from *Pseudo-Matthew*, Salome does her test and then cries out, "It has never been heard or thought of that anyone should have her breasts full of milk and that the birth of a son should show his mother to be a virgin. But there has been no spilling of blood in his birth, no pain in bringing him forth. A virgin has conceived, a virgin has brought forth, and a virgin she remains" (Virgo peperit et postquam peperit uirgo esse perdurat) (*Ps.-Matt.* 13:3).[12] In both of these cases, the narrative of Salome's test serves to confirm what has already been indicated by the statements regarding whether Mary is Joseph's wife or not—her undefiled state.

Before leaving Mary, we can briefly review a few more examples of how text transmission was interwoven with interpretation. One of the first impulses writers of the second century faced was to expand on the biblical narrative—indeed, one of the longest sections of the *Prot. James* is devoted to Mary's own birth and, especially, the stories regarding her parents Joachim and Anna. Particularly telling is the subsequent development of such stories: take, for example, the contrast between the openings of the *Prot. James*, the Latin sixth–seventh-century *Ps.-Matt.*, and the ninth-century adaptation of *Ps.-Matt.* found in the *Libellus de nativitate sanctae Mariae*.

> In the "Histories of the Twelve Tribes of Israel" Joachim was a very rich man, and he brought all his gifts to the Lord. . . .
>
> —*Prot. James* 1:1

> In those days there was a man in Israel, Joachim by name, of the tribe of Judah. . . .
>
> —*Ps.-Matt.* 1:1

> The blessed and very glorious Mary, ever-virgin, was born of royal lineage and of the family of David.
>
> —*Libellus* 1:1[13]

The contrast seen here is important: the story found in the second-century *Prot. James*, which emphasizes Mary's Jewish background and only later attempts to demonstrate in a graphic way her virginity, is dramatically different in its opening from that found in the *Libellus*, which from the very start applies doctrinal epithets to Mary (e.g., "ever-virgin," "the Virgin," or the "Virgin of the Lord").

A final passage, so important for later liturgy, is worth highlighting in the stories about Mary and the birth of Jesus. There can scarcely be a more important passage for subsequent liturgy than the "Magnificat" (found in Luke 1:46–55). Here again we find textual variants that may shed light on the subsequent history of the passage and its use. In particular, note the very opening of the passage: "And Mary said, 'My soul magnifies the Lord'" (καὶ εἶπεν Μαριαμ Μεγαλύνει ἡ ψυχὴ μου τὸν κύριον) (Luke 1:46). This is the reading found in all of the Greek witnesses to the passage and nearly all of the versional and patristic witnesses. However, in some old Latin manuscripts, we read that *Elizabeth* is actually the speaker in this verse: instead of the Latin *et ait Maria Magnificat anima mea Dominum*, these Old Latin texts read *et ait Elisabel* [or Elisabet or Elisabeth] *magnificat anima mea Dominum*.[14] Such a variant is surely hard to explain given the subsequent history of this hymn, and it is found in at least three Old Latin manuscripts dating from the fourth, fifth, and seventh centuries along with the Armenian translation of Irenaeus *Against Heresies* 4.7.1, Niceta, bishop of Remesiana, and in Jerome's remark about variant readings here in his Latin translation of Origen's *Commentary on Luke*.[15] Could it be that Elizabeth was the original reading? This makes better transcriptional sense—the name would have then been changed to Mary during the rise of Marian devotion—but the external evidence certainly favors Mary and thus it becomes all the more difficult to explain why some scribes (particularly in the Latin west?) might have Elizabeth say this magnificat. Interestingly, in the *Prot. James*, it is the midwife who comes the closest to saying the beginning of the magnificat, not Mary or Elizabeth: "And the midwife said, 'My soul is magnified today, for my eyes have seen wonderful things; for salvation is born to Israel'" (καὶ εἶπεν ἡ μαῖα ἐμεγαλύνθη ἡ ψυχή μου σήμερον . . .) (*Prot. James* 19:2). Instead of "midwife," some of the Syriac witnesses and the Ethiopic version here simply read "woman," allowing for the possibility that the saying could be attributed to Mary or to Elizabeth.

What I want to suggest is this: Throughout the expansions on the story of Mary, we find evidence that the stories were told in light of present circumstances and that the development of Marian devotion can be seen both in these retellings and also in the textual variants of a single text as it is copied and translated by different scribes.[16] My goal here is not to sort out the direction of the changes in these cases; rather, it is to suggest that the variant readings betray doctrinal—both Christological and Mariological—disputes that center on Mary's purity, her virginity, and the state of her relationship to Joseph at various stages in the narrative. In each of these cases, we find witnesses to the development of ideas about Mary in the apocryphal and patristic literatures of the second century and beyond.

Amid all of the retellings, I conclude this section with the words of Ambrose, who develops and encapsulates the virginal Mary (and, strikingly, her connection to books!):

> She was a virgin not only in body but also in mind, who stained the sincerity of its disposition by no guile, who was humble in heart, grave in speech, prudent in mind, sparing of words, studious in reading, resting her hope not un uncertain riches, but on the prayer of the poor, intent on work, modest in discourse; wont to seek not man but God as the judge of her thoughts, to injure no one, to have goodwill towards all, to rise up before her elders, not to envy her equals, to avoid boastfulness, to follow reason, to love virtue.
>
> —*De Virginibus* 2.2.7

> Moreover, she seemed to herself to be less alone when she was alone. For how should she be alone, who had with her so many books, so many archangels, so many prophets?
>
> —*De Vir.* 2.2.10

Such a description of Mary's character, actions, and purity moves well beyond the very words of scripture. We find ourselves here in the hermetical imaginary, so to speak, an interpretive impulse that needs only the hint of a textual authority ("a virgin") to develop a description of Mary and the pure virginal ideal—and once again the figure of the ascetic female reader comes to the fore, here in the person of Mary.

Mary Magdalene: Apostle, Saint, and Prostitute

If Mary the Mother of Jesus comes to be the opposite of Eve as a female character, Mary Magdalene becomes an amalgam of both images.[17] Like Mary the Mother, Mary Magdalene represents life in stark contrast to Eve's representation of death: "In paradise," writes Gregory the Great, "a woman gave death to man; now from the tomb a woman announces life to men and tells the words of the Life-giver just as a woman (Eve) told the words of the death-bearing serpent" (*Homily* 25).[18]

In the case of Mary Magdalene, the traditions that follow the explicit mentions of her in the Gospels conflate various narratives. These conflations lead to the image of Mary Magdalene as the woman taken in adultery and the sexual sinner who has repented and intersect with debates about her role as an apostle. Apart from the brief identification of Mary Magdalene as the one "from whom seven demons had gone out" (Luke 8:2), the appearance of Mary in the Gospels of the New Testament is exclusively related to the scenes of Jesus's death, burial, and resurrection (Matt. 27:55–56, 61; 28:1; Mark 15:40–41, 47; 16:1, 9; Luke 24:10; John 19:25; 20:1, 11, 16, 18). Take the well-known ending narrative of the Gospel of Mark: Mary Magdalene, along with Mary the mother of James, and Salome, bring spices to anoint Jesus's body and, arriving at the tomb, they wonder who might roll away the stone for them. They arrive to find the stone already rolled away and they enter into the tomb and find a man in a white robe, who tells them, "You see Jesus of Nazareth, who was crucified. He has risen, he is not here; see the place where they laid him. But go, tell his disciples and Peter that he is going before you to Galilee; there you will see him, as he told you" (Mark 16:6–7). But the women fled the tomb and "said nothing to any one for they were afraid" (Mark 16:8). This is the ending of the Gospel of Mark best attested by all of our earliest manuscripts: fourth-century Codices Sinaiticus and Vaticanus end here, as do some of the Old Latin manuscripts, the

Syriac palimpsest from Sinai, and the earliest church father. But beginning in the seventh century, we see an addition to the ending of the Gospel of Mark in a wide array of versions (e.g., Latin, Syriac, Coptic, Ethiopic): "But they reported all the things they had been told to Peter and those with him. And after this, Jesus himself sent out by means of them, from east to west, the sacred and imperishable message/proclamation of eternal salvation" (Mark 16, shorter ending); furthermore, a longer ending, following upon Mark 16:8 comes to be part of the tradition in the majority of Greek witnesses and appears as early as Irenaeus and the Diatessaron. Its uses of non-Markan vocabulary suggests to most scholars that this longer ending, although well known, was not original.[19]

Instructive for our purposes is the explicit role Mary Magdalene plays in this longer ending: "Now when he rose early on the first day of the week, he appeared first to Mary Magdalene, from whom he had cast out seven demons. She went and told the others who had been with him who were mourning and weeping. But when they heard that he was alive and had been seen by her, they did not believe" (Mark 16:9–11). There are some manuscripts (e.g., the fifth-century Codex Bezae's first scribe) that modify the ending of this passage by adding "and they did not believe *her*" (*και ουκ επιστευσαν αυτη*)—if there was any question about Mary Magdalene's role as witness to and messenger of the resurrection, this codex strives to eliminate it. What ensues in the following verses is subsequent appearances to two anonymous figures and then to the eleven disciples.

These various endings to Mark, along with the textual variants within them, betray a central issue in the depiction of Mary Magdalene in early Christian literature. Although she plays a minor role in the Gospels, she comes to be central in all of the canonical gospel accounts of the death and resurrection (and especially in the empty tomb narratives). But we begin to see traces of a controversy about her role as witness to the resurrection and, in particular, her role in comparison to that of Peter. Both the shorter and longer endings of the Gospel of Mark, in different ways, serve to minimize her role. And such tensions find their most vivid early representation in the final saying in the Coptic *Gospel of Thomas*, a text with likely second-century origins: "Simon Peter said to them, 'Let Mary leave us, for women are not worthy of life.' Jesus said, 'I myself shall lead her in order to make her male, so that she too may become a living spirit resembling you males. For every woman who will make herself male will enter the kingdom of heaven'" (*GThomas* 114).[20] This stands in marked contrast to other references to Mary in the Nag Hammadi corpus. Take, for example, the Gospel of Philip: "There were three who always walked with the Lord: Mary his mother and her sister and Magdalene, the one who was called his companion . . . His sister and his mother and his companion were each a Mary" (*GPhilip* 59). Further on, in a passage now made famous by Dan Brown's *The Da Vinci Code*, a passage filled with lacunae seems to suggest a debate among Jesus's followers about his love for Mary Magdalene. A few lines after the mention of Mary Magdalene by name, we find: "They said to him, 'Why do you love her more than all of us?' The savior answered and said to them, 'Why do I not love you like her?'" (*GPhilip* 64). Whereas in the Gospel of Philip, Mary Magdalene appears as the "companion" of Jesus, in the *Gospel of Peter*, she is identified as the "disciple" of Jesus.

The fullest exposition of her roles as disciple and apostle appears in the *Gospel of Mary* (not to be confused with the *Prot. James*, which sometimes goes under the name *Gospel of Mary*), extant in two third-century Greek manuscripts (*P.Ryl.* 463 and *P.Oxy.* 3525) and a fifth-century Coptic codex (Codex Berolinensis 8525).[21] This is a text where Mary Magdalene is a teacher and even Peter invites her to teach: "Peter said to Mary, 'Sister, we know that the Savior loved you more than all other women. Tell us the words of the Savior that you remember, the things which you know that we do not because we have not heard them.' Mary responded, 'I will teach you about what is hidden from you.' And she began to speak these words to them" (*GMary* 6). As the text continues, Mary relays visions and teachings of the savior. Upon concluding, some of the disciples contest whether she has relayed Jesus's teachings and whether he could have spoken to her privately, but Levi answers, speaking directly to Peter, "'Peter, you have always been a wrathful person. Now I see you contending against the woman like the Adversaries. For if the Savior made her worthy, who are you then for your part to reject her? Assuredly, the Savior's knowledge of her is completely reliable. That is why he loved her more than us'" (*GMary* 10:7–10). Although the text betrays a controversy, it seeks above all to confirm Mary Magdalene's role as apostle and teacher.

Where is the image of Mary Magdalene as a prostitute in all of these retellings? It is in the sixth-century West that we begin to find Mary Magdalene associated with the sinful woman of Luke 7:36–50 and sometimes with the woman taken in adultery from John 7:53–8:11.[22] It is in the image of Mary Magdalene as prostitute or an adulterous woman that we find the fullest expression of the recasting of a female character in negative sexualized form. It is also where we see the work that interpreters did with the story of Mary Magdalene, who appears in all four canonical gospels but is nowhere a fully developed character: To make sense of her character as well as the multiple stories of unnamed sinful women, interpreters rewrote the texts by conflating different stories. Or, put differently, the textual transmission becomes inflected by the oral circulation of conflated, expanded, and edited stories. Because many of these stories emerge in a time period beyond our primary concern here and because they have been so well examined, I will not rehearse them here. But it is worth emphasizing that Mary Magdalene provides the example par excellence of the sexualizing of a female character along with her repentance and subordination. The images that come to be attached to her iconography depict her as either a sinner or a penitent saint. And the numerous depictions of Mary in the act of reading range from the virginal contemplative to the voluptuous and sensual woman.

Eve, Mary the mother of Jesus, and Mary Magdalene are three female characters who come to play a significant role in emergent discourses about gender, virginity, and asceticism. In the retelling of each of their stories, scribes, interpreters, and readers embellished, modified, and expanded the narratives about them. Such a practice shows one of the many ways in which stories about women were used "to think with": to wrestle with issues of Christian practice and belief required attending to the very representation of women in early Christian texts. Before turning to another famous female character—Thecla—I want to suggest that the textual variants we have considered thus far are best understood alongside a series of other variants from New Testament texts, variants that have received attention in recent years by scholars interested in the history of women in early Christianity.

"Minor" Female Characters

Mary and Martha

The story of Mary and Martha found in Luke 10:38–42 came to have significant use as a paradigm for two approaches to the Christian life—the ascetic/contemplative and the active/service. What I want to address here briefly are two variants that appear in the textual tradition of this story—first a variant in the opening verse, which begins the story:

> As they were going along their way, he came into a certain village; a woman named Martha *received him* (ὑπεδέξατο αὐτόν).
>
> —found in P⁴⁵, P⁷⁵, Codex Vaticanus, and the Sahidic Coptic version

A wide array of diverse textual witnesses contain, however, a longer reading, saying that "Martha received him into her house" (εἰς τὴν οἰκίαν, apparently in P³, Codex Sinaiticus, and others; εἰς τὴν οἰκίαν αὐτῆς in the first corrector of Codex Sinaiticus and the second corrector of Codex C; εἰς τὴν οἶκον αὐτης found in Codex Alexandrinus, Codex Bezae, the Freer Gospel Codex, a number of other important Greek manuscripts, as well as the Latin and Syriac versions). For a moment, let us consider the history of transmission here. The shorter reading has the more ancient witnesses in its favor, whereas the longer reading has the majority, as well as diversity, of witnesses. The transcriptional process is equally difficult: we might wonder, for starters, why scribes would add in the words "into her house" if they were not there originally. To clarify: exactly what is meant by the somewhat ambiguous "received him" or "welcomed him"? The same verb used here for "receive" is that used to describe conception: "For just as a woman receives the unformed seed of her husband (ὥσπερ γὰρ σπορὰν ἀνδρὸς ἀμόρφωτον ὑποδεξαμένη γυνή) and after a period of time brings forth a perfect human being, so too the Church, one might say, constantly conceiving those who take refuge in the word, and shaping them according to the likeness of form of Christ, after a certain time makes them citizens of that blessed age" (Methodius, *Symposium* 8.6). Is it possible that scribes considered the shorter reading "bold and bare" and therefore added the words "into her house"?[23] Or, is it possible that the words "into her house" were original and scribes removed them because of the implications? We cannot resolve this issue—for simple lack of sufficient evidence—but both readings have implications for the erotic overtones of the passage.

In the second verse of the narrative, another variant appears that has significance for our purposes and here the main variant consists simply of the addition or omission of a relative pronoun as well as an "also." In some manuscripts, we find "And she [i.e., Martha] had a sister called Mary, who also sat at the feet of the Lord and listened to his word"; others read, "And she had a sister called Mary also sitting at the feet . . ."; more significantly, others omit the *also/and*: "And she had a sister called Mary who sat at the Lord's feet. . . ." The absence of *also* suggests that Mary is the only listener here and accentuates the difference between Mary and Martha. Furthermore, it implies a unique and special connection between Mary and Jesus. As we shall see, there is a strikingly similar passage in the *Acts of Paul and Thecla* in which Thecla sits at the feet of Paul; and in a very similar way, variants exist there that diverge precisely in the depiction of Thecla *by herself* or Thecla *along with others* listening to Paul.

The Woman Taken in Adultery

Writing around the year 415 CE, Augustine of Hippo claims that "certain persons of scant faith—or better, I believe, enemies of the true faith—fearing their wives be given impunity in sinning, removed from their manuscripts the Lord's act of kindness toward the adulteress as if the Lord had given them permission to do so" (*De adulterinis conjugiis* 7.6). Here we have one of those rare instances when a literary reference to variant readings—in this case, the excision of the story of the woman taken in adultery (John 7:53–8:11)—can be placed alongside the evidence from our extant manuscripts. The rich afterlife of the story—in which the Pharisees bring a "woman caught in adultery" to Jesus to test him, and he refuses to condemn her—goes well beyond the eleven scant verses, and the textual history is remarkably fluid. In fact, our earliest and best witnesses to the Gospel of John do not contain the pericope; when it does appear in fourth- and fifth-century codices, its location varies. Jennifer Knust's recent work on this pericope has shown, rightly to my mind, that "the *pericope adulterae* experienced a particularly complex transmission history."[24] Furthermore,

Knust argues compellingly that the transmissional history of this story can be understood especially well within the context of "the development of anti-Jewish imperial policy," and she details the textual variants within the story to show the anti-Jewish tendencies of such variants.[25]

There is no need to rehearse all of her arguments here; rather, I want to make a simpler point. The possible use of the story within the discourse of anti-Judaism does not mitigate against reading the appearance or omission of the story more directly in light of Augustine's claims. As we have already seen, textual variants in the stories about women demonstrate that these stories were read both as a "model of" and a "model for" reality—to use the language of Clifford Geertz.[26] And Augustine's comment suggests precisely this: people were excising the story out of a fear that their wives might think the story provided too much permissiveness. The interaction between reading, interpretation, and behavior is unmistakable here.

Women in Thessalonica

Another series of variants, which have received fair attention, appear in chapter 17 of the book of Acts and they have to do with the descriptions of women converts in Thessalonica.[27] On three occasions, the women are identified:

> Some of them were persuaded and joined Paul and Silas, as did a great many of the devout Greeks and not a few of the leading women (γυναικῶν τε τῶν πρώτων οὐκ ὀλίγαι).
>
> —Acts 17:4

> Many of them therefore believed, including not a few Greek women and men of high standing (τῶν Ἑλληνίδων γυναικῶν τῶν εὐσχημόνων καὶ ἀνδρῶν οὐκ ὀλίγοι).
>
> —Acts 17:12

> But some of them joined him and became believers, including Dionysius the Areopagite and a woman named Damaris (καὶ γυνὴ ὀνόματι Δάμαρις), and others with them.
>
> —Acts 17: 34

What is striking is that on each of these occasions, the "Western" version of the text provides a different reading. In the first case, Codex

Bezae and old Latin versions read, "not a few of the wives of the leading men" instead of "not a few leading women"! It is a very small difference in the Greek (the nominative γυναίκες instead of the genitive) that effects a radically different sense. In the second instance, the passage "devout Greeks and not a few of the leading women" is written by the first corrector of Codex Bezae as "Greeks and men of high standing and their wives (Ελληνων και των ευσχημονων ανδρες και γυναικες ικανοι επιστευσαν)." In the third case, Codex Bezae omits the mention of Damaris altogether, but other manuscripts insert a single word (τίμια = honored) so that Damaris is an honored woman. These are subtle changes textually, but they have significant implications for interpretation. I am not suggesting here that an "egalitarian" text has been reformulated into one that promotes subordination; rather, that the different readings may well betray different conceptions about the roles of women and permit the text to function toward different ends.

Junia/Junias

In the well-known conclusion to Paul's letter to the church at Rome, he thanks his co-workers: Phoebe, Prisca and Aquila, Mary, Ampliatus, Urbanus, Tryphaena and Tryphosa, and many others. Relevant to our interests here is the following passage: "Greet Andronicus and Junia/Junias (Ἰουνιᾶν), my relatives and my fellow prisoners; they are prominent among the apostles (ἐπίσημοι ἐν τοῖς ἀποστόλοις) and they were in Christ before me (Rom. 16:7). The issue here is rather simple: Does the name *Iounian* refer to a man (Junias) or a woman (Junia)? The declension of the name allows for either one, but whereas the name Junia was common in antiquity, Junias is entirely unattested. Scholars have long noted that the history of interpretation is quite striking. Until the medieval period, commentators assumed that Paul was referring to a woman, but then a marked shift takes place and commentators begin arguing that the referent is a man.[28] Recently, Eldon Epp has written extensively on the variants attached to the name Junia/Junias, considering carefully both the lexical form of the name Junia or Junias and the history of interpretation.[29] Epp's conclusion "is simple and straightforward: *there was an apostle Junia.*"[30]

1 Corinthians 14:34–35: The Silencing of Women

"Let women be silent"—thus begins a passage whose transmission history has received more attention than any other variants we are considering here.[31] In the midst of a lengthy section about spiritual gifts—namely, speaking in tongues and prophecy—we find in the textual tradition of Paul's first letter to the church at Corinth two verses that appear in different locations in different manuscripts. These are verses 34 and 35: "Let the women keep silent in the *ekklesia*. For they are not permitted to speak, but they should be subordinate just as the law says. If there is anything they desire to know, let them ask their husbands at home, for it is shameful for them to speak in *ekklesia*" (1 Cor. 14:34–35). The textual problem here has to do with the location of the verses: some manuscripts have these verses embedded within the chapter, and others place them at the end of the chapter after verse 40, suggesting that there may have been confusion among scribes about the correct location of the verses. Roaming verses such as these sometimes indicate a passage that had been inserted in a margin at some point in the transmission of the passage; subsequent scribes then insert the verses into different locations. Nearly all scholars now consider the verses an interpolation into Paul's letter.

What has been less studied is a variant within the verses. Codex Alexandrinus—recall the fifth-century biblical codex with whose reading of 1 Clement 21:7 we began—produces what appears to be a unique reading. Instead of leaving the passage "let them be submissive or subordinate" without referent, this scribe adds the words "to their husbands" (or "to men"—τοῖς ἀνδροις) so that the passage becomes explicit about women being subordinate to their husbands. (And it is worth recalling that this apparently unique reading is found in the only early Christian manuscript that names, albeit much later, a female scribe!) There are, of course, plenty of literary parallels for the notion that women should be subordinate to their husbands. One especially explicit example appears in the recently published collection of documents from the Coptic village Jeme in Upper Egypt; we find the following inscribed on an ostracon (a fragment of pottery): "If you still do not teach this man's wife that she agree to obey him like every woman and do his bidding, know that I shall excommunicate you as long as she continues to be in this disturbed state. I have written this once again to you!"[32]

Conclusions

The goal of this chapter has been to illustrate what happens to female characters—named or unnamed, minor or major—in early Christian literature during the course of the reproduction and interpretation of their stories. How can we read the flexibility—indeed, elasticity—of their textual traditions? To say that there was a deliberate attempt to control women, to limit their activities, and to silence and subordinate them in each case would be going beyond what our evidence allows. Rather, I suggest that we read these texts and their multiple variations as illuminative of how copying and interpretation worked in tandem with one another.

"First among All Women"
The Story of Thecla in Textual Transmission and Iconographic Remains

I shall not lay any stress on the example of a few women who, from having received a masculine education, have acquired courage and resolution. . . . These . . . may be reckoned exceptions, and are not all heroes as well as heroines exceptional to general rules? I wish to see women neither heroines nor brutes; but reasonable creatures.

—Mary Wollstonecraft, 1792

Now, having heard you all sufficiently contesting in word, I pronounce victors and I crown—Thecla with a greater and thicker crown as the first among you, having shone forth more magnificently.

—Methodius, *Symposium* 11.1

Saint Thekla is pretty much the patron saint of "wow."

—Suzanne, blogger

A MONG ALL THE FEMALE CHARACTERS FROM EARLY CHRISTIAN literature, Thecla stands out as altogether unique—for her reception as a protomartyr, even though she does not die a martyr's death; for her literary traditions and active cultus that emerged early in late antiquity (particularly in the East); and for the richness of our documentary and visual remains of her cult. Although Tertullian complains that women have wrongly taken the example of Thecla as license to baptize and to teach (*De Bapt.* 17), Methodius cloaks Thecla "with a larger and thicker crown, as the chief of you, and as having shone with greater luster than the rest" (*Symp.* 11.1); Jerome claims that Thecla will be there to meet Eustochium in heaven (*Ep.* 22.41); Gregory of Nazianzen calls her the "holy and illustrious virgin" (*Orationes* 21.22); Gregory of Nyssa claims his sister Macrina was given the secret name "Thecla" even before her birth (*Vita Macrina* 3); and the anonymous writer of the fifth-century *Life and Miracles of Saint Thecla* begins his text by identifying Thecla as a protomartyr second in order only to Stephen: "She was first among all women (πρώτη δὲ πασῶν γυναικῶν), so that Stephen might be the leader of men struggling for and through Christ, and Thecla of women" (*LM* 1.15–17). By the fourth century, even a stone carver labels the boat carrying Paul on a sarcophagus relief "Thecla."[1]

But such literary remnants of Thecla veneration are just the smallest hint of a cult that appears to have appealed widely and long throughout the Mediterranean. As we have already seen, Egeria comments specifically on her stop at Seleucia's Saint Thecla church (*Peregrinatio Aetheriae* 23.2), which is possibly the earliest site associated with the Thecla cult. Soon other sites in Asia Minor, Egypt, Syria, Rome, and later Spain had their own Thecla churches, catacombs, and monasteries. In spite of the mixed regard for the *Apocryphal Acts* in the nineteenth and early twentieth centuries, there has been a steady stream of treatments of the second-century narrative, the Thecla cult, and the visual and archaeological remains related to Thecla.[2] And Thecla appropriation and veneration in contemporary religious circles, too, has witnessed a revival in recent years—perhaps inspired by the feminist movements of the late twentieth century. Among the many claims to Thecla today, Thecla appears as the "patron saint of 'wow,'" from a blogger who finds Thekla "amazing," "a friend of Saint Paul the apostle, a rebellious teenager and young adult devoted to God, defying not just the will of her pagan parents, but the patronistic government of Iconium and Antioch, and one of the first protomar-tyrs for Christ. . . . She embodies everything that makes her a truly Awesome woman."[3]

Given the extensive treatment that the second-century literary *Acts of Paul and Thecla* has received, as well as the Thecla cult in late antiquity, I see no reason to rehearse such developments here. Rather, I return to the dual interests of this book—women and books—to highlight two underexplored features of the Thecla tradition: (1) how the textual transmission of the second-century *APT* comes to rewrite and refashion the figure of Thecla, and (2) the association of the char-acter of Thecla with books in literature and art. By shifting our atten-tion to Thecla in this chapter and to other female characters from the *Apocryphal Acts of the Apostles* in the next, I hope to show that the transformations that biblical characters underwent—in textual transmission—are also evident in nonbiblical female characters. Combined, these transformations illustrate one manifestation of the sexual/textual politics in late antiquity, just as the emergence of the ideal female ascetic reader could be another. Furthermore, the textual contestations over female characters—their roles, their bodies, sexu-ality and asceticism, and their erotic depictions—betray controversies that circulated in which women served as the medium and locus on which the discourse of paradox hinged.

Transforming the Body of Thecla

As is the case with all of the female characters we have explored so far, the figure of Thecla underwent transformation in literary retellings, paraphrases, and expansions of the second-century *APT*.[4,5] The out-line of the second-century narrative is by now well known: Paul comes to Iconium and is welcomed into the house of Onesiphorus, where he begins preaching his message of continence, chastity, and purity (chaps. 1–6). A certain Thecla, "sitting at the window close by," hears him speak and she is so taken by his words praising chastity and self-control that she proceeds to cut off her engagement to her betrothed, Thamyris (7–10). Thamyris stirs up officials to bring Paul to trial because he has "deceived the city of the Iconians" and Thecla, in particular, after which Paul is sent to prison (11–17). Thecla, "by night," bribes the jailer and goes to Paul in prison, where she is found by her family and Thamyris, who subsequently inform the governor who brings them both before the tribunal, sentencing Paul to be flogged and thrown out of the city and Thecla to be burned (18–21). The fire, however, does not "touch her" and Thecla is saved (22). Thecla searches for Paul and finds him in a tomb with Onesiphorus and his family, whereupon she declares to Paul that she desires to cut her hair and follow him and asks him to baptize her, to which he responds, "be patient" (23–25). Paul then takes Thecla with him to Antioch, where she is immediately accosted by "a certain Syrian" named Alexander, and although she remains pure and manages to shame Alexander, she is taken again to the governor who condemns her to the wild beasts (26–27). While waiting to be thrown to the beasts, she is housed by "Queen Tryphaena" (whose dead daughter has spoken to her in a dream asking her to care for Thecla) and then thrown to the beasts, who proceed to "lay down at her feet" (28–33). In what might well be regarded as the climax of the story, Thecla notices a pool in the midst of the arena, throws herself in it, and baptizes herself (34). Subsequent attempts to kill her are similarly unsuccessful and the story concludes with Thecla dressing as a man, searching for and finding Paul in Myra, and finally "she went to Seleucia and enlightened many by the word of God; then she rested in a glorious sleep" (35–43).

Later endings to the *APT* highlight the dissatisfaction with the brief ending of the *APT* and betray the developing cult. Some Greek manuscripts continue after "Seleucia" and claim that she lives in a cave for seventy-two years when "certain men" come "to corrupt her," but she "entered into the rock alive and went underground. And she departed to Rome to see Paul and found that he had fallen asleep. And after staying there a short time, she rested in glorious sleep and she is buried about two or three stadia from the tomb of her master Paul" (thereby legitimating Rome as a cult center for Thecla veneration).[6] A much longer ending appears in another Greek manuscript and includes further trials she undergoes and miracles she performs, and finally concludes with her fleeing into the rock from "the lawless men" (but without a mention of Rome here). Both of these endings reflect subsequent appropriations of the Thecla story and are interwoven with her developing cult veneration.

Other retellings of the Thecla narrative similarly illuminate the use and transformation of the second-century narrative. Scott Johnson's study of the fifth-century paraphrase of *APT*, found in the *Life* portion of *The Life and Miracles of Saint Thecla*, has highlighted several key developments in the literary expansion of the story of Thecla: (1) the opening "encratic beatitudes" in the second-century narrative have been "de-asceticized" by the author of *LM*; (2) in the scene at the window when Thecla first hears Paul speaking, the author of *LM* has emphasized Thecla as a hearer and not a seer of Paul; (3) the author of *LM* reworks portions of *APT* to highlight the orthodoxy of Thecla in the Trinitarian language of the fourth century; (4) in the important prison scene from *APT*, where Thecla is found "bound to Paul in affection," the author of *LM* diffuses the erotic element by including a long speech by Paul in which Paul extols Thecla's piety and faith; (5) the baptismal scene is expanded to emphasize her readiness for martyrdom.[7]

In this last scene, I would extend Johnson's analysis even further. The phrase Thecla uses in *LM* for her baptism is "On this day I am baptized (ὑστέρα ἡμέρᾳ βαπτίζομαι)". Dagron notes that there are a number of diverse variants here, some of which excise Thecla's claim to baptism in this scene. It is not a coincidence that one of the most hotly contested features to the Thecla story comes to appear in the fifth-century paraphrase—Tertullian, in other words, was not alone in his concerns about the story being taken to support women's rights to baptize. Indeed, later writers who use the Thecla narrative seem consistently either to omit the baptismal scene altogether or distance Thecla as actor—take, for just one example, the fifth- or sixth-century pseudo-Chrysostom homily. Here Thecla's baptism is entirely omitted.

What is striking and informative is that precisely where we see subsequent retellings, paraphrases, or sermons transforming the narrative and figure of the second century, we find similar textual variants in the copying of the *APT* itself. In other words, textual transformation does not take place just in appropriations of Thecla but in the very work of scribes who copied and translated the *APT*. We have already seen this in the endings that scribes added. But I turn now to some examples taken from the *APT* of key passages that betray subsequent debates and discomfort with aspects of the second-century narrative. At certain junctures in the story, particularly where the erotic element comes to the fore, some scribes correct or corrupt—to use textual-critical terms—their texts by modifying or eliminating that very eroticism.

The first instance is found in Paul's opening sermon in Onesiphorus's house. Paul has just arrived in Iconium, and when Onesiphorus learns this, he goes out to meet Paul and invites him into his home. Paul's speech has parallels with Matthew's and Luke's beatitudes, but they take on both Pauline and ascetic overtones.

> Blessed are the pure in heart (οἱ καθαροὶ τῇ καρδία),
>   for they shall see God.
> Blessed are they who have kept their flesh pure
>   (οἱ ἁγνὴν τὴν σάρκα τηρήσαντες), for they
>   shall become a temple of God.
> Blessed are the self-controlled (οἱ ἐγκρατεῖς), for to
>   them will God speak.
> Blessed are they who have renounced this world
>   (οἱ ἀποταχάμενοι τῷ κοσμῷ τούτῳ), for they
>   shall be well pleasing unto God.
> Blessed are they who have wives as if they had them
>   not (οἱ ἔχοντες γυναίκας ὡς μὴ ἔχοντες), for they
>   shall be heirs to God.
>
>   —APT 5

Purity, renunciation, and self-control: these are the qualities worthy of blessing throughout the *Apocryphal Acts*. Egkrateia (ἐγκράτεια), which in earlier Greek classical literature, as well as Jewish Greek writing, meant *temperance* or *self-control*, throughout the *Apocryphal Acts* designates sexual abstinence or celibacy. The Latin translations further extend this meaning of ἐγκράτεια by using the term *abstinentes*.[8]

Paul's speech continues with themes that are less specifically ascetic: "Blessed are they who fear God, for they shall become angels of God. Blessed are they who tremble at the words of God, for they shall be comforted. Blessed are they who have received the wisdom of Jesus Christ, for they shall be called sons of the Most High," and so forth. The climax of Paul's speech, however, is concerned with bodies: "Blessed are the bodies of the virgins (τὰ σώματα τῶν παρθένων), for they shall be well pleasing to God, and shall not lose the reward of their purity" (ἁγνείας) (6). This last blessing is particularly striking: in light of the renunciation, transcendence, or transformation of the body in early Christian asceticism, the affirmation of the bodies (σώματα) of the virgins is rather peculiar; moreover, it is found in our best witnesses to the Greek text, as well as in the sixth-century Coptic papyrus in Heidelberg. Although it may be that this blessing is linked to Pauline notions of bodies as temples of the Holy Spirit (and this is supported by earlier statements in "Paul's" speech in Onesiphorus's house), it is precisely here that we find evidence of a textual contest over the virginal body: some scribes have re-formed the text by adding two words. In several eleventh- and twelfth-century Greek manuscripts, the text reads, "Blessed are the bodies and spirits/souls/breath (τὰ πνεύματα) of the virgins" rather than "Blessed are the bodies of the virgins." Likewise, the Syriac has "blessed are the bodies and the souls [*ruah*] of the virgins," and the Armenian has "souls and bodies of the virgins."[9] The addition of these words tempers the blessing of the body. Even more striking is a reading found in a fifteenth-century Latin manuscript in which "the bodies" are eliminated altogether and replaced with beati spiritus virginum. However we choose to translate *spiritus*—breath, soul, spirit—it is the incorporeal part of the body. Such variant readings betray a textual contest over the bodies of virgins.[10]

Thecla is transfixed by Paul's speech. She stays at her window, listening "night and day," watching the women and virgins going in to Paul. Her betrothed, Thamyris, comes looking for her, and her mother bemoans Thecla's state: "She sticks to the window like a spider, is moved by his words, and gripped by a new desire and a fearful passion; for the maiden hangs upon the things he says and is taken captive" (9). Once again, "a new desire and a fearful passion (ἐπιθυμία καινῇ καὶ πάθει δεινῷ)" is odd or, at the very least, paradoxical language in a text so overtly promoting celibacy. Evidently, it was also problematic for some scribes and translators. Some Greek manuscripts replace καινή (new) with δεινή (strange), clarifying that Thecla's desire for Paul is of a different kind from her desire for her betrothed. In one Latin manuscript,[11] "and a fearful passion" has been replaced with *atque nouae doctrinae*—a phrase that certainly carries little of the overtly erotic overtones of "a new desire and a fearful passion." In Conybeare's translation of the Armenian, the erotic element is excised altogether: "She strains her eyes to gaze upon a strange man, and hearkens to his words as if they were pleasing, though they are illusive and vain and disgusting."

Another contest over words takes place when Thecla visits Paul in prison—the erotic climax, if you will, of the entire story. Some time has passed since Paul's initial speech in Onesiphorus's house; by now, Thecla, thoroughly "gripped by a new desire," has severed ties with her fiancé. In his anger, Thamyris brings Paul before the authorities, claiming that "he has destroyed the city of the Iconians, and my betrothed, so that she will not have me" (15). After a brief exchange, the governor has Paul bound and "led off to prison until he should find leisure to give him a hearing" (18). As we can expect, Thecla searches for Paul. After bribing the doorkeeper (apparently she was locked in her room), Thecla goes to the prison. There she bribes the jailer, and then, we read, she "went in to Paul and sat at his feet and heard [him proclaim] the mighty acts of God. And Paul feared nothing, but comported himself with full confidence in God; and her faith was increased, as she kissed his fetters" (18). Before long, Thamyris and others come looking for Thecla and find her in the prison, "so to speak [or "in a certain way"], bound with him in affection" (19). It is impossible to miss the erotic language here: τρόπον τινὰ συνδεδεμένην τῇ στοργῇ.

The erotic image was not lost on the scribes who copied the passage. One of the scribes who added τὰ πνεύματα (the spirits) in the passage considered previously has here chosen to eliminate the whole phrase "in a certain way bound with him in affection." Simple haplography—that is, the possibility that the scribe simply skipped a line accidentally in the process of copying—cannot explain the omission. Rather, I would suggest that this omission is quite deliberate; it removes the erotic element with its potential dangers. No longer can readers (or hearers) "misread" or "misconstrue" the passage as suggesting an erotic embrace between Paul and Thecla; the purity of the passage, and the relationship, is preserved.

The versional evidence is even more striking in this instance, though not altogether uniform. For the phrase "so to speak, bound with him in affection," the Latin readings found in various manuscripts are as follows: "as though joined to his feet" (*quasi colligatam ad pedes eius*); "sitting by Paul's feet" (*Pauli pedibus assidentem*); "listening to God's teaching from Paul" (*doctrinam dei a Paulo audientem*); "sitting at the feet of Paul, joined in the desire of Christ" (*eam sedentem ad pedes Pauli, colligatam desiderio Christi*). Talk about cleaning up the story! But one Latin scribe, surprisingly, goes in the opposite direction, daringly describing Thecla as "having been bound with him in some kind of affection" (*quodam affectu eidem copulatam*).

The Syriac and Armenian versions appear to approach the problem from a different direction. Perhaps in response to the Greek narrative's problematic notion that Thecla was found alone with Paul in prison—and in a compromising position—the Syriac and Armenian translations make it clear that others were in the prison, thus preserving some sense of propriety. The Syriac, for example, reads, "And they went, as the doorkeeper told them, and found her sitting at Paul's feet, she and many persons, and they were listening to the great things of the Most High."[12] The Armenian reads, "So they went and found her as the doorkeeper told them; they came and found her sitting at the feet of Paul, and saw several other people as well who were listening to the great things of Christ."[13] The textual instability and narrative expansions or clarifications do not seem to be arbitrary here; multiple readings reveal ambivalences about the image of Thecla with Paul.

Another example occurs at a crucial juncture. Woven throughout the *APT* is the notion of transgressing gender boundaries. This motif or image is by now quite familiar from our early Christian materials (and we will return to it again in the next chapter): the *Passion of Perpetua*, for example, in which Perpetua is "stripped naked and becomes a man"; Jesus's closing statement in the *Gospel of Thomas*, "I will make Mary male"; the *Sayings of the Desert Mothers* that play with this notion; the quasi-transvestite narratives of Eugenia, Mary/Marinus, Pelagia, and others; Augustine's mother, who is manly in her faith; and so forth.[14] In the *APT*, Thecla's desire to bend genders pushes the limits of ancient gender constructions. At different points, she proposes to cut her hair short, wear a man's tunic, and follow Paul wherever he goes. The first declaration of her desire follows her visit to Paul in prison. By this time, Thecla's refusal to marry Thamyris has caused an uproar in town. When she is found in prison with Paul, the governor (apparently in an effort to keep some measure of peace) brings Paul and Thecla to trial. He asks her, "Why do you not marry Thamyris according to the law of the Iconians?" She remains silent, whereupon her mother cries out, "Burn the lawless one! Burn her that is no bride in the midst of the theater, that all the women who have been taught by this man may be afraid" (20). The governor then sentences Paul to be flogged and sent out of the city, and he condemns Thecla to be burned.

Thecla, however, survives the fire; indeed, "the fire did not touch her" (22). She is therefore released, and once again she seeks out Paul.

She finds him with Onesiphorus and his wife and children, praying and fasting in a tomb. Her arrival is the cause for joy: "Within the tomb there was much love, Paul rejoicing, and Onesiphorus and all of them" (25). Then Thecla makes her proposition: "I will cut my hair short and follow you wherever you go," but Paul denies her, saying, "The season is unfavorable, and you are comely (εὔμορφος). May no other temptation take hold of you, worse than the first, and you not endure it but play the coward." Thecla replies, "Only give me the seal in Christ, and temptation will not touch me." And Paul says, "Thecla, have patience and you will receive the water" (25). Note the adjective *comely—εὔμορφος—*well formed. The gender ambiguity of this word is significant: εὔμορφος is an adjective of two endings, masculine and neuter, where the masculine doubles for the feminine. Such gender ambiguity serves to emphasize exactly what Thecla is requesting— that she become like a man. Such subtlety was not lost on the scribes. The same scribes who amended the passages quoted previously have taken it upon themselves here to reemphasize Thecla's womanhood: They insert the word γυνή—γυνή εὔμορφος (a comely woman). If there was any doubt about Thecla's ability to transcend or transgress gender boundaries, these scribes eliminate it. On a small scale, we find here a process similar to that identified by Stephen Davis in his recent article on intertextuality in the stories of "transvestite saints," in which he argues that these "legends themselves never quite allow their readers to forget that the transvestite saint is still a woman by nature."[15]

I offer one final example of engendered textual variants, appearing this time in the scene of Thecla's persecution in the arena. "When she had finished her prayer, she turned and saw a great pit full of water, and said: 'Now it is time for me to wash.' And she threw herself in, saying: 'In the name of Jesus Christ I baptize myself on the last day!'" (34). We have some independent help in understanding how this particular passage might have been interpreted, for Tertullian admonishes those who take "Thecla's example as a license for women's teaching and baptizing," arguing that this text was written not by Paul but by a presbyter in Asia who was removed from office when his authorship was discovered (*De Baptismo* 17). Although there remain significant questions about Tertullian's report, what is interesting here for my purposes is that the problem of Thecla baptizing herself can be (and was) solved textually quite easily.[16] Some Latin manuscripts simply excise the whole passage: "And she threw herself in, saying: 'In the name of Jesus Christ I baptize myself on the last day!'" Others use not a reflexive construction but rather a simple passive, so that Thecla declares not "I baptize myself" but "I am baptized (*ego baptizor*)". The Syriac and Armenian also use a simple passive construction, supporting the removal of Thecla's own agency.

In these passages, I would argue that we see scribes emphasizing the incorporeal aspect of virgins, excising erotically suggestive passages, and reaffirming Thecla's inability to transcend her female body. Blessing the bodies of virgins was as problematic as depicting them bound in affection with an apostle and/or able to become like a man. In each case, the effort to circumscribe and control the virginal body is paramount. Carlin Barton has illuminated "the paradox of the eye" in Roman antiquity.[17] I suggest a similar paradox here. It is precisely because the body is both powerful and vulnerable that we find it so hotly contested in early Christian books. Books, likewise, were a powerful resource and arena for debates about the human body among early Christians, and perhaps because of their power, they were vulnerable to corruption and manipulation. Not only could they be erased and reinscribed—reused as palimpsests—but their words could also be altered in the process of copying and translation.

Thecla and Books

If Thecla's body comes to be refashioned in the transmission of the second-century *APT* (Thecla in the book), her image also undergoes a transformation with regard to her connection to books (Thecla and books). One of the interesting features to the development of Thecla veneration is the emergence of a tradition that associates Thecla with books. Although the iconography of Thecla most commonly depicts her with wild beasts around her—as we find especially in the ampullae associated with her cultic sites—there are a number of images of Thecla with books. Take, for example, the mosaic of female saints from the beautiful Byzantine Katholikon at Hosios Loukas. In the center of this lunette, located on the western wall, just to the right of the entrance to the church, we find Constantine and Helen. Moving clockwise, we find Saints Agatha, Eugenia, Febronia, Anastasia, and Thecla (next to Constantine). What is striking is that Thecla is the only saint here with a book (and cross) in her hand. And if this image is not sufficient to convince us that there is something unusual about Thecla here, across the entrance on the other western wall lunette we find the mosaic of Saints Juliana, Marina, Euphemia, Barbara, Catherine, and Irene, and not one of these saints holds a book. Even more striking is that the image of the book in Thecla's hand is identical to the image of a book in Paul's hand in an arch just opposite. Why, then, is Thecla the one female saint with a book? It may well be that she is the only saint considered apostolic and that is the end of the story— and the appearance of only Thecla and Mary Magdalene with books in the later church of Kalambaka in Thessaly may well support this. But I think there is more to the depiction.

In the second-century *APT*, books play virtually no role. At the very outset of the narrative, Paul comes into Iconium with Demas and Hermogenes, whom "he loved greatly, so that he sought to make sweet to them all the words of the Lord" (*APT* 1). Only later manuscript tradition adds the following after "Lord": "of the teachings and interpretations of the Gospel."[18] In Paul's opening

FIGURE 5.1. Mosaic lunette from western wall of Hosios Loukas Katholikon. Mount Helikon, Greece. Courtesy of author.

speeches at Onesiphorus's house, there is no mention of the Gospel; Paul speaks, and Thecla hears. But such absences did not prevent later images from inserting the Gospel into the story. Take, for example, the image found on a fifth-century Roman ivory plaque from a casket.

Here we see Thecla gazing from her window (or rooftop?) at Paul, who preaches with scroll in hand. The image is quite similar to the much later scene in the Thecla altar from Tarragona, Spain, where Paul holds a book—here a codex—in his right hand while Thecla gazes from her window, although here the sight lines make it clear that Thecla hears Paul but does not see him.[19]

As the *APT* continues, Thecla later teaches Tryphaena the word of God, and the text concludes with Thecla enlightening "many in the word of God"; subsequent endings added to the second-century narrative include the miracle of her escape into the rock and being transported to Rome, but books still do not appear. There is just one passage in the second-century narrative in its earliest form that mentions the Gospel—nearly at the end when Thecla goes one last time to find

FIGURE 5.2. Ivory panel detail of Paul and Thecla. Courtesy of Erich Lessing/Art Resource.

Paul and says to him, "I have received the bath, Paul; for he who has worked with you for the Gospel has also worked with me for my baptism" (Ἔλαβον τὸ λουτρόν, Παῦλε. Ὁ γὰρ σοὶ συνεργήσας εἰς τὸ εὐαγγέλιον κἀμοὶ συνήργησεν εἰς τὸ λούσασθαι). Thecla then declares to Paul that she is going to Iconium, and he responds with his "commission": "Go and teach the word of God!" (Ὕπαγε καὶ δίδασκε τὸν λόγον τοῦ θεοῦ) (*APT* 40–41). In this brief exchange, Thecla recognizes Paul working for the Gospel (although it is hardly clear that this refers to a book per se), and Paul commissions Thecla. It is here we see the beginnings of Thecla's role as teacher, but this is not sufficient to explain a subsequent connection between Thecla and books (recall that Irene is also depicted as a teacher and yet her image does not come to be associated with books).

The earliest textual source that begins to expand the image of Thecla as teacher is the third-century *Symposium* of Methodius. We can now unpack this source further.[20] Methodius depicts Thecla as the winner in the contest of words between the women arguing the merits of virginity; furthermore, on three occasions in particular he notes her intellect, the first of which appears just before Thecla begins her lengthy speech:

> Thecla said, "It is my turn after her to continue the contests; and I rejoice, since I too have the favoring wisdom of words (τὴν σοφίαν τῶν λόγων), perceiving that I am, like a harp, inwardly attuned, and prepared to speak with elegance and propriety." Arete [replies]: "I most willingly hail thy readiness, O Thecla, in which I confide to give me fitting discourse, in accordance with thy powers; since thou wilt yield to none in universal philosophy and instruction, instructed by Paul in what is fitting to say of evangelical and divine doctrine (φιλοσοφίας τε γὰρ τῆς ἐγκυκλίου καὶ παιδείας οὐδενὸς ἐστερήσεις, τῆς εὐαγγελικῆς τε αὖ καὶ θείας, τί χρὴ καὶ λέγειν, παρὰ Παύλῳ σεσοφισμένην)."
>
> —*Symp.* 7.9

Methodius here has taken the image of Paul working on behalf of God and teaching the Gospel and attached this explicitly to Thecla— here Paul instructs Thecla and now Thecla is imbued with wisdom and philosophy. At the conclusion of Thecla's speech, we have a discussion between Euboulius (aka Methodius) and Gregorion about the merits of Thecla's speech and this discussion confirms the claims made before she speaks:

> Euboulius: How bravely and magnificently, O Gregorion, has Thecla debated!
> Gregorion: What, then, would you have said, if you had listened to herself, speaking fluently, and with easy expression, with much grace and pleasure? So that she was admired by everyone who attended, her language blossoming with words, as she set forth intelligently, and in fact picturesquely, the subjects on which she spoke, her countenance suffused with the blush of modesty; for she is altogether brilliant in body and soul (ὅλη γὰρ εἶναι πέφυκε λευκὴ καὶ σῶμα καὶ ψυχήν).
> Euboulius: Rightly do you say this, Gregorion, and none of these things is false; for I knew her wisdom also from other noble actions, and what sort of things she succeeded in speaking, giving proof of supreme love to Christ; and how glorious she often appeared in meeting the chief conflicts of the martyrs, procuring for herself a zeal equal to her courage, and a strength of body equal to the wisdom of her counsels (ἴσην τῇ προθυμίᾳ τὴν σπουδὴν κεκτημένη καὶ τῇ ἀκμῇ τῶν βουλευμάτων τὴν ῥώμην τοῦ σώματος).
>
> —*Symp.* 8.17

"Brilliant in body and soul," "strength of body equal to [her] wisdom"—such images extend the dual aspect of Thecla's career, as protomartyr and teacher, well beyond the *APT*, and although books do not specifically appear in the *Symposium*, we certainly have Thecla connected to intellectual life.

In the fifth-century *Life and Miracles*, Thecla is connected to books in three key chapters, two of which serve to legitimate the author's collection itself. In fact, these are passages that say less about Thecla and more about the rhetorical construction of the author: in the first instance, Thecla appears to the author while he is writing and "She took from [his] hand the tablet (ἀφαιρεῖσθαί μου τῆς χειρὸς τὴν τετράδα)"; then, after appearing to read, she gave the author an approving smile, thereby authorizing his collection (*Mir.* 31).[21] Near the end of the work, the author inserts another miracle related to Thecla's approval: in this case, Thecla appears to him at night "and offers always a book or a parchment to me (βιβλίον τί μοι πάντως ἢ χάρτην ὤρεγεν)" (*Mir.* 41); again here, Thecla offers the author her approval of his work. In one of the *Miracles*, Thecla performs a

miracle of giving literacy to a certain Xenarchis—a striking confir-
mation not just of Thecla's ability to heal but also of her own literacy
and intellect. Some person—"whether a man or a woman" the author
is not able to say—gave Xenarchis a book and "the book was the Gospel (τὸ δὲ βιβλίον εὐαγγέλοιν ἦν)". When she takes hold of the
book, despite her apparent illiteracy, "she began to read (ἄρχεται καὶ
ἀναγιγνώσκειν)", an astonishing miracle to the women around her
(*Mir.* 45). Although we cannot press this story too far, the *Miracles*
do attest to a greater attention to literacy, authorial composition, and
Thecla as both healer and intellectual than we find in the *APT*. And
this makes good sense given the emergence of ascetic women
readers—at least in literary and iconographic representation—in the
fourth century and later. Derek Krueger's attention to the role of
Thecla as patron of the author of the *Miracles* has highlighted well
the image of Thecla as a patron saint of letters;[22] however, I want to
press the connection between Thecla and books further.

FIGURE 5.3. Painting of Adam, Eve, Paul, and Thecla from the dome of
the Chapel of Peace. Fifth to sixth centuries. El Bagawat, Egypt. Courtesy
of Ken Parry.

Strikingly, the images we find of Thecla in the *Life and Miracles* appear at nearly the same time period as the most important visual imagery we have for Thecla with a book—that of the painting from the Chapel of the Peace in Egypt. To my mind, indeed, the most fascinating iconography related to Thecla, writing, and books is that found in this fifth- or sixth-century chapel at El-Bagawat in the Kharga Oasis, Egypt. Although Ahmed Fakhry's initial publication of the necropolis included photographs of the painting of Paul and Thecla in the Chapel of Peace, more recent publications and photographs—particularly those of Stephen Davis—lend themselves to a very different interpretation.[23]

Moving from left to right across the image, found on the dome of the chapel, we find Adam and Eve with the serpent coiled around a palm between them; then comes Thecla and Paul, and just beyond Paul is Mary with a dove (Holy Spirit). The name of each of these figures is inscribed just above them higher on the dome, so there is no ambiguity here about identification. The image, however, can be read in multiple ways, now that we have observed the transformation of female biblical characters and the multiple images of Thecla. Take, for example, the proximity of Eve and Thecla (sinner and saint) or the symmetry between Eve and Mary (all the more fitting given Eve is the bringer of death and Mary the bringer of life). But now we can turn to the key scene for us—that of Thecla and Paul. Fakhry described the scene as follows:

> Paul and Thekla . . . sit facing one another on folding stools with legs crossed. Paul wears a white robe and has a shawl put over his head. He holds in his right hand a pen and in his left hand there is an object which might be the ink-pot. . . . He tries to write in a book held between the hands of Thekla. Thekla wears a green dress whose folds are drawn in either dark green or red lines. Her blonde hair falls in curls over her shoulders, the white long veil is put over her head and falls at the sides.[24]

Central to Fakhry's interpretation are Paul's and Thecla's hands. According to Fakhry, Thecla holds the tablet and offers Paul a writing surface, and Paul writes: a passive Thecla, an active Paul. However, Stephen Davis has recently offered a different—and, in my view, far more persuasive—description of the scene:

> On the south side of the dome (above the doorway), the two figures sit facing each other. . . . [Thecla's] eyes are cast down toward her lap where she holds a yellow book or a writing tablet. Thecla writes in the book with a pen, while Paul sits across from her on the right, gesturing toward the book with a pointing stick he holds in his hand.[25]

The difference here concerns how one interprets the two implements Thecla and Paul hold in their hands—that Thecla also holds a stylus-shaped implement seems clear from close examination of the painting itself. If so, then this appears to be the earliest image of Thecla with a book. Do we also here have a sense of Thecla as a writer or a scribe? If so, might we read the image in concert with the tradition about Codex Alexandrinus, with which we began? Although the colophon naming Thecla as scribe of that fifth-century codex is much later, it is difficult to imagine where the tradition developed if there was not already a tradition about Thecla as scribe.

Conclusion

The richness of the Thecla traditions provides an important focus for any treatment of women and books in early Christianity. If, as Mary Wollstonecraft argued long ago, "every individual is . . . a world in itself,"[26] Thecla is precisely such a world. And she returns us again to books and bodies. The textual transmission of the *APT* highlights the refashioning of bodies, ascetic and erotic, while the subsequent development of the story of Thecla offers a window into the early stages of images of women with books—a precursor, if you will, to the contemplative woman of the Middle Ages absorbed in reading.

Contesting the Ascetic Language of Eros

Textual Fluidity in the Apocryphal Acts of the Apostles

A new monk arrives at the monastery. He is assigned to help the other monks in copying the old texts by hand. He notices, however, that they are copying copies, not the original books. So, the new monk goes to the head monk to ask him about this. He points out that if there was an error in the first copy, that error would be continued in all of the other copies. The head monk says, "We have been copying from the copies for centuries, but you make a good point, my son." So, he goes down into the cellar with one of the copies to check it against the original. Hours later, nobody has seen him. So, one of the monks goes downstairs to look for him. He hears sobbing coming from the back of the cellar and finds the old monk leaning over one of the original books crying. He asks what's wrong. The old monk sobs, "The word is celebrate!*"*

—Anonymous joke

"IT IS GOOD FOR A MAN NOT TO TOUCH A WOMAN," THE CONGREGA-
tion at Corinth wrote to Paul sometime in the middle of the first
century (1 Cor. 7:1). Paul's response to their statement, which betrayed
a debate among themselves about the comparative virtues of marriage
and celibacy, was hardly the end of the controversy. In fact, his response
(found in 1 Cor. 7) "proved sufficiently elastic to enable exegetes to
express their varied ascetic preferences while expounding a text that
they considered immutable and eternally valid."[1] One striking feature
of the debates about marriage, asceticism, and celibacy is the appearance of textual variants in the books of the New Testament as well as a
host of other early Christian texts that intersect well with these debates;
in fact, in some cases, variants betray quite well how debates about
ideology and praxis—in this case, the theory and practice of asceticism—made their way into the transmission of early Christian texts.
Even though we do not have textual support for the scenario imagined
in the preceding joke—*celebrate* or *celibate?*—there have been attempts
to bring together a number of ascetically oriented variant readings
(e.g., the addition of "and fasting" at Mark 9:29; variants related to John
the Baptist's diet) found in New Testament texts.[2] My focus in this
chapter, however, is specifically on sexual asceticism, and the sexual/
textual politics that emerged in the midst of debates about celibacy.[3]

Asceticism and the New Testament: Debating Marriage and Celibacy

Christians such as Clement of Alexandria, writing against opponents
both libertine and ascetic, took a broadly middle ground in the celi-
bacy/marriage debates: "We bless sexual abstinence in those to whom
this condition has been given by God, but we also marvel at mo-
nogamy and the holiness of a single marriage (ἡμεῖς εὐνουχίαν μὲν
καὶ οἷς τοῦτο δεδώρηται ὑπὸ θεοῦ μακαρίζομεν, μονογαμίαν δὲ
καὶ τὴν περὶ τὸν ἕνα γάμον σεμνότητα θαυμάζομεν) (*Strom.*
3.1.4).[4] Epiphanius likewise catalogs the sexual sins of heretics—
either by their claims that marriage is from the devil (e.g., Encratites)
or by being altogether too licentious (e.g., Carpocratians)—in his
well-known *Panarion*. Likewise, Jerome, Augustine, Ambrose, John
Chrysostom, and Pelagius (among numerous others) write extensively on the comparative merits of marriage versus celibacy, and in

each case, their claims betray widespread debate. To explain why and how Christians come to develop a discourse privileging virginity over marriage goes beyond my aim here;[5] rather, I hope to demonstrate that the ongoing debates about celibacy find their way into the transmission of early Christian literature.

Such debates, however, were not simply about interpreting Paul, though interpretation of scripture was a central component (imagine the hermeneutical athletics necessary for ascetically minded interpreters of the passage "Be fruitful and multiply!").[6] The debates went beyond interpretation to the very words of individual texts and passages. Indeed, a wide array of textual variants suggests that a malleable, "living" text played an important role in shaping and explaining diverse interpretations, which could then make their way back into the transmission of the text. In many cases, we simply cannot know whether a variant was introduced by scribes or editors to "resolve" some hermeneutical problem or whether the fact that there were different readings led to divergent interpretations. But divergent readings certainly aided the proliferation of distinct interpretations. Consider, for example, Clement of Alexandria's radical claim that Paul was married—all the more surprising given the subsequent interpretation of Paul's attitude toward marriage and his claims about his own status as unmarried: "Paul," Clement writes, "did not hesitate to greet his *syzygos* (i.e., *wife*) in one of his letters" (*Strom.* 3.6.53), a reference to Philippians 4:3 where Paul addresses his "true yokefellow (γνήσιε σύζυγε)". Clement (and later Origen) understood Paul's *syzygos* as his wife, not an implausible translation of the term; modern interpreters and translators have argued that either it should be read as a proper name (Syzygos), a code for the congregation as a whole, or a likeminded companion of Paul.[7]

The debate between Jerome and Helvidius over the virginity of Mary is particularly illuminating in this regard. Helvidius—about whom we know nothing apart from Jerome's treatise—apparently ranked virginity below marriage and argued that Mary bore children subsequent to Jesus. And much of his argument appears to have depended on very careful readings of gospel narratives and, in some cases, upon specific variant readings. About the year 383 CE, Jerome responds to Helvidius, calling on "God the Father to show that the mother of His Son, who was a mother before she was a bride, continued a Virgin after her son was born" and claiming that he will "adduce the actual words of Scripture (*ipsa Scripturarum verba ponenda sunt*)" to support his position (*Against Helvidius* 2). When Jerome comes to "proving" that Joseph did not touch Mary, he does indeed bring scripture to bear:

> You [i.e., Helvidius] cannot for shame say Joseph did not know of [the miraculous events prophesying Jesus's birth], for Luke tells us, "His father and mother were marveling at the things which were spoken concerning him." And yet you with marvelous effrontery contend that the reading of the Greek manuscripts is corrupt (*Graecis codicibus falsata contendas*), although it is that which nearly all the Greek writers have left us in their books, and not only so, but several of the Latin writers have taken the words in the same way. Nor need we now consider the variations in the copies, since the whole record both of the Old and New Testament has since that time been translated into Latin, and we must believe that the water of the fountain flows purer than that of the stream.[8]
>
> (*Against Helvidius* 8)

The passage at issue is Luke 2:33, where we find, indeed, two principal divergent readings in a variety of Greek manuscripts and versions.

> And his father and mother were marveling at the things that were said about him (καὶ ἦν ὁ πατὴρ αὐτοῦ καὶ ἡ μήτηρ θαυμάζοντες ἐπὶ τοῖς λαλουμένοις περὶ αὐτοῦ).
>   —Attested in important and diverse witnesses such as the fourth-century Codices Sinaiticus and Vaticanus, Codex Bezae, the Freer Gospel Codex, a number of important minuscules, and Latin, Syriac, and Coptic versions

> And Joseph and his mother were marveling at the things that were said about him (καὶ ἦν Ἰωσὴφ καὶ ἡ μήτηρ . . .).
>   —Found in a number of uncial manuscripts, Family 13, the majority text, old Latin and vulgate manuscripts, and also in some Syriac and Bohairic Coptic versions; with just the addition of the definite article before "Joseph" this is also the reading found in the fifth-century Codex Alexandrinus

On the surface, the problem is simple: Is Joseph Jesus's father? And, if so, in what sense? But more critical is the nature of Joseph's relationship to Mary. Thus, what reading better protects Mary's purity and chastity? Helvidius, apparently, preferred (or simply used) the latter reading ("Joseph") and Jerome clearly favors the former reading. Although Jerome argues in favor of the reading most textual critics find has better claims to originality, the issue for us is less about determining originality than highlighting the way in which debates about virginity and celibacy—here through the perpetual virginity of Mary—depended on the very words of scripture. In other words, the debate here highlights one of the ways scripture is deployed in an argument. Whereas Jerome's text seems at odds with what he wants to argue (i.e., that Joseph and Mary never consummated their marriage and they both remained virgins), the more crucial point for him is that Joseph knew about the specialness of Jesus and therefore would never have imagined touching Mary.

The Language of Paradox: Eroticism and Asceticism

> *. . . the affinity between asceticism and narrative lies in their common interest and investment in temptation.*
>
> —Geoffrey Harpham, *Ascetic Imperative*, 67

As we have already seen in our look at the textual tradition of the *Acts of Paul and Thecla*, the striking and paradoxical language of eroticism in the service of an ascetic message could sometimes be contested in the transmission of texts. The best visual analogy for the process here is the censorship of art that is considered too pornographic—the covering of naked genitals in the Sistine Chapel is just one of the most well-known examples. The Thecla tradition does not stand alone in this respect—indeed, the transmission of other texts leaves traces of concern about erotic language. Recall our discussion of the Mary and Martha story in chapter 4 where the textual variants surrounding Martha's "welcome" of Jesus may well bear traces of the concern for the appropriate relationship between them. Appearances—especially appearances that emerge from paradoxical language—can compromise the message. Here a few examples mostly taken from the *Acts of Thomas* and the *Acts of Andrew* will suffice, I hope, to demonstrate my point and open possibilities for further study.

Acts of Thomas

The *Apocryphal Acts Thomas*, a text likely written originally in Syriac in the third century, has, like the *APT*, prominent women at the center of several narratives: thus, for example, the flute-girl plays a central role in Act One (chaps. 1–16) and Mygdonia is a lead character in Acts Nine to Eleven (82–138); throughout, other women appear and the storyline depends on them.[9] One of the important characteristics of the *AT* is its strong advocacy of asceticism, leading some scholars to argue variously for a Manichean or Encratite background to the text. That the *Apocryphal Acts* were contested among the orthodox and the Manicheans, we have come to recognize well; take, for example, the unmitigated praise for the women of the *Apocryphal Acts* in Manichean Psalms:

> A despiser (κατα φρονεῖν) of the body (σῶμα) is Thecla, the lover of God. A shamer of the serpent is Maximilla the faithful (πιστός). A receiver of good news is Iphidama her sister also. . . . A champion in the fight (ἀγών) is Aristobula the enduring one. A giver of Light . . . is Eubula the noble woman (εὐγενής), drawing the heart of the prefect (ἡγεμών). A . . . that loves [her] master is Drusiane, the lover of God. . . .
>
> —*Psalms of Heracleides 25–32*[10]

This representation of these women, as we shall see, is only one side of their reception history. Note in particular how the blessing on the bodies at the outset of *APT* has here been transformed into the image of Thecla as a despiser of bodies. But while we might focus our attention on how debates about heresy collided (or colluded) with those about women—indeed, Virginia Burrus has shown us well how the "orthodox virgin has her counterpart in the figure of the heretical harlot"—we do well also to regard the *AT* as part of the fabric of what Peter Brown has called the "wild and wooly" Syrian asceticism of late antiquity.[11]

In the opening narrative, Judas Thomas is instructed to leave Jerusalem and go to India; he sails with the "merchant Abban" to a city called Andrapolis, where there is a wedding. Abban and Thomas decide to go to the wedding and while they are there, a "Hebrew," "a flute-girl, holding her flute in her hand, went round them all; and when she came to the place where the apostle was she stood over him, playing the flute over his head a long time" (ἔστη ἀπάνω αὐτοῦ καταυλοῦσα πρὸς τὴν κεφαλὴν αὐτοῦ ὥραν πολλήν) (AT 5). The image here is suggestive and the text carefully goes on to indicate that Thomas does not actually look at her: "And as the apostle looked to the ground (αὐτοῦ δὲ εἰς τὴν γῆν ἀφορῶντος), one of the cup-bearers stretched forth his hand and struck him. And the apostle, having raised his eyes (ἐμβλέψας), looked at the man who had struck him" (AT 6). Thomas then proceeds to sing a hymn about the "maiden [who] is the daughter of light"; immediately afterward, he concludes his song, which the text tells us was in Hebrew and only the flute-girl could understand him. Although she plays the flute now for others at the party, she

> repeatedly looked back and gazed at him (ἀφεώρα καὶ ἀπέβλεπεν). For she loved (ἠγάπησεν) him as one belonging to her race, and he was also beautiful in appearance above all who were there. And when the flute-girl had finished her flute-playing, she sat down opposite him, and looked steadily at him (ἀφορῶσα καὶ ἀτενίζουσα εἰς αὐτόν). But he looked at no one at all, neither did he pay attention to anyone, but kept his eyes only on the ground (αὐτὸς δέ ὅλως εἰς οὐδένα ἀφεώρα οὐδὲ προσεῖχεν τινι, εἰ μὴ μόνον εἰς τὴν γῆν ἔχων τοὺς οφθαλμοὺς αὐτοῦ προσεῖχεν).
>
> —AT 8

What should we make of the focus here on the gaze? The flute-girl plays the flute around his head, but he does not look at her; she gazes steadily at him after he sings, but he keeps his eyes focused on the ground. Given the significance of sight in antiquity, and in particular the gaze, the attention here on eyes is important.[12] Most instructive is that the gaze in these passages comes to be a site of textual variants. In the first instance, some Greek manuscripts apparently simply delete the passage that has her playing the flute "around his head"; in the flute-girl's gazing at Thomas with such focus, we find a series of variants that serve to minimize the emphasis on the gaze or omit it altogether. The Syriac likewise works especially to emphasize that Thomas's gaze stays away from the flute-girl. In the first instance after she plays "over him," the Syriac inserts "Judas did not lift up his face, but was looking all the while on the ground."[13]

The story of Mygdonia later in the AT provides some key variants that share much with what we have seen in the story of Thecla.

Mygdonia, like Thecla, comes to hear the apostle, in this case Judas Thomas, preach a sermon about meekness, temperance, and holiness, though the sermon is less explicitly ascetic than what we find in the *APT*. When he concludes, Mygdonia throws herself at his feet and beseeches him, "Care for me and pray for me, that the mercy of God, whom you preach, may come upon me and I become his dwelling place and be joined in the prayer and in the hope and in the faith in him" (καὶ καταλλαγῶ ἐν τῇ εὐχῇ καὶ τῇ ἐλίδι καὶ τῇ πίστει αὐτοῦ) (*AT* 87). The Syriac, on the other hand, reads the passage somewhat differently: Mygdonia falls down at his feet and begs him to pray for her so that, she says, "I may become a handmaiden of Him, and that I too may be united with you in prayer and in hope and in thanks-giving, and that I too may become a holy temple and He may dwell in me." Given the implications of the language of unification that we have already seen (recall Thecla bound up in Paul's fetters), I do not think it is insignificant that there are two different readings here, and the Syriac may well be the earlier text.

As the tension in the narrative begins to mount—Mygdonia converts to Thomas's message of celibacy and refuses to have intercourse with her husband Charisius—there are several variants in passages about nakedness. For example, Mygdonia prays that she will be able to withstand Charisius's "shamelessness" and then she takes "herself, veiled, to her bed"; at least one manuscript, however, omits that she is veiled. In the subsequent narrative, it becomes clear why the veil is important (and the Syriac indicates that after she prays, "she covered herself and lay down") (*AT* 97). Immediately following, the Greek and Syriac read (respectively): "Having eaten, Charisius came near her" and "Karish, as soon as he had eaten, came and stood over her, and took off his clothes." Naked or covered—the appearance is quite different and the key issue here is whether Mygdonia sees Charisius's/Karish's nakedness. The same manuscript that omits "veil" in the Greek also omits Charisius "came near her"; and in the Syriac, the covering becomes quite clear. It is worth setting these variants against a later passage—the scene of Mygdonia's baptism. Here Mygdonia stands "before the apostle with uncovered head" and the apostle asks "the nurse (Marcia) to undress her and put around her a linen dress" (*AT* 121). In the Syriac, however, the apostle instructs Narkia/Marcia "to anoint her and to put a cloth round her loins," a reading that removes the image of a naked Mygdonia (even temporarily) before Thomas.

Margaret Miles has identified the multiple interpretations of "naked baptism" by Christian writers (e.g., stripping off the old life in imitation of Christ; leaving the world; death and rebirth; a reference to "naked and unashamed" from Genesis; "quasi-martyrdom"; "stripping off the body"; and evocative of the bridal chamber);[14] behind such attention to and interpretations of the practice and the ideology behind it, I would suggest, lurks an a priori need to explain that which is problematic. If this is the case, it is not surprising to find that baptismal scenes, with attendant nakedness, become ripe for textual manipulation. Consider here also the passage from the *Apocryphal Acts of John*, in which Drusiana's dead body is stripped by her would-be lover and the variant readings about the clothing left on her body: Is she stripped to some sort of "doubly fringed" undergarment (δικρόσσιον) or to a "shroud" (καρκάλιον)? The former term is found, with great variation in orthography, in most manuscripts of the passage, and the latter just in one manuscript. It may well be, as Junod and Kaestli argue, that the appearance of the latter term is an attempt to eliminate the rare term *dikrossion* and not an attempt at moralizing, but the effect certainly is one that clarifies and resolves ambiguity about her nakedness. The concern with seeing nakedness appears a few chapters later, when Andronicus comes to Drusiana's grave and finds Callimachus and Fortunatus dead (νεκρούς) or naked (γυμνούς)—the manuscripts here offer two very different texts.

A final variant is worth consideration in the *AT*'s Greek version of Mygdonia's speech to Charisius (her rejected husband) just following her baptism by Thomas; throughout her speech, she compares her (former) marriage to Charisius to her present marriage to Jesus: "That bridal chamber is taken down, but this remains forever. That bed was spread with coverings, but this with love and faith" (*AT*, Act 10). We can note here again the erotic language co-opted in the service of celibacy: ἐκείνη ἡ κλίνη πάρεσιν κατέστρωται, αὕτη δὲ στοργῇ τε καὶ πίστει. Likewise, we find the absence of the passage in one of the Greek witnesses. There is a close parallel to this scene in the *Acts of Peter*. Here we find two competing readings in the passage regarding Albinus's feelings toward Xantippe (his wife who has just rejected him): Is he "raging like a mad man and passionately loving (ἐρῶν) Xantippe" or "suffering and raging like a mad man after/for Xantippe" (*AP* 34)?

Each of these can be viewed alongside the case of Thecla's longing for Paul. While it would be going too far to say that such passages were changed because of their erotic imagery, nevertheless, the readings produced by the various manuscripts permit quite different interpretations. Recently, Derek Krueger has discussed the following story found only in the Latin version of John Moschos's *Spiritual Meadow*: Abba Stephen the Cappadocian is in the church when he sees two naked anchorites about to enter the church; Stephen begs them to take him with them when they are about to depart, but they refuse.[15] Although we cannot know precisely why this story does not appear in some of the manuscripts of the *Spiritual Meadow*, Krueger's suggestion that the story "inhabits the liminal space between the erotic and its sublimation" may be one piece to the puzzle.[16] Indeed, the excision of such a story fits well with what is beginning to come into focus: narratives of desire, especially those with particularly erotic overtones, appear to be especially vulnerable to textual corruptions/corrections.

Acts of Andrew

The *Apocryphal Acts of Andrew* is similarly tantalizingly full of divergent readings that intersect with eroticism and asceticism, though the textual remains here permit only glimpses of the malleable textual tradition. For the story of Maximilla that is relevant to our study, the primary witnesses are three medieval Greek witnesses, two of which must certainly come from the same recension and the third of which is fragmentary; in addition, sections of the *AA* are found in Gregory's *Epitome* and other retellings.[17] That there was a controversy about this text, and especially its Manichean tendencies (or use by Manicheans), is evident in the fifth-century Evodius of Uzzala's recasting of the story of Eucleia. Moreover, his recasting highlights debates not only about the overarching message of the book but also about the character of Maximilla herself. According to *AA*, Maximilla tries to ward off her husband Ageates's sexual advances by offering him her maid Eucleia. The story here tells of a wanton, demanding, and boastful Eucleia, and an exonerable and chaste Maximilla. Note, however, how Evodius tells the story:

> Observe, in the Acts of Leucius which he wrote under the name of the apostles, what manner of things you accept about Maximilla the wife of Egetes: who, refusing to pay her due to her husband (though the

apostle had said "Let the husband pay the due to the wife and likewise the wife to the husband"), imposed her maid Euclia upon her husband, decking her out, as it is there written, with wicked enticements and paintings, and substituted her as deputy for herself at night, so that he in ignorance used her as his wife.[18]

Here Maximilla has become disobedient of scripture, opportunistic, and deceptive. The picture is entirely changed. Controversy precisely about this narrative may explain, too, why the passages from *AA* found in Epiphanius the Monk do not include the story and likewise why it is missing from the *Laudatio's* excerpts.

On another occasion, a small textual change effects a very different sense, much like what we found in the *Acts of Paul and Thecla*. Recall the variants in the *APT* related to who is in the prison when Thecla is found there—just Thecla or Thecla with many others. Similarly, in *AA*, after one of Andrew's speeches there are two versions of his audience:

> And after he had spoken (ὁμιλήσας) with the brethren (ἀδελφοῖς) for some time, he sent each one (ἕκαστον) away to their home saying to them (αὐτοῖς), "Neither are you are ever forsaken by me, servants (δοῦλοι) of Christ, because of the love in him, nor will I be forsaken by you because of that mediation." And each went away to his house (καὶ ἀπηλλάγη ἕκαστος εἰς τὰ αὐτοῦ).
>
> —*AA* 34, ms. V

> And after speaking to the women for a long time (καὶ δὴ προσομιλήσαντος αὐταῖς ἐπὶ πολλὰς ὥρας τλος ἀπέπεμψατο αὐτὰς εἰρηκώς), at last he sent them away, saying, "Go in peace, for you know well, maidservants of the Lord (δοῦλαι τοῦ κυρίου), that neither are you ever forsaken by me because of the love in him, nor will I be forsaken by you because of that mediation.
>
> —*AA* 34, mss. H, S

The effects of these two brief narratives are different. In the first, the audience is a general one, though one might infer even that it is a male audience. For the second, it is specifically a female audience, and Andrew speaks more directly toward them.

In another passage, a simple omission serves to obscure the erotic implications. Recall that in the *APT*, there were textual changes at the moment when Thecla is found kissing Paul's fetters in the prison.

In *AA*, there is also textual variation in at least one instance of kissing, once again in the prison. Maximilla, along with Iphidama, goes to meet Andrew in the prison and upon finding him there, "she placed his hands on her eyes, and then brought [them] to her mouth and kissed [them] (καὶ τὰς χεῖρας αὐτοῦ εἰς τὰς ἰδίας ὄψεις θεῖσα καὶ τῷ στόματι προσφέρουσα κατεφίλει). The variant here is a simple one: in the Vatican manuscript, the final word—*kissed*—is missing. We might well argue that bringing the hands to her mouth already implies kissing, but the precise language is absent. Even if we recognize that greeting with a kiss is a very early Christian practice, the appearance of variants at these moments suggests, or rather illustrates what we know from other sources—namely, that the Christian kiss was a controversial practice.[19] In addition to this passage from *AA* and that from *APT*, the *Acts of John* also contains a "kissing" scene that is omitted in a number of key manuscripts.[20]

Transvestite Female Saints/Manly Women

Few features of the landscape of female asceticism in late antiquity have received as much attention in recent years as the idea of the "manly woman" or the appearance of "transvestite saints."[21] The concluding verse of the Coptic *Gospel of Thomas*—"I will make Mary male . . ."— is but the most famous example of women being "made" male. Ancient texts are replete with the image of "manly women"—virtuous, pious, and faithful; and the attribution extends from Olympias and Monica, the mother of Augustine, to the women of the *Apocryphal Acts* and *Sayings of the Desert Mothers*. How we should understand this motif in relationship to the notion of transvestite saints continues to be questioned. Recall Thecla, who "sewed her mantle into a cloak after the fashion of men (σχήματι ἀνδρικῷ), and went off to Myra, and found Paul . . ." (*APT* 40). Or the later story of Basilina, "who desired all the more to see the holy elder with her own eyes, and planned to put on masculine attire and visit him in the laura . . . [but] he sent word to her: 'Know that, even if you come, you will not see me'" (Cyril of Scythopolis, *Lives of the Monks of Palestine* 219.20).[22]

Although we know that the paradoxical metaphor of the manly woman appears with some frequency as a positive attribution in Christian ascetic literature, we also know that the related (but distinct) tradition of transvestite saints came to be contested, as Canon 62 from the Council in Trullo of 692 CE shows:

> We decree that no man should wear feminine attire, nor any woman that which suits men . . . (μηδένα ἄνδρα γυναικείαν στολὴν ἐνδιδύσκεσθαι, ἢ γυναῖκα τὴν ἀνδράσιν ἁρμόδιον; *ne ullus vir muliebri veste, vel ulla mulier veste virili induatur*).
>
> —*Council of Trullo, ca. 692, canon 62*[23]

Tracing both images—the manly woman and the transvestite female saint—goes well beyond my goal (and has been done by other scholars); rather, I return again to texts and bodies to explore several instances in which the language and the "practice" of transvestitism becomes textually contested. Each of them should be placed alongside the image of Thecla cutting her hair and Paul's deferral of that act, which we discussed in the previous chapter.

Consider the following passages from the *AA*. Andrew speaks to Maximilla and urges her to withstand her husband's pressures:

> I would also say the following, "Well done, O nature (φύσις), you who are saved even though you were not strong and you did not hide. Well done, O soul (ψυχή), crying out what you have suffered and returning to yourself. Well done, O man (ἄνθρωπε), learning what is not yours and pressing on to what is yours. . . . If, man (ἄνθρωπε), you understand all these things in yourself, that you are immaterial, holy, light, kin of the unbegotten, mindly, heavenly, transparent, pure, superior to flesh, superior to the world. . . ."
>
> —*AA* 38

To be sure, the term *anthrope* here could simply be translated "human being," which sets it alongside nature and soul, but the full force of Maximilla as a man, not just a human being, is apparent further in Andrew's speech: "I beg you, therefore, the wise man, that your noble mind continue steadfast (δέομαί σου οὖν τοῦ φρονίμου ἀνδρὸς ὅπος διαμείνῃ εὔοψις νοῦς) (*AA* 41). These passages serve to emphasize, as we found in *APT*, that in being superior to the body, being chaste and pure, Maximilla has become "manly." It is striking, however, that both of these passages are found only in a single manuscript, the Vatican Greek manuscript of *AA*. Furthermore, we would do well to add here the variants to Maximilla's disguise just a few chapters later: Does Maximilla go out disguised as Andrew (i.e., does she take on the form of a man, the form of the apostle himself), or does the Lord go before her in the form of Andrew (*AA* 46)? These two readings appear in different manuscripts. The change is miniature—the variant consists merely of the case ending of *Andrew*, nominative or genitive—but the effect is quite different. It is worthwhile remembering, too, that our manuscripts here are all much later than the Council of Trullo, which instructed women not to dress as men.

In the *Passion of Perpetua and Felicitas*, there is a well-known vision of Perpetua the day before she was to be thrown into the arena with the beasts. In her vision, "an Egyptian" "of vicious appearance" comes out to fight with her, and then there appears a second "handsome young man" as her assistant. Suddenly, her "clothes were stripped off" and, she says, "I was a man" (*et expoliata sum, et facta sum masculus*) (*Pass. Perp.* 10).[24] Again in this instance, the textual tradition exhibits a range of variants precisely at this point, from "I was stripped, a man" to "I was stripped and was made." Both of these eliminate the notion of "becoming male." Though we may not determine scribal intentions, the diversity of readings created by scribes functions to destabilize the text and permit an even wider range of interpretations.

A third and final example appears in the sayings of the desert mother Sarah—"It is I who am a man, you who are women."[25] The textual tradition of the *Sayings of the Desert Fathers*, in their various collected forms, is notoriously difficult and complex. However, it is worth noting that this particular saying only appears in some of the manuscripts with the collected sayings, and not in others. Much more work would need to be done to look systematically at how the collections were produced and what kinds of patterns of inclusion and exclusion we might detect in different manuscripts. For now, we can simply note that the saying is somewhat unstable in the tradition.

Conclusion

It is fitting to conclude this chapter with stories of women becoming men/manly, for if the metaphor has any one meaning in late antiquity it is that of the body being perfected. Why should women become male? To demonstrate their mastery of their bodies and the discipline of their souls and their bodies. How better to show the possibilities that asceticism allowed than to take those characters most in need of perfection—women—and show their transformation? Alongside the notion of perfecting the body through asceticism, there appears a perfection of the text. Texts, like bodies, are ripe for corruption; the discipline of the body can be matched—or even constructed—through disciplining the text. Books and bodies, we are reminded once again, are vulnerable and powerful and thus great care must be taken to get the words and the flesh right. Put differently, a text, especially a hand-inscribed manuscript, was always open to erasure and reinscription, correction or corruption; so, too, the body was endlessly malleable and reformable. The crux for an emergent discourse of Christian asceticism was tying the two corporealities together.

Conclusion

We do not wish to imitate, we wish to perfect. . . .

—Kenneth Clark, *The Nude*

Instead of veering between deconstruction and transcendence, we could try another train of speculations: that "women" is indeed an unstable category, that this instability has a historical foundation, and that feminism is the site of the systematic fighting-out of that instability—which need not worry us.

—Denise Riley, *"Am I That Name?"*

WORDS DRIFT AND ARE REWRITTEN; BODIES ARE UNSTABLE AND transformed; the malleable word and body are fraught with danger as well as the potential for perfection—such images encapsulate the themes of this book. Throughout, my interest has been in uncovering a palimpsestuous narrative, one that reveals the layering inherent in any writing and rewriting of a text as well as the formation and reformation of the body. Nowhere, I would argue, are such intertwined efforts in late ancient Christianity as apparent as in the stories about women, asceticism, and sexuality. From such a metaphorical notion of the palimpsest, it seems only appropriate to turn in conclusion to a material palimpsest—namely, the Syriac palimpsest from St. Catherine's Monastery in Sinai.

In January 1892, the twins Agnes Lewis and Margaret Gibson, scholars of Semitic languages from Cambridge, made their first of many trips to Saint Catherine's Monastery in Sinai.[1] The primary aim of their visit was to study the manuscripts in the library and to photograph the Syriac codex of the Apology of Aristides discovered earlier by James Rendel Harris. But their most significant discovery on this trip took place not by rummaging through the monastic library; rather, it happened through the daily routine of dining. At least, that is how the story has been told and retold (even by me!) until recently. I quote here at length from the story as told by Lewis and Gibson's biographer, A. Whigham Price, in 1985:

> Hospitality in an *all-male community*, though cordial, is apt to be of a somewhat *rough-and-ready kind*. At St. Catherine's, meals tended to be served on the firm principle that one eats to live, and no more. *Butterdishes*, for instance, were scorned: when, at breakfast, butter was required, it was simply planked down on an old sheet of discarded manuscript, and put thus on the table. After all, vellum is a tough material, and will resist grease for at least the period of one meal; and its use reduces the washing up. Such, at any rate, was the monks' normal custom, and they saw no reason to vary it for their *feminine visitors*. They had been so long out of the world that they had forgotten that *women attach considerable importance to such trifles*. So the butter for the twins' meals appeared on the same ersatz tableware. Our *heroines* were somewhat disconcerted but, as *well-bred women*, naturally made no comment.
>
> Agnes, indeed, saw in such unusual arrangements an excellent opportunity to combine study with eating, to blend intellectual refreshment with the somewhat clumsy methods prescribed by the Lord for refuelling the human frame. Hence, it soon became her custom to scrutinise the *"butterdish"* with an unobtrusive scholarly eye, to see whether it offered anything of interest. As a rule it did not; but one morning the grubby sheet proved to be a fragment of a *palimpsest*, and at the edge of the "dish," disappearing under the lump of butter, was a line or two of the underwriting—clearly visible—which she at once recognised as a verse of the Gospels. This happened to be in

Syriac, Agnes' newly-acquired language (and therefore one in which she happened to be especially interested at that moment). Tactful and casually-worded enquiries, after the meal, led her to a certain basket in the glory-hole where they had been working. There, she found a complete Syriac palimpsest of three hundred and fifty-eight pages, the leaves of which were mostly glued together by dirt and damp—so firmly, indeed, that the least force used to separate them resulted in instant crumbling. . . .

When the pages were dry enough to examine, Agnes scrutinised them carefully under her lens. After a few minutes, she straightened her back and reported excitedly that while the upper (or more recent) writing seemed to contain an account—*very well-thumbed in places!*—of the lives of *certain rather frisky women saints*, the underlying and more ancient script was evidently a copy of the four Gospels of a very early date indeed.[2]

This is a story worth unpacking, for "it entirely lacks plausibility" as Janet Soskice has recently shown.[3] I myself accepted the basic outline of the story (with the exception of Price's affect), though I looked in vain for any evidence of the story of the "butterdish" in Agnes Lewis's own writings; thus, in what follows I am partly palimpsesting myself.

The immediate interest of the palimpsest for the Cambridge scholars, as Price suggests, lay in the underwriting—the four Gospels dated to the fifth or even late fourth centuries; here was what came to be called the Sinaitic Syriac manuscript of the Gospels, a codex whose readings have been important in this study. Transcribing and publishing the upper writing of the palimpsest, the eighth-century copy of the lives of so-called frisky women saints, was prepared some eight years later by Agnes Lewis. Lewis herself notes the asymmetry of value between the under and upper writing: "Although these 'Select Narratives' cannot pretend to much value when compared with the ancient Gospel-text which underlies them, and which has been preserved for their sakes alone during eleven centuries, and though it would be a difficult task to sift the few grains of historical truth which they contain from their bushels of imaginative chaff, they are not without some literary beauty."[4]

But the story of this manuscript illustrates well the multiple meanings inherent in my title *The Gendered Palimpsest*, for the

Syriac manuscript is a palimpsest in the codicological sense, and the highly gendered and multilayered narrative attached to its discovery is surely palimpsestuous.[5] Price's telling of the event casts the characters as "rough-and-ready" men—the monks of St. Catherine's who, Price winks, appeared to have thoroughly enjoyed reading the lives of the "frisky women saints"—and the monks' "feminine visitors," "well-bred women" who attached "considerable importance to the trifles" of dishware. Likewise, the narrative produced by both Price and Lewis in 1900 highlighted the asymmetry of the two layers of the palimpsest itself: the gospels produced by the male evangelists far outweighed in importance the "imaginative chaff" of those lives of "frisky women."[6]

Yet to some extent, the palimpsest itself bears witness to a different hierarchy: old gospel texts reused for the lives of exemplary

FIGURE C.1. Sinaitic Syriac Palimpsest, folio 12b. Syriac Gospel underwriting. Late fourth to early fifth centuries. *Lives of Holy Women* upper writing. Eighth century. Digital reproduction from Arthur Hjelt, *Syrus Sinaiticus*, Helsingfors, 1930.

women saints—a palimpsest engendered in multiple senses. The "lives" of Thecla, Eugenia, Mary/Marinus, Euphrosyne, Onesima, Drusis, Barbara, Mary (slave of Tertullius), Irene, Euphemia, Sophia, Cyprian, and Justa are written over the gospels of Matthew, Mark, Luke, and John.

Thus, we find in this palimpsest Thecla written above—on top of—Mark; Eugenia on top of Mark, Luke, and Matthew; Euphrosyne on top of Matthew and Luke; Pelagia on top of Mark; and so forth. And the colophon itself offers the scribe's rationale: "I, the mean one, and the sinner, John the Stylite, of the monastery of Beth-Mari-Qanun in the town of Ma'arath Kaukab of Antioch, by the mercy of God, I have written this book for the profit of myself, of my brethren, and of those who are neighbors to it."[7] We have, then, a codex that began as a Gospel codex, reused by John the Stylite to inscribe the stories of women saints for the benefit of himself and his fellow monks, found again in the nineteenth century by two women scholars from Cambridge, whose find comes to be told and retold in the twentieth century. Attending every layer to the history of this manuscript is gender and its construction, the representation of books and bodies. In the Sinaitic palimpsest, we have a vivid example of a palimpsest (en)gendered—created and gendered in its first creation, gendered in its late-nineteenth-century context, and gendered in a late-twentieth-century reading of the narrative of its find. As such, it forms a fitting counterpart (and book end) to the story of Codex Alexandrinus with which we began.

Women and writing, writing and women: unfortunately, it is simply impossible—not to mention undesirable—to conclude with a simplistic historical narrative that might suggest that women were once involved in the writing process but have long since been forgotten; or to imply that there was back in the reaches of time some equality between men and women that then gave way to subordination. Rather, I conclude where I began with the weave of image and word: with Mitchell, I argue that "knowledge [is] a social product, a matter of dialogue between different versions of the world, including different languages, ideologies, and modes of representation";[8] extending the work of Margaret Miles and Kenneth Clark, I see the ancient (and modern) desire and quest for perfection attending not just the body but also the book; and with Denise Riley, I find that our sources indeed betray the instability of the "category" woman at every turn. We find in our early Christian literature multiple engagements with different modes of ordering, of understanding, of comprehending the world—a virtually endless series of "fantasy echoes." The unstable and malleable word and flesh, book and body, open to a dynamic world of complexity, debate, and paradox.

Notes

Introduction

Chapter epigraphs. For the Greek text and translation (with my own modifi-cations) of 1 Clement, I rely on the edition of Bart D. Ehrman, *The Apostolic Fathers*, vol. 2, Loeb Classical Library (Cambridge, Mass.: Harvard University Press, 2003), with frequent comparison to the following editions: Andreas Lindemann, *Die Clemensbriefe* (Tübingen, Germany: Mohr-Siebeck, 1992), and Horacio E. Lona, *Der erste Clemensbrief* (Göttingen, Germany: Vanden-hoeck and Ruprecht, 1998).

Quoted in Bruce M. Metzger, "Explicit References in the Works of Ori-gen to Variant Readings in New Testament Manuscripts," in *Biblical and Patristic Studies in Memory of Robert Pierce Casey*, ed. J. Neville Birdsall and Robert W. Thomson (Freiburg, Germany: Herder, 1963), 78–79; Greek edition: GCS *Origenes* X, 387, 28.

Joan W. Scott, "Fantasy Echo: History and the Construction of Identity," *Critical Inquiry* 27 (2001): 287.

Books and Bodies section epigraphs. Jorge Luis Borges, prologue to his "Cat-alog of the Exhibition Books from Spain," in *Selected Non-Fictions, Jorge Luis Borges*, ed. Eliot Weinberger, trans. Esther Allen, Suzanne Jill Levine, and Eliot Weinberger (New York: Penguin Books, 1999), 445.

John Fuller quoted in A. S. Byatt, *On Histories and Stories: Selected Essays* (Cambridge, Mass.: Harvard University Press, 2001), 43.

1. John Dagenais, *The Ethics of Reading in Manuscript Culture: Glossing the* Libro de Buen Amor (Princeton, N.J.: Princeton University Press, 1994), 16.

2. Greek text: Otto Stählin and Ludwig Früchtel, *Clemens Alexandrinus*, II, GCS 52 (Berlin: Akademie Verlag, 1960), 296.

3. Alexandrinus is sometimes considered the best witness to the original of 1 Clement (Ehrman, *Apostolic Fathers*, 30), but its singularity combined with the diversity of the other witnesses might suggest otherwise in this particular instance.

4. Scot McKendrick, "The Codex Alexandrinus or the Dangers of Being a Named Manuscript," in *The Bible as Book: The Transmission of the Greek Text*, ed. Scot McKendrick and Orlaith A. O'Sullivan (London: British Library, 2003), 1.

5. B. H. Cowper, ed., *Codex Alexandrinus. He Kaine Diatheke. Novum Testamentum Graece: ex antiquissimo Codice Alexandrino a C. G. Woide olim descriptum* (London: Williams and Norgate, 1860), xiv; on its canonical status, at least in some circles, see also Michael W. Holmes, ed., *The Apostolic Fathers*, 3rd ed. (Grand Rapids, Mich.: Baker Academic, 2007); likewise, Bart D. Ehrman has shown that Didymus the Blind considered 1 Clement canonical: "The New Testament Canon of Didymus the Blind," *VC* 37 (1983): 1–21.

6. For an Egyptian origin, see F. G. Kenyon, *The Codex Alexandrinus in Reduced Photographic Facsimile: New Testament and Clementine Epistles* (London: British Museum, 1909), 7; for Constantinople, see especially, F. C. Burkitt, "Codex 'Alexandrinus,'" *JTS* 11 (1909–1910): 603–606; for Ephesus, see most recently the proposal of Scot McKendrick, "Codex Alexandrinus," 9–10.

7. I discuss the history of Codex Alexandrinus in my *Guardians of Letters: Literacy, Power, and the Transmitters of Early Christian Literature* (New York: Oxford University Press, 2000), 50–51; what follows appears there in fuller detail.

8. For the note, see the photographic facsimile by Edward M. Thompson, *Facsimile of the Codex Alexandrinus*, 4 vols. (London: Trustees of the British Museum, 1879–1883).

9. Just under the Arabic note appears what seems to be Bentley's translation of the note: memorant hunc librum scriptus fuisse manu Thecla Martyris (H. J. M. Milne and T. C. Skeat, *The Codex Sinaiticus and the Codex Alexandrinus*, 2nd ed. [London: British Museum, 1955], 36).

10. These comments are found in two separate letter, dated, respectively, January 30, 1624, and February 27, 1627, and found in *The Negotiations of Sir Thomas Roe, in His Embassy to Ottoman Porte, from the*

Year 1621–1628 Inclusive (London, 1740), p. 335, letter 241, and p. 618, letter 448.

11. C. L. Hulbert-Powell, *John James Wettstein, 1693–1754* (London: SPCK Publishing, 1938), 101; J. J. Wettstein, *Prolegomena ad Novi Testamenti* (Amsterdam: R. & J. Wetstenios and G. Smith, 1730), 11. Interestingly, the suggestion of a female scribe is absent from the 1751 edition. (I am grateful to Zachary Yuzwa for tracking this down.)

12. B. H. Cowper, *Codex Alexandrinus*, xx.

13. McKendrick, "Codex Alexandrinus," 5.

14. Tova Rosen, *Unveiling Eve: Reading Gender in Medieval Hebrew Literature* (Philadelphia: University of Pennsylvania Press, 2003), 114.

15. Some of what follows is drawn from my "Engendering Palimpsests: Reading the Textual Tradition of the Acts of Paul and Thecla," in *The Early Christian Book*, ed. William Klingshirn and Linda Safran (Washington, D.C.: Catholic University of America Press, 2007), 177–193.

16. Maureen Tilley, *The Bible in Christian North Africa: The Donatist World* (Minneapolis, Minn.: Fortress Press, 1997), 64.

17. Brian Stock, *Augustine the Reader: Mediation, Self-Knowledge, and the Ethics of Interpretation* (Cambridge, Mass.: Harvard University Press, 1996), 109; the decisive moment is found in Augustine's *Confessions* 8.12.

18. Palladius, *Historia Lausiaca* 8; my translation is based on the Greek text found in Dom Cuthbert Butler, *The Lausiac History of Palladius*, vol. 2, Text and Studies 6 (Cambridge: Cambridge University Press, 1904); English translation available in Robert T. Meyer, trans., *Palladius: The Lausiac History*, ACW 34 (New York: Paulist Press, 1964).

19. Dagenais, *Ethics of Reading in Manuscript Culture*, xvii.

20. Bruce M. Metzger, *The Text of the New Testament: Its Transmission, Corruption, and Restoration* (New York: Oxford University Press, 1992), 17–18.

21. H. G. Evelyn White, *The Monasteries of the Wadi 'N Natrun* (New York: Metropolitan Museum of Art, 1926), xlv; see also William Wright, *Catalogue of Syriac Manuscripts in the British Museum Acquired since the Year 1838* (London: Trustees of the British Museum), no. 328, 274.

22. On writing as ascetic devotion, see especially Derek Krueger, "Writing as Devotion: Hagiographical Composition and the Cult of the Saints in Theodoret of Cyrrhus and Cyril of Scythopolis," *Church History* 66 (1997): 707–719; and ibid., "Hagiography as an Ascetic Practice in the Early Christian East," *Journal of Religion* 79 (1999): 216–232.

23. Dennis R. MacDonald, trans., *The Acts of Andrew and the Acts of Andrew and Matthias in the City of the Cannibals* (Atlanta: Scholars Press, 1990), 282; see also Kate Cooper, "The Patristic Period," in *The Blackwell*

Companion to the Bible and Culture, ed. John F. A. Sawyer (Oxford: Wiley-Blackwell, 2006), 33; on the "magical use" of scripture see E. A. Judge, "The Magical Use of Scripture in the Papyri," in *Perspectives on Language and Text: Essays and Poems in Honor of Francis I. Andersen's Sixtieth Birthday, July 28, 1985,* ed. Edgar W. Conrad and Edward G. Newing (Winona Lake, Ind.: Eisenbrauns, 1987), 339–349.

24. W. J. T. Mitchell, *Iconology: Image, Text, Ideology* (Chicago: University of Chicago Press, 1986), 8.

25. Annette Kuhn, *The Power of the Image: Essays on Representation and Sexuality* (London: Routledge, 1985), 10.

26. Emily A. Hemelrijk, *Matrona Docta: Educated Women in the Roman Élite from Cornelia to Julia Domna* (London: Routledge, 1999), 35.

27. Epiphanius, preface to his *Panarion,* found in Philip R. Amidon, trans., *The* Panarion *of St. Epiphanius, Bishop of Salamis : Selected Passages* (New York: Oxford University Press, 1990), 21.

28. See "The Letter-Writer" from David Roberts, *Egypt and Nubia* (London: Moon, 1846–1849).

29. Quoted in Mitchell, *Iconology,* 40.

30. Patricia Cox Miller, *The Poetry of Thought in Late Antiquity: Essays in Imagination and Religion* (Aldershot, England: Ashgate, 2001), 5.

31. Mitchell, *Iconology,* 43.

32. Scott, "Fantasy Echo," 304.

33. *Oxford English Dictionary* (Oxford: Oxford University Press, 2008).

34. Sarah Dillon, *The Palimpsest: Literature, Criticism, Theory* (London: Continuum, 2007), 3.

Part I

1. Terry G. Wilfong, *Women of Jeme: Lives in a Coptic Town in Late Antique Egypt* (Ann Arbor: University of Michigan Press, 2002), 76.

2. On Jewish attitudes toward women studying, see especially Judith Romney Wegner, *Chattel or Person? The Status of Women in the Mishnah* (New York: Oxford University Press, 1988), 161ff and 193ff.

3. On the general subject of women's education during this time, see F. A. Beck, "The Schooling of Girls in Ancient Greece," *Classicum* 9 (1978): 1–9; Susan Cole, "Could Greek Women Read and Write?" in *Reflections of Women in Antiquity,* ed. Helen P. Foley (New York: Gordon and Breach Science Publishers, 1981), 219–245; and S. B. Pomeroy, "'Technikai kai Mousikai': The Education of Women in the Fourth Century and in the Hellenistic Period," *American Journal of Ancient History* 2 (1977): 51–68; and

most recently and most helpfully, Raffaella Cribiore, *Gymnastics of the Mind: Greek Education in Hellenistic and Roman Egypt* (Princeton, N.J.: Princeton University Press, 2001), esp. 74–101.

4. See, e.g., the numerous papyri letters that exhibit illiterate women in families in which the men were literate (for example, *P.Mich.* ix.554; *P.Fayum* 100; *P.Oxy.* xvii.2134; *P.Amh.* ii.102; *P.Tebt.* ii.399).

5. As do men as well. See Cole, "Could Greek Women Read and Write?," 234; Rita Calderini, "Gli *agrammatoi* nell'Egitto Greco-romano," *Aegyptus* 30 (1950): 14–41; H. C. Youtie, "Because They Do Not Know Letters," *ZPE* 19 (1975): 101–108.

6. Cole, "Could Greek Women Read and Write?," 235.

7. *Gymnastics of the Mind*, 90n63.

8. *Women of Jeme*, 75–76.

9. William Harris, *Ancient Literacy* (Cambridge, Mass.: Harvard University Press, 1989), 314.

10. Jane Rowlandson, "Gender and Cultural Identity in Roman Egypt," in *Women's Influence on Classical Civilization*, ed. Fiona McHardy and Eireann Marshall (London: Routlege, 2004), 151–166, see esp. 158.

Chapter 1

Chapter epigraph. Ann Bergren, *Weaving Truth: Essays on Language and the Female in Greek Thought* (Cambridge, Mass.: Center for Hellenic Studies, 2008), 250.

1. Anthony Tuck, "Stories at the Loom: Patterned Textiles and the Recitation of Myth in Euripides," *Arethusa* 42 (2009): 151–159, esp. 152 for quotation.

2. See Raymond J. Starr, "The Circulation of Literary Texts in the Roman World," *CQ* 37 (1987): 213–223; Felix Reichmann, "The Book Trade at the Time of the Roman Empire," *Library Quarterly* 8 (1938): 40–76; A. F. Norman, "The Book Trade in Fourth-Century Antioch," *Journal of Hellenic Studies* 80 (1960): 122–126; and Kim Haines-Eitzen, *Guardians of Letters: Literacy, Power, and the Transmitters of Early Christian Literature* (New York: Oxford University Press, 2000), 1; see also Myles McDonnell, "Writing, Copying, and Autograph Manuscripts in Ancient Rome," *CQ* 46 (1996): 469–491.

3. Mary R. Lefkowitz, "Did Ancient Women Write Novels," in *"Women Like This: New Perspectives on Jewish Women in the Greco-Roman World*, ed. Amy-Jill Levine (Atlanta: Scholars Press, 1991), 199–219, quotation on 199; Roger S. Bagnall and Raffaella Cribiore, *Women's Letters from Ancient Egypt, 300 BC–AD 800* (Ann Arbor: University of Michigan Press, 2006), 7.

4. Alison Beach, *Women as Scribes: Book Production and Monastic Reform in Twelfth-Century Bavaria* (Cambridge: Cambridge University Press, 2004): "I begin with the conviction that it is impossible to determine the sex of a scribe based on any supposed inherent difference in the handwriting of men and women" (5).

5. See Jane Snyder's *The Woman and the Lyre: Women Writers in Classical Greece and Rome* (Carbondale: Southern Illinois University Press, 1989); for other collections treating ancient women writers, see especially Laurie J. Churchill, Phyllis R. Brown, and Jane E. Jeffrey, eds., *Women Writing Latin: From Roman Antiquity to Early Modern Europe,* vol. 1, *Women Writing Latin in Roman Antiquity, Late Antiquity, and the Early Christian Era* (New York: Routledge, 2002); Jane Stevenson, *Women Latin Poets: Language, Gender, and Authority, from Antiquity to the Eighteenth Century* (Oxford: Oxford University Press, 2005); and Peter Dronke, *Women Writers of the Middle Ages: A Critical Study of Texts from Perpetua to Margeurite Porete* (Cambridge: Cambridge University Press, 1984); see also Emily A. Hemelrijk, *Matrona Docta: Educated Women in the Roman Elite from Cornelia to Julia Domna* (London: Routledge, 1999).

6. Ross S. Kraemer, "Women's Authorship of Jewish and Christian Literature in the Greco-Roman Period," in *"Women Like This,"* ed. Amy-Jill Levine, 221–242.

7. Dronke, *Women Writers,* 1. On the issue of authorship, see the balanced and helpful treatment by Ross Kraemer and Shira Lander, who offer a corrective of many of the assumptions behind Dronke's claims as well as an excellent bibliography: "Perpetua and Felicitas," in *The Early Christian World,* vol. 2, ed. Philip Esler (London: Routledge, 2000), 1048–1068.

8. Ronald Heine, *Montanist Oracles and Testimonia* (Macon, Ga.: Mercer University Press, 1989), 124–126; see also Ross Kraemer, *Women's Religions in the Greco-Roman World: A Sourcebook* (Oxford: Oxford University Press, 2004), 93–94.

9. For the translation I am relying on Snyder, *The Woman and the Lyre,* 137–138; for the Latin text along with a translation see Elizabeth A. Clark and Diane F. Hatch, *The Golden Bough, The Oaken Cross: The Virgilian Cento of Faltonia Betitia Proba* (Chico, Calif.: Scholars Press, 1981); for a critical edition, see *Poetae Christiani Minores,* ed. C. Schenkl, CSEL 16 (Vienna: Tempsky, 1888); on Proba see also Kraemer, "Women's Authorship," 221; and Danuta R. Shanzer, "The Anonymous *Carmen contra paganos* and the Date and Identity of the Centonist Proba," *Revue des Etudes Augustiniennes* 32 (1986): 232–248, and "The Date and Identity of the Centonist Proba," *Recherches Augustiniennes* 27 (1994): 75–96.

10. Snyder, *The Woman and the Lyre*, 139–141.

11. On the late fourth-century dating, see especially E. D. Hunt, "The Date of *Itinerarium Egeriae*," *Studia Patristica* 38 (2001): 401–416. The literature on Egeria is substantial. Worth noting especially is Hagith Sivan, "Who Was Egeria? Piety and Pilgrimage in the Age of Gratian," *HTR* 81 (1988): 59–72. Worth noting, too, is the debate between Laurie Douglass and Jas' Elsner on whether the earlier pilgrim of Bordeaux may have been a woman: Laurie Douglass, "A New Look at the *Itinerarium Burdigalense*," *JECS* 4 (1999): 313–334; Jas' Elsner, "The *Itinerarium Burdigalense*: Politics and Salvation in the Geography of Constantine's Empire," *JRS* 90 (2000): 181–195.

12. For the text and a helpful introduction, see John Wilkinson, *Egeria's Travels to the Holy Land: Newly Translated with Supporting Documents and Notes*, rev. ed. (Jerusalem: Ariel Publishing House, 1981).

13. As Leo Spitzer suggests in "The Epic Style of the Pilgrim Aetheria," *Comparative Literature* 1 (1949): 249.

14. Snyder, *The Woman and the Lyre*, 150.

15. Bagnall and Cribiore, *Women's Letters*, 368–370.

16. Jerome, *Ep.* 127, 7; J. N. D. Kelly, *Jerome: His Life, Writings, and Controversies* (London: Duckworth, 1975), 80–81; Peter Brown, *The Body and Society: Men, Women, and Sexual Renunciation in Early Christianity* (New York: Columbia University Press, 1988), 366.

17. Jerome, *Ep.* 127, 7.

18. It was through Marcella's preestablished circle of ascetic women that Jerome initially made contact with women that would become his friends for the duration of his life. See Elizabeth A. Clark, *Jerome, Chrysostom, and Friends: Essays and Translations*, Studies in Women and Religion 2 (New York: Edwin Mellen Press, 1979), 44; see also Jerome, *Ep.* 47.3.

19. Obsecras litteris et suppliciter deprecaris, ut tibi scribam, immo rescribam, quomodo vivere debeas et viduitis coronam inlaeso pudicitiae nomine conservare (F. A. Wright, trans., *Select Letters of St. Jerome* [London: Heinemann, Ltd., 1933]).

20. NPNF, s.s. (Christian Literature Publishing Company, 1893).

21. See the English translation of the Latin text in Benedicta Ward, *Harlots of the Desert: A Study of Repentance in Early Monastic Sources* (Kalamazoo, Mich.: Cistercian Publications, 1987), 69–70; for the Syriac version—"Pelagia wrote down on a wax tablet a passionate and moving message with a plea concerning her salvation"—see Sebastian P. Brock and Susan Ashbrook Harvey, trans., *Holy Women of the Syrian Orient* (Berkeley: University of California Press, 1987), chap. 20, p. 48.

22. Brock and Harvey, *Holy Women of the Syrian Orient*.

23. Alban Butler, *Lives of the Fathers, Martyrs, and Other Principle Saints*, vol. 3 (Dublin: James Duffy, 1866); also available online, accessed October 2, 2010, http://www.bartleby.com/210/3/132.html.

24. For the Greek text, see the edition of Denys Gorce, *Vie de Sainte Mélanie*, SC 90 (Paris: Éditions du Cerf, 1962).

25. See Alix Barbet and Claude Vibert-Guigue, *Les peintures des nécropoeis romaines d'Abila et du Nord de la Jordanie*, 2 vols. (Beirut: Institut français d'archéologie du Proche-Orint, 1988–1994); and Alan Millard, *Reading and Writing in the Time of Jesus* (New York: New York University Press, 2000), 64.

26. For what follows, see my fuller treatment of the evidence for female scribes in *Guardians of Letters*, 41–52; for a later period see most recently Alison I. Beach, *Women as Scribes*.

27. See Dom Cuthbert Butler's edition, *The Lausiac History of Palladius*, vol. 1 (Cambridge: Cambridge University Press, 1989), 150.

28. For more examples, see my *Guardians of Letters*, 44ff. I also treat there the more problematic example from Juvenal in his *Satires*.

29. Henry A. Sanders, *The New Testament Manuscripts in the Freer Collection. Part I. The Washington Manuscript of the Four Gospels* (New York: Macmillan Company, 1918), 3.

30. *Women's Letters*, 48–54, 59–67.

31. See Natalie Kampen, *Image and Status: Roman Working Women in Ostia* (Berlin: Mann, 1981), 157; Eve D'Ambra, "Mourning and the Making of Ancestors in the Testamentum Relief," *American Journal of Archaeology* 99 (1995): 667–681.

32. W. E. Crum and H. G. Evelyn White, *The Monastery of Epiphanius at Thebes*, pt. 2 (New York: Metropolitan Museum of Art, 1926); see also Terry G. Wilfong, *Women of Jeme: Lives in a Coptic Town in Late Antique Egypt* (Ann Arbor: University of Michigan Press, 2002), 112.

33. See especially Riet van Bremen, *The Limits of Participation: Women and Civic Life in the Greek East in the Hellenistic and Roman Periods* (Amsterdam: J. C. Gieben, 1996); on women as literary patrons, see Hemelrijk, *Matrona Docta*, 97–145; for the Christian context, see Elizabeth A. Clark, "Patrons, Not Priests: Gender and Power in Late Ancient Christianity," *Gender and History* 2 (1990): 253–273; on literary patronage more broadly, see Ruurd R. Nauta, *Poetry for Patrons: Literary Communication in the Age of Domitian* (Leiden, the Netherlands: Brill, 2002).

34. On the production and transmission of Jerome's writings, see especially Paulo Evaristo Arns, *La Technique du livre d'après Saint Jérôme* (Paris, E. De Boccard, 1953); on the women around Jerome, see also Philip Rousseau,

"'Learned Women' and the Development of a Christian Culture in Late Antiquity," *Symbolae Osloenses* 70 (1995): 116–147.

Chapter 2

Chapter epigraphs. Greek: SC 90 (1962); English ed. (with occasional modifications): Elizabeth A. Clark, *The Life of Melania the Younger: Introduction, Translation, and Commentary* (New York: Edwin Mellen Press, 1984).

Hélène Cixous, *Three Steps on the Ladder of Writing*, trans. Sarah Cornell and Susan Sellers (New York: Columbia University Press, 1994).

Exemplary Women Readers epigraph. Adrienne Rich, *On Lies, Secrets, and Silence: Selected Prose 1966–1978* (New York: W. W. Norton, 1979), 38.

1. Robert J. White, trans., *The Interpretation of Dreams (Oneirocritica) by Artemidorus* (Park Ridge, N.J.: Noyes Press, 1975).

2. Compare Jeremiah 17:1 where it is the sins of the people written on their hearts: "The sin of Judah is written with an iron pen; with a diamond point it is engraved on the tablet of their hearts, and on the horns of their altars."

3. See especially Bernard M. W. Knox, "Silent Reading in Antiquity," *GRBS* 9 (1968): 421–435; J. Balough, "Voces Paginarum: Beiträge zur Geschichte des lauten Lesens und Schreibens," *Philologus* 82 (1927): 84–109, 202–240.

4. Taken from Benedicta Ward's translation of the Latin *Vitae Patrum* (PL 73, cols. 851–1024) in her *The Desert Fathers: Sayings of the Early Christian Monks* (London: Penguin Books, 2003).

5. Benedicta Ward, *The Sayings of the Desert Fathers: The Alphabetical Collection* (Kalamazoo, Mich.: Cistercian Publications, 1975), 58.

6. Elizabeth A. Clark, *Reading Renunciation: Asceticism and Scripture in Early Christianity* (Princeton, N.J.: Princeton University Press, 1999), 57.

7. The discussion of Douglas Burton-Christie on the ambivalence toward books among the desert fathers remains one of the best: "While there can be no doubt that the written word occupied a significant place in the life of the desert monks, there is evidence that many of the desert fathers believed that too much reliance on books, even the most sacred, could lead to trouble" (*The Word in the Desert: Scripture and the Quest for Holiness in Early Christian Monasticism* [New York: Oxford University Press, 1993], 115 and, more broadly, 111–117); on the early Christian preference for orality, the passage from Papias quoted by Eusebius has been cited: "For I did not suppose that what I received from books would benefit me as much as that from a living and surviving voice" (*HE* 3.29).

8. I leave aside the possible example of the addressee of the second Johannine epistle; although the author addresses the epistle "to the elect lady," it seems most likely that this is a metaphor for a congregation (2 John 1, 5, 13).

9. The Greek text is taken from Bart D. Ehrman, *The Apostolic Fathers*, vol. 2 (Cambridge, Mass.: Harvard University Press, 2003). I have modified Ehrman's translation.

10. See the singular reading πορνείας in the fifteenth-century Codex Athous.

11. For a fuller discussion of the papyrus and these claims, see Susanna Elm, "An Alleged Book-Theft in Fourth-Century Egypt: P. Lips. 43," *Studia Patristica* 18 (1989): 209–215, esp. 211.

12. I am grateful to Kim Bowes for pointing me toward this reference.

13. English edition: O. M. Dalton, *The Letters of Sidonius*, vol. 1 (Oxford: Clarendon Press, 1915); Latin edition: André Loyen, ed. and trans., *Sidoine Apolinaire, Poèmes et Lettres*, vol. 2, *Lettres* (Paris: Budé, 1970).

14. I have generally followed the English translations in the NPNF, with comparison to the *Select Letters of St. Jerome*, trans. R. A. Wright (London: Heinemann, 1933) and to the Latin as found in CSEL 54.

15. Roger Chartier, *The Order of Books: Readers, Authors, and Libraries in Europe between the Fourteenth and Eighteenth Centuries*, trans. Lydia G. Cochrane (Stanford, Calif.: Stanford University Press), viii.

16. NPNF, s.s. vol. 3; for the listing of various letters to women, especially helpful is the collection of texts found in Kevin Madigan and Carolyn Osiek, eds., *Ordained Women in the Early Church: A Documentary History* (Baltimore, Md.: Johns Hopkins University Press, 2005). Note especially that the reference to Theodoret of Cyrrhus's letters follows the convention of adding "*Sirm*" when referring to letters found in the collection of Jacques Sirmond (1642). See more recently the edition of Yvan Azema, *Theodoret de Cyr: Correspondence*, SC 98 (Paris: Éditions du Cerf, 1964).

17. Quoted in Madigan and Osiek, eds., *Ordained Women in the Early Church*, 57.

18. Translation taken from Virginia Woods Callahan, trans., *Saint Gregory of Nyssa Ascetical Works* (Washington, D.C.: The Catholic University of America Press, 1967), 165.

19. Ronald E. Heine, trans., *Gregory of Nyssa's Treatise on the Inscriptions of the Psalms* (Oxford: Clarendon Press, 1995); for the Greek, see Jacobus McDonough and Paulus Alexander, *Gregorii Nysseni Opera* 5 (Leiden, the Netherlands: E. J. Brill, 1962), 29.

20. Greek text: Dom Cuthbert Butler, *The Lausiac History of Palladius*, vol. 2 (Cambridge: Cambridge University Press, 1904); English translation:

Robert T. Meyer, trans., *Palladius: The Lausiac History* (New York: Paulist, 1964).

21. The secondary literature on fasting is vast: see especially Teresa M. Shaw, *The Burden of the Flesh: Fasting and Sexuality in Early Christianity* (Minneapolis, Minn.: Fortress Press, 1998); Caroline Walker Bynum, *Holy Feast and Holy Fast: The Religious Significance of Food to Medieval Women* (Berkeley: University of California Press, 1987).

22. See Sebastian P. Brock and Susan Ashbrook Harvey, trans., *Holy Women of the Syrian Orient* (Berkeley: University of California Press), 154–155.

23. For all of these lives, see Agnes Smith Lewis, *Select Narratives of Holy Women from the Syro-Antiochene or Sinai Palimpsest as Written above the Old Syriac by John the Stylite of Beth-Mari Qanūn in AD 778* (London: C. J. Clay and Sons, 1900).

24. See especially the following passage: "One thing specially pleased me. I received from this holy man the copies of Abgar's letter to the Lord, and the Lord's letter to Abgar, which he had read to us. I have copies of them at home, but even so it is much better to have been given them there by him. And it may be that what we have at home is not so complete, because what I was given here is certainly longer. So, dearest ladies, you yourselves must read them when I come home, if such is the will of Jesus our God" (19.19 in John Wilkinson, *Egeria's Travels to the Holy Land: Newly Translated with Supporting Documents and Notes*, rev. ed. [Jerusalem: Ariel Publishing House, 1981]).

25. Kate Flint, *The Woman Reader 1837–1914* (Oxford: Clarendon Press, 1993), 18.

26. Rich, *On Lies, Secrets and Silence*, 43; see also Alice Walker, *In Search of our Mothers' Gardens: Womanist Prose* (San Diego, Calif.: Harcourt Brace, 1983), esp. 66–70.

27. Katha Pollitt, *The Mind-Body Problem: Poems* (New York: Random House, 2009), 42–43.

Chapter 3

Chapter epigraphs. W. R. Greg, "False Morality of Lady Novelists," *National Review* 8 (1859): 144; quoted in Kate Flint, *The Woman Reader 1837-1914* (Oxford: Clarendon Press, 1993), 4.

Edgar J. Goodspeed, "The Acts of Paul and Thecla," *The Biblical World* 17 (1901): 185–190.

Romance Writers of America, "About the Romance Genre," accessed August 28, 2009, http://www.rwanational.org/cs/the_romance_genre.

1. For a critical study of the modern romance novel, see especially Janice Radway, *Reading the Romance: Women, Patriarchy, and Popular Literature* (Chapel Hill: University of North Carolina Press, 1984).

2. Romance Writers of America, press release, accessed August 29, 2009, http://www.rwanational.org/cs/pressroom.

3. This chapter is a revision of my essay "The Apocryphal Acts of the Apostles on Papyrus: Revisiting the Question of Readership and Audience," in *New Testament Manuscripts: Their Texts and Their World*, ed. Thomas J. Kraus and Tobias Nicklas (Leiden, the Netherlands: E. J. Brill, 2006), 293–304. I am grateful for the permission to include a revised version of the essay here.

4. Stevan L. Davies, *The Revolt of the Widows: The Social World of the Apocryphal Acts* (Carbondale: Southern Illinois University Press, 1980), 95–96.

5. Virginia Burrus, *Chastity as Autonomy: Women in the Stories of Apocryphal Acts*, Studies in Women and Religion 23 (Lewiston, N.Y.: Edwin Mellen Press, 1987), 108.

6. Jan N. Bremmer, "The Novel and the Apocryphal Acts: Place, Time and Readership," in *Groningen Colloquia on the Novel 9*, ed. H. Hofmann and M. Zimmerman (Groningen, the Netherlands: Egbert Forsten, 1998), 157–180, esp. 176.

7. Stephen J. Davis, *The Cult of St. Thecla: A Tradition of Women's Piety in Late Antiquity*, Oxford Early Christian Studies (Oxford: Oxford University Press, 2001), 12–13. Although Davis acknowledges the notion of a female audience/readership (and he uses both terms without distinction), he does seem to side with the testimony of Tertullian to conclude that the *Acts of Paul and Thecla* "did in fact have an early audience among women" (12).

8. William Harris, *Ancient Literacy* (Cambridge, Mass.: Harvard University Press, 1989).

9. See, for example, the articles collected in J. H. Humphrey, ed., *Literacy in the Roman World*, Journal of Roman Archaeology Supplementary Series 3 (Ann Arbor, Mich.: Journal of Roman Archeology, 1991); Rosalind Thomas, *Literacy and Orality in Ancient Greece* (Cambridge: Cambridge University Press, 1992); Janet Watson, ed., *Speaking Volumes: Orality and Literacy in the Greek and Roman World* (Leiden, the Netherlands: Brill, 2001); Alan Millard, *Reading and Writing in the Time of Jesus* (New York: New York University Press, 2000).

10. Simon Goldhill, *Foucault's Virginity: Ancient Erotic Fiction and the History of Sexuality* (Cambridge: Cambridge University Press, 1995); Kate Cooper, *The Virgin and the Bride: Idealized Womanhood in Late Antiquity* (Cambridge, Mass.: Harvard University Press, 1996).

11. Jeremy W. Barrier, *The Acts of Paul and Thecla: A Critical Introduction and Commentary* (Tübingen: Mohr Siebeck, 2009), 21.

12. Susan A. Stephens, "Who Read Ancient Novels?" and Ewen Bowie, "The Readership of Greek Novels in the Ancient World," both in James Tatum, ed., *The Search for the Ancient Novel* (Baltimore, Md.: Johns Hopkins University Press, 1994), 405–418 and 436–459, respectively; more recently, in their collection of the papyrological remains of ancient Greek novels, Susan A. Stephens and John J. Winkler address issues of authorship and readership briefly (*Ancient Greek Novels, The Fragments: Introduction, Text, Translation, and Commentary* [Princeton, N.J.: Princeton University Press, 1995], esp. 9ff.).

13. Stephens, "Who Read Ancient Novels?," 413.

14. Stephens and Winkler, *Ancient Greek Novels*, 9–10.

15. Ibid., 10.

16. See especially his treatment of reading practices in *The Order of Books: Readers, Authors, and Libraries in Europe between the Fourteenth and Eighteenth Centuries*, trans. Lydia G. Cochrane (Stanford, Calif.: Stanford University Press, 1994), esp. 1–23; his engagement with the work of D. F. McKenzie in *On the Edge of the Cliff: History, Languages, and Practices*, trans. Lydia Cochrane (Baltimore, Md.: Johns Hopkins Press, 1997), 81–89; and his assessment of the notion of "popular literature" in *Forms and Meanings: Texts, Performances, and Audiences from Codex to Computer* (Philadelphia: University of Pennsylvania Press, 1995). Some of the themes from Chartier's work are also picked up in James J. O'Donnell, *Avatars of the Word: From Papyrus to Cyberspace* (Cambridge, Mass.: Harvard University Press, 1998).

17. Eric Turner, *Greek Papyri: An Introduction* (Oxford: Clarendon Press, 1968), 92; and his "Scribes and Scholars of Oxyrhynchus," *MPER* 5 (1955): 141–149.

18. Colin H. Roberts, *Manuscript, Society and Belief in Early Christian Egypt* (London: Oxford University Press, 1979).

19. These figures must remain preliminary, because some still unidentified papyri may well be remains of apocryphal acts materials. My figures were collected in large part from the edition of *Clavis Apocryphorum Novi Testmanti* by M. Geerard, CCSA (Turnhout, Belgium: Brepols,1992). The thirteen consist of *P.Oxy.* 849 (*Acts of Peter*); *P.Oxy.* 851 (*Acts of Andrew*); *P Oxy.* 850 (*Acts of John*); *P.Hamb.bil.* 1; *P.Oxy.* 1602; *P.Oxy.* 6; *P.Michigan* 1317, 3788; *P.Berlin* 13893; *P.Ant. I.*13; *P.Fackelmann, no.* 3; *P.Bodmer X* (all for the *Acts of Paul*).

20. There continues to be a debate about the original language of the *Acts of Thomas*. Han J. W. Drijvers agreed with a widely held view that "the Ath came into being at the beginning of the 3rd century in East Syria, and

were originally composed in Syriac" ("The Acts of Thomas," in Edgar Hennecke and Wilhelm Schneemelcher, ed., *The New Testament Apocrypha*, vol. 2 [Cambridge: James Clarke & Co. Ltd., 1992], 323). On the other hand, A. F. J. Klijn has more recently argued (in his translation of the Syriac text) that the Greek text "represents an earlier tradition of the contents" of the *Acts of Thomas* (*The Acts of Thomas: Introduction, Text and Commentary*, 2nd rev. ed [Leiden, the Netherlands: Brill, 2003], 8–9). Elsewhere, Klijn writes of his decision to focus in his edition on the Syriac text. He wanted to emphasize the "Syriac origin of the Ath," but he had to make continual reference to the Greek manuscripts because their texts are "much better than the various Syriac texts." Thus, he concludes, "The Greek text shows that this work was written in an environment in which at least the Syriac language was well known. It appears that sometimes the Greek cannot be understood without the help of the Syriac version. We have to conclude that the work was written in a bilingual environment" ("The Acts of Thomas Revisited," in *The Apocryphal Acts of Thomas*, ed. Jan N. Bremmer [Leuven, Belgium: Peters, 2001], 1–10, esp. 4).

21. *The Cult of St. Thecla* (2001).

22. Colin H. Roberts, ed. and trans., *The Antinoopolis Papyri*, vol. I (London: Egypt Exploration Society, 1950), 27.

23. The textual unity of all of the *Apocryphal Acts* is a subject of enormous complexity and still requires much research, although there is a wide-ranging bibliography on this subject. For brief introductions to the problems associated with each of the texts, see the edition of Hennecke-Schneemelcher, *New Testament Apocrypha*, vol. 2.

24. The standard edition is that by Michel Testuz, *Papyrus Bodmer X-XII* (Cologny-Genève: Bibliothèque Bodmer, 1959).

25. The most recent study of III Corinthians is that of Vahan Hovhanessian (*Third Corinthians: Reclaiming Paul for Christian Orthodoxy* [New York: Peter Lang, 2000]), who argues "that manuscript evidence, Patristic references, and the content, style and theology of the two documents point to 3 Cor having an origin independent of AP" (48). See also A. F. J. Klijn, "The Apocryphal Correspondence between Paul and the Corinthians," *VC* 17 (1963): 2–23; Willy Rordorf, "Hérésie et Orthodoxie selon la Correspondance apocryphe entre les Corinthiens et l'Apôtre Paul," *Cahiers de la Revue de Théologie et de Philosophie* 17 (1993): 21–63.

26. The new reassessment of this interesting codex, based on a new photographic edition, will likely correct the views of Eric Turner (*Typology of the Early Codex* [Philadelphia: University of Pennsylvania Press, 1977], 79–81), Testuz, and me (*Guardians of Letters: Literacy, Power, and the*

Transmitters of Early Christian Literature [New York: Oxford University Press, 2000], 96–104) regarding the precise hands and codices involved in this composite; see also Tobias Nicklas and Tommy Wasserman, "Theologische Linien im *Codex Bodmer Miscellani?*" in *New Testament Manuscripts: Their Texts and Their World*, ed. Thomas J. Kraus and Tobias Nicklas (Leiden, the Netherlands: Brill, 2006), 161–188.

27. See the plate provided in *P. Oxy.*, vol. 2. The editors describe the hand as follows: "The handwriting is a medium-sized upright uncial of a common third to fourth century type. Had the material used been papyrus, we should have been more disposed to assign it to the late third than to the fourth century, but since vellum was not commonly used in Egypt until the fourth century, it is safer to attribute the fragment to the period from Diocletian to Constantine" (7).

28. *P. Oxy. 850*, 12.

29. M. Gronewald, "Einige Fackelmann Papyri," *ZPE* 28 (1978): 274–276.

30. *P.Ant.* I, 26.

31. E. Turner, *Greek Manuscripts of the Ancient World* (Princeton, N.J.: Princeton University Press, 1971), 3ff.

32. *P. Ant.* I, 27.

33. *Guardians of Letters*, 67.

34. I am currently working on a project related to miniature codices (and I am grateful for the suggestions and help of Thomas Kraus, Malcolm Choat, and AnneMarie Luijendijk). For now, see further on the form and function of early Christian books my "Textual Communities in Late Antique Christianity," in Philip Rousseau, ed., *A Companion to Late Antiquity* (Chichester, UK: Wiley-Blackwell, 2009), 246–257.

35. *Forms and Meanings*, 88.

Part II

1. The best introductions to the field of New Testament textual criticism are Bruce M. Metzger and Bart D. Ehrman, *The Text of the New Testament: Its Transmission, Corruption, and Restoration*, 4th ed. (New York: Oxford University Press, 2005), see esp. 300ff for a discussion of these criteria; Kurt and Barbara Aland, *The Text of the New Testament: An Introduction to the Critical Editions and to the Theory and Practice of Modern Textual Criticism*, trans. Erroll F. Rhodes (Grand Rapids, Mich.: Eerdmans, 1987); and the more advanced volume by D. C. Parker, *An Introduction to the New Testament Manuscripts and Their Texts* (Cambridge: Cambridge University Press,

2008); for Latin texts, see James E. G. Zetzel, *Latin Textual Criticism in Antiquity* (New York: Arno Press, 1981); still important and relevant is L. D. Reynolds and N. G. Wilson, *Scribes and Scholars: A Guide to the Transmission of Greek and Latin Literature*, 2nd ed. (Oxford: Clarendon Press, 1974).

2. W. K. Wimsatt, Jr. and M. C. Beardsley, "The Intentional Fallacy," *The Sewanee Review* 54 (1946): 468–488.

3. Walter Benjamin, "The Work of Art in the Age of Mechanical Reproduction," in his *Illuminations*, ed. Hannah Arendt, trans. Harry Zohn (New York: Schocken Books, 1968), 218–219.

4. *Writing and Holiness: The Practice of Authorship in the Early Christian East* (Philadelphia: University of Pennsylvania Press, 2004).

5. Claudia Rapp, "Christians and Their Manuscripts in the Greek East in the Fourth Century," in *Scritture, libri e testi nelle aree provinciali di Bisanzio. Atti del seminario di Erice (18–25 settembre 1988)*, ed. Guglielmo Cavallo, Giuseppe de Gregorio, and Marilena Maniaci (Spoleto: Centro Italiano di Studi Sull'alto Medioevo, 1991), 141.

6. D. C. Parker, *The Living Text of the Gospels* (Cambridge: Cambridge University Press, 1997), 204.

7. Richard Wagner, *My Life* (1939; repr. New York: Dodd, Mead, and Company, 1911), 42.

8. Ibid, 42–43 (emphasis mine).

9. Michel Foucault, *This Is Not a Pipe*, trans. and ed. James Harkness (Berkeley: University of California Press, 1983), 44.

10. Take, for example, Ross Kraemer's work on the apocryphal work *Joseph and Aseneth*; she shows that of the two main recensions of that work, "the longer text appears concerned to subordinate a reading of Aseneth as angelic to her role as Joseph's pre-ordained wife" (*When Aseneth Met Joseph: A Late Antique Tale of the Biblical Patriarch and His Egyptian Wife, Reconsidered* [New York: Oxford University Press, 1998], 80); similarly, Tal Ilan attends to "censorship" of female characters in the manuscript and interpretative traditions of rabbinic literature (*Mine and Yours Are Hers: Retrieving Women's History from Rabbinic Literature* [Leiden: Brill, 1997]).

Chapter 4

Chapter epigraphs. Brian Stock, *Listening for the Text: On the Uses of the Past* (Baltimore, Md.: Johns Hopkins University Press, 1990), 112.

J. Hillis Miller, "Narrative," in *Critical Terms for Literary Study*, 2nd ed., ed. Frank Lentricchia and Thomas McLaughlin (Chicago: University of Chicago Press, 1995), 66.

1. In my opinion, the best treatment of the importance of storytelling remains that of Averil Cameron, *Christianity and the Rhetoric of Empire: The Development of Christian Discourse,* Sather Classical Lectures 55 (Berkeley: University of California Press, 1991); see also Claudia Rapp, "Storytelling as Spiritual Communication in Early Greek Hagiography: The Use of Diegesis," *JECS* 6 (1988): 431–448.

2. For both passages, I am drawing from James Robinson, *The Nag Hammadi Library* (San Francisco: HarperSanFrancisco, 1990).

3. For the same notion elsewhere in the Talmud, see Shabbat 146a and Abodah Zarah 22b.

4. Michel Testuz, *Papyrus Bodmer VII–IX* (Cologny-Genève: Bibliothèque Bodmer, 1959); see also my *Guardians of Letters: Literacy, Power, and the Transmitters of Early Christian Literature* (New York: Oxford University Press, 2000), 96–104; on the codex more generally, see James M. Robinson, *The Pachomian Monastic Library at the Chester Beatty Library and the Bibliothèque Bodmer,* Institute for Antiquity and Christianity, Occasional Papers 19 (Claremont, Calif.: Institute for Antiquity and Christianity, 1990).

5. *Guardians of Letters,* 102–104; see also Tommy Wasserman, "Papyrus 72 and the *Bodmer Miscellaneous Codex*," *NTS* 51 (2005): 137–154. I continue to find Wasserman's attempts to find a unity to the contents of this codex under the broad theme "theological" uncompelling.

6. See the Akathistos hymn for both of these images.

7. A good introductory article on Mary in the New Testament is that of Vasiliki Limberis in *Women in Scripture: A Dictionary of Named and Unnamed Women in the Hebrew Bible, the Apocryphal/Deuterocanonical Books, and the New Testament,* ed. Carol Meyers, Toni Craven, and Ross S. Kraemer (Boston: Houghton Mifflin Co., 2000), 116–119; on the development of the cult of Mary, see Hilda Graef, *Mary: A History of Doctrine and Devotion* (Westminster, Md.: Christian Classics, 1985); Vasiliki Limberis, *Divine Heiress: The Virgin Mary and the Creation of Christian Constantinople* (London: Routledge, 1994).

8. See especially Bart Ehrman, *The Orthodox Corruption of Scripture* (Oxford: Oxford University Press, 1993), 54–55, 58–59.

9. For the critical edition of *Prot. James,* I am using Emile de Strycker, *La forme la plus ancienne du Protévangile de Jacques. Recherches sur le Papyrus Bodmer 5 avec une édition critique du texte et une traduction annotée* (Brussels: Société des Bollandistes, 1961).

10. See Elliott's inclusion of the passages from the Arabic Infancy Gospel and also the ninth-century Leabhar Breac in his *A Synopsis of the Apocryphal Nativity and Infancy Narratives* (Leiden, the Netherlands: Brill, 2006), 69–70.

11. For a treatment of Mary in the Akathistos hymn, see Leena Mari Peltomaa, *The Image of the Virgin Mary in the Akathistos Hymn* (Leiden, the Netherlands: Brill, 2001); see also her translation of the hymn on 2–19.

12. The most recent critical edition of *Pseudo-Matthew*, which Elliott follows, is that of Jan Gijsel and Rita Beyers, eds., *Libri de Nativitate Mariae*, 2 vols., CCSA 9, 10 (Turnhout, Belgium: Brepols, 1997).

13. I am depending upon the very helpful volume by J. K. Elliott, *A Synopsis of the Apocryphal Nativity and Infancy Narratives*.

14. See E. S. Buchanan, *The Four Gospels from the Codex Veronensis (b). Being the first complete edition of the Evangeliarium Purpureum in the Cathedral Library at Verona. With an introduction descriptive of the MS and two facsimiles* (Oxford: Clarendon, 1911); on this particular variant see also R. Laurentin, "Traces d'allusions Etymologiques en Luc 1–2," *Biblica* 38 (1957): 1–23, esp. 15–17; J. Rendel Harris, "Mary or Elisabeth," *Expository Times* 41 (1929/1930): 266–267 and 42 (1930/1931): 188–190.

15. See Bruce Metzger, *A Textual Commentary on the Greek New Testament*, 2nd ed. (London: United Bible Societies, 1995), 109; and his "Explicit References in the Works of Origen to Variant Readings in New Testament Manuscripts," in *Biblical and Patristic Studies in Memory of Robert Pierce Casey*, ed. J. Neville Birdsall and Robert W. Thomson (Freiburg, Germany: Herder, 1963), 78–95, esp. 85–86.

16. I have not dealt here with the issue of gender identification in Marian devotion. There might be some textual evidence in the variants of the Lukan magnificat that bear this up: see, for example, "henceforth all generations will call me blessed" in contrast to the readings found in Didymus and the reading in *Prot. James* 12.2: "Who am I that all the women of the earth bless me?"

17. On the figure of Mary Magdalene in the Gospels and beyond, see especially Ann Graham Brock, *Mary Magdalene, the First Apostle: The Struggle for Authority*, Harvard Theological Studies 51 (Cambridge, Mass.: Harvard University Press, 2003); Deirdre Good, ed., *Mariam, the Magdalen, and the Mother* (Bloomington: Indiana University Press, 2005); Susan Haskins, *Mary Magdalen: Myth and Metaphor* (New York: Riverhead Books, 1995); Karen L. King, *The Gospel of Mary of Magdala: Jesus and the First Woman Apostle* (Santa Rosa, Calif.: Polebridge Press, 2003); a good general article on the depiction of Mary Magdalene as a prostitute is found in Jane Schaberg, "How Mary Magdalene Became a Whore," *Bible Review* 8 (1992): 30–37, 51–52; see also her *The Resurrection of Mary Magdalene: Legends, Apocrypha, and the Christian Testament* (New York: Continuum, 2002).

18. PL 76, col. 1194; Benedicta Ward, *Harlots of the Desert: A Study of Repentance in Early Monastic Sources* (Kalamazoo, Mich.: Cistercian Publications, 1975), 14.

19. See especially, Bruce M. Metzger and Bart D. Ehrman, *Text of the New Testament: Its Transmission, Corruption, and Restoration,* 4th ed. (New York: Oxford University Press, 2005), 322–327; D. C. Parker, *An Introduction to the New Testament Manuscripts and Their Texts* (Cambridge: Cambridge University Press, 2008), 341–342 and his *The Living Text of the Gospels* (Cambridge: Cambridge University Press, 1997), 124–147; James A. Kelhoffer, *Miracle and Mission: The Authentication of Missionaries and Their Message in the Longer Ending of Mark* (Tübingen, Germany: Mohr Siebeck, 2000); Paul L. Danove, *The End of Mark's Story: A Methodological Study* (Leiden, the Netherlands: Brill, 1993).

20. See the translation by Thomas O. Lambdin in Robinson, ed., *The Nag Hammadi Library;* much has been written on this particular saying, but see especially Elizabeth Castelli, "'I Will Make Mary Male': Pieties of the Body and Gender Transformation of Christian Women in Late Antiquity," in *Body Guards: The Cultural Politics of Gender Ambiguity,* ed. Julie Epstein and Kristina Straub (New York: Routledge, 1991), 29–49.

21. Although there continues to be some debate about whether the Coptic Gospel of Mary from Nag Hammadi refers to Mary Magdalene or Mary the mother of Jesus, the evidence to my mind tilts decidedly toward Mary Magdalene; see especially King, *The Gospel of Mary of Magdala.* For the opposing view, see especially Stephen Shoemaker who argues for Mary the mother of Jesus ("Jesus' Gnostic Mom: Mary of Nazareth and the 'Gnostic Mary' Traditions," in Good, *Mariam, the Magdalen, and the Mother,* 153–182; "A Case of Mistaken Identity? Naming the Gnostic Mary," in *Which Mary? The Marys of Early Christian Tradition,* ed. F. Stanley Jones, SBL Symposium Series 19 [Atlanta: Society of Biblical Literature, 2002], 5–30; "Rethinking the 'Gnostic Mary': Mary of Nazareth and Mary of Magdala in Early Christian Tradition," *JECS* 9 [2001]: 555–595; and his *Ancient Traditions of the Virgin Mary's Dormition and Assumption,* Oxford Early Christian Studies [New York: Oxford University Press, 2002], esp. chap. 4); in favor of Mary Magdalene is J. Kevin Coyle, "Mary Magdalene in Manichaeism?" *Le Museon* 104 (1991): 39–55.

22. And also sometimes with Mary of Bethany (John 11:1–12:8; Luke 10:38–42).

23. Metzger, *Textual Commentary,* 129.

24. Jennifer Knust, "Early Christian Re-Writing and the History of the *Pericope Adulterae,*" *JECS* 14 (2006): 489; see also her article, "Jesus, an Adulteress, and the Development of a Christian Scripture," in *A Tall*

Order: Writing the Social History of the Ancient World. Essays in Honor of William V. Harris, ed. Jean-Jacques Aubert and Zsuzsanna Várhelyi (Munich: K. G. Saur, 2005), 59–84; see also Larry J. Kreitzer and Deborah W. Rooke, eds., *Ciphers in the Sand: Interpretations of the Woman Taken in Adultery (John 7.53–8.11)* (Sheffield, UK: Sheffield Academic Press, 2000).

25. Knust, "Early Christian Re-Writing," 533.

26. Clifford Geertz, "Religion as a Cultural System," in his *The Interpretation of Cultures* (New York: Basic Books, 1973), 93.

27. On these variants, see especially Ben Witherington, "The Anti-Feminist Tendencies of the 'Western' Text in Acts," *JBL* 103 (1984): 82–84; Eldon Jay Epp, *The Theological Tendency of Codex Bezae Cantabrigiensis in Acts* (Cambridge: Cambridge University Press, 1966).

28. See especially the brief article by Bernadette Brooton, "'Junia . . . Outstanding among the Apostles' (Romans 16:7)," in *Women Priests: A Catholic Commentary on the Vatican Declaration*, ed. Leonard Swidler and Arlene Swidler (New York: Paulist Press, 1977), 141–144.

29. Eldon Jay Epp, "Text-Critical, Exegetical, and Socio-Cultural Factors Affecting the Junia/Junias Variation in Romans 16:7," in *New Testament Textual Criticism and Exegesis: Festschrift for J. Delobel*, ed. A. Denaux (Leuven, Belgium: Leuven University Press/Peeters, 2002), 227–291; and his *Junia: The First Woman Apostle* (Minneapolis: Fortress Press, 2005); see also his "Minor Textual Variants in Romans 16:7," in *Transmission and Reception: New Testament Text-Critical and Exegetical Studies*, ed. J. W. Childers and D. C. Parker (Piscataway, N.J.: Gorgias Press, 2006), 123–141; see also John Thorley, "Junia, a Woman Apostle," *NovT* 38 (1996): 18–29.

30. Epp, *Junia*, 80.

31. See especially Antoinette Clark Wire, *The Corinthian Women Prophets: A Reconstruction through Paul's Rhetoric* (Minneapolis: Fortress Press, 1990), 149–158, 229–232; Philip B. Payne, "Fuldensis, Sigla for Variants in Vaticanus, and 1 Cor 14.34-5," *NTS* 41 (1995): 240–242; ibid., "Ms. 88 as Evidence for a Text without 1 Cor 14:34-5," *NTS* 44 (1998): 152–158; ibid., "The Text-Critical Function of the Umlauts in Vaticanus, with Special Attention to 1 Corinthians 14:34–35: A Response to J. Edward Miller," *JSNT* 27 (2004): 105–112; Jacobus Hendrik Petzer, "Reconsidering the Silent Women of Corinth: A Note on 1 Corinthians 14:34–35," *Theologia Evangelica* 26 (1993): 132–138.

32. *O.Crum*, Ad 13; Terry G. Wilfong, *Women of Jeme: Lives in a Coptic Town in Late Antique Egypt* (Ann Arbor: University of Michigan Press, 2002), 79.

Chapter 5

Chapter epigraphs. Mary Wollstonecraft, *A Vindication of the Rights of Woman*, ed. Deidre Shauna Lynch (New York: W. W. Norton, 2009), 82–83n5.

"St. Thekla: A Good Woman Will Not Be Kept Down," accessed August 31, 2009, http://iconnewmedianetwork.com/2007/12/11/saint-thekla-a-good-woman-will-not-be-kept-down/.

1. David R. Cartlidge and J. Keith Elliott, *Art and the Christian Apocrypha* (London: Routledge, 2001), 148.

2. The bibliography here is significant, but most important for the cult is Stephen J. Davis, *The Cult of Saint Thecla: A Tradition of Women's Piety in Late Antiquity.* Oxford Early Christian Texts (Oxford: Oxford University Press, 2001); see also Leonie Hayne, "Thecla and the Church Fathers," *VC* 48 (1994), 209–218; on the cults at Rome and Seleucia, see Kate Cooper, "A Saint in Exile: The Early Medieval Thecla at Rome and Meriamlik," *Hagiographica* 2 (1995): 1–23; a helpful rehearsal of the testimonies to Paul and Thecla is found in Bernhard Pick, *The Apocryphal Acts of Paul, Peter, John, Andrew and Thomas* (Chicago: Open Court Press, 1909), 8–13; on the *Life and Miracles*, see Gilbert Dagron's edition, *Vie et miracle de Sainte Thecle* (Brussels: Societe des Bollandistes, 1978); Scott Fitzgerald Johnson, *The Life and Miracles of Thekla: A Literary Study* (Washington, D.C.: Center for Hellenic Studies, 2006); for a treatment of Thecla art, see especially Claudia Nauerth and Rüdiger Warns, *Thekla: Ihre Bilder in der früchristlichen Kunst* (Wiesbaden, Germany: Otto Harrassowitz, 1981). Two most recent studies are especially worth noting: Ross Kraemer, *Unreliable Witnesses: Religion, Gender, and History in the Greco-Roman Mediterranean* (New York: Oxford University Press, 2011), and B. Diane Lipsett, *Desiring Conversion: Hermas, Thecla, Aseneth* (New York: Oxford University Press, 2011).

3. "St. Thekla: A Good Woman Will Not Be Kept Down."

4. Some of what follows appeared in my article "Engendering Palimpsests: Reading the Textual Tradition of the Acts of Paul and Thecla," in *The Early Christian Book*, ed. William E. Klingshirn and Linda Safran (Washington, D.C.: The Catholic University of America Press, 2007), 177–193.

5. English translations of these works are best found in vol. 2 of Edgar Hennecke, Wilhelm Schneemelcher, and R. McL. Wilson, eds., *New Testament Apocrypha* (Cambridge: James Clark and Co.; Louisville, Ky.: Westminster, 1992), and J. K. Elliott, *The Apocryphal New Testament: A Collection of Apocryphal Christian Literature in an English Translation* (Oxford: Oxford University Press, 1993). For the Acts of Paul and Thecla, on which I focus, the standard critical edition continues to be that of Richard A. Lipsius, Maximilian Bonnet, and Constantin von Tischendorf, eds., *Acta Apostolorum*

Apocrypha, vol. 1 (Leipzig, Germany: Hermann Mendelssohn, 1891). A new critical edition is needed, particularly one that would incorporate all of the manuscripts identified in Maurice Geerard, *Clavis Apocryphorum Novi Testamenti* (Turnhout, Belgium: Brepols, 1992); the recent commentary and translation by Jeremy W. Barrier does not, unfortunately, offer a proper critical edition but includes textual notes: *The Acts of Paul and Thecla: A Critical Introduction and Commentary* (Tübingen: Mohr Siebeck, 2009).

6. J. K. Elliott's edition includes both of these endings: *The Apocryphal New Testament,* 372–374.

7. Johnson, *Life and Miracles,* 15–66.

8. Similarly, as Elizabeth Clark has pointed out, Jerome's Latin translations of the Pastorals "pressed verses in an ascetic direction" by, for example, rendering the Greek *sophrosune* (sound-mindedness and/or self-control) "as *castitas* or as *incorruptio*" (Clark, *Reading Renunciation: Asceticism and Scripture in Early Christianity* [Princeton, N.J.: Princeton University Press, 1999], 166).

9. For the Armenian, I am depending upon the translation of Frederick Cornwallis Conybeare, ed., *The Apology and Acts of Apollonius and Other Monuments of Early Christianity* (London: Swan Sonnenschein, 1894).

10. Such variants may also be attempts to harmonize this text with the gospel texts, particularly Pauline, Matthean, and Lukan passages; I am grateful to Georgia Frank for reminding me of this scribal tendency and the likelihood that scribes copying the *Apocryphal Acts* in this instance may have been influenced by their knowledge of canonical passages.

11. Identified by Oscar von Gebhardt as "m" in his *Passio S. Theclae virginis: die lateinischen Übersetzungen der Acta Pauli et Theclae nebst Fragmenten, Auszügen und Beilagen* (Leipzig: J. C. Hinrichs, 1902).

12. William Wright, *Apocryphal Acts of the Apostles,* vol. 2 (London: Williams and Norgate, 1871; repr. Hildesheim, Germany: Georg Olms, 1990; and Piscataway, N.J.: Gorgias Press, 2005), 126. I depend here on the 1990 reprinted edition, which comprises two volumes bound in one with original pagination.

13. Conybeare, *Apology and Acts of Apollonius,* 70–71.

14. Again, there is extensive bibliography on "transvestite saints" as well as motifs of the manly woman. See especially Elizabeth Castelli, "'I Will Make Mary Male': Pieties of the Body and Gender Transformation of Christian Women in Late Antiquity," in *Body Guards: The Cultural Politics of Gender Ambiguity,* ed. Julia Epstein and Kristina Straub (New York: Routledge, 1991), 29–49; Evelyne Patlagean, "L'histoire de la femme déguisée en moine et l'évolution de la sainteté féminine à Byzance," *Studi Medievali* 3(17) (1976): 597–623; John Anson, "The Female Transvestite in Early

Monasticism: Origin and Development of a Motif," *Viator: Medieval and Renaissance Studies* 5 (1974): 1–32; and Susan Ashbrook Harvey, "Women in Early Byzantine Hagiography: Reversing the Story," in *That Gentle Strength: Historical Perspectives on Women in Christianity*, ed. Lynda L. Coon, Katherine J. Haldane, and Elisabeth W. Sommer (Richmond: University Press of Virginia, 1990), 36–59.

15. Stephen J. Davis, "Crossed Texts, Crossed Sex: Intertextuality and Gender in Early Christian Legends of Holy Women Disguised as Men," *JECS* 10 (2002): 29.

16. For an excellent discussion of the problems pertaining to the passage in Tertullian, see now most recently Ross Kraemer, *Unreliable Witnesses*, 117–120.

17. Carlin A. Barton, *The Sorrows of the Ancient Romans: The Gladiator and the Monster* (Princeton, N.J.: Princeton University Press, 1993), esp. 91–95: "The eye realized the polarization that magnetized Roman culture during this period: the operation, concurrently, of the extremes of power and powerlessness" (93); "it was the paradox of heightened power and heightened vulnerability that made the eye especially fascinating: it injured and was injured simultaneously" (94).

18. See Lipsius et al. for manuscripts and Schneemelcher's note on this passage.

19. The image has been reproduced a number of places: see Nauerth and Warns, *Thekla*, 85ff.; Nauerth and Warns also note the similarity, p. 86; Pedro de Palol and Max Hirmer, *Early Medieval Art in Spain* (New York: H. N. Abrams, 1967), n. 251.

20. For the Greek text, I am dependent on G. Nathanael Bonwetsch, *Methodius*, GCS 27 (Leipzig: J. C. Hinrichs, 1917); see also Herbert Musurillo's *Méthode d'Olympe Le Banquet*, SC 95 (Paris: Éditions du Cerf, 1963); English translations can be found in Musurillo, *The Symposium, A Treatise on Chastity*, ACW 27 (Westminster, Md.: Newman Press, 1958), and by William R. Clark in ANF 6 (Grand Rapids, Mich.: Eerdmans, 1951). Helpful secondary sources include the recent work by M. Benedetta Zorzi, "The Use of the Terms ἁγνεία, παρθενία, σωφροσύνη, and ἐγκράτεια in the *Symposium* of Methodius of Olympus," *VC* 63 (2009): 138–168; Alexander Bril, "Plato and the Sympotic Form in the *Symposium* of St. Methodius of Olympus," *Zeitschrift für Antikes Christentum* 9 (2005): 279–302.

21. On this chapter as authorizing the work of the author, see especially, Johnson, *Life and Miracles*, 118–120.

22. Derek Krueger, *Writing and Holiness: The Practice of Authorship in the Early Christian East* (Philadelphia: University of Pennsylvania Press), 79–92.

23. Ahmed Fakhry, *The Necropolis of el-Bagawāt in Kharga Oasis* (Cairo: Government Press, 1951); Stephen Davis, *The Cult of St. Thecla*, esp. 153–158. I am grateful to Davis for sharing his photographs with me; when this book went to press, Oxford University Press found Ken Perry's photographs (for which I am also grateful) clearer to reproduce.

24. Fakhry, *Necropolis*, 78.

25. Davis, *Cult of Saint Thecla*, 157. I am grateful to Stephen Davis for corresponding with me about his interpretation of the image.

26. *Vindication*, 57.

Chapter 6

Chapter epigraph. This joke has circulated among textual critics in recent years and each time the version is a bit different. Accessed August 31, 2009, http://www.seejokes.com/Joke/See/Religion/52/New-Monk.html.

The Language of Paradox epigraph. Geoffrey Galt Harpham, *The Ascetic Imperative in Culture and Criticism* (Chicago: University of Chicago Press, 1987), 67.

1. Elizabeth Clark, *Reading Renunciation: Asceticism and Scripture in Early Christianity* (Princeton, N.J.: Princeton University Press, 1999), 259.

2. Text variants that have to do with broader ascetic practices (e.g., fasting, John the Baptist's diet) have been dealt with by others. In Mark 9:29, for example, when the disciples ask why they were unable to cast a demon out of a boy, Jesus replies, "This kind [of demon] cannot be driven out by anything but prayer"; to this verse, a host of manuscripts add "and fasting." Remarkably, this reading seems to appear in our earliest papyrus fragment of the Gospel of Mark, P[45], alongside a strong list of Greek manuscripts and Latin, Syriac, and Coptic versions. This longer reading, in fact, could be the original one; so originally the text would have said "prayer and fasting" were required to cast out the demon. The dual actions of prayer and fasting are well known (e.g., Luke 2:37, 5:33; Acts 13:3, 14:23). Variants attached to food appear elsewhere in the textual record. At Matthew 22:4 in the parable about the marriage feast, the king calls to his servants saying, "Tell those who are invited, behold, I have made ready my dinner, my oxen and my fat calves are killed, and everything is ready; come to the marriage feast." Again in the Sinaitic Syriac manuscript, we find an unusual— apparently unique—reading that omits the passage about oxen and fat calves in the marriage feast. Epiphanius has a rather unusual record, too, of what the Gospel of the Ebionites says about John the Baptist's diet (i.e., that

it was exclusively vegetarian). See Bruce M. Metzger and Bart D. Ehrman, *The Text of the New Testament: Its Transmission, Corruption, and Restoration*, 4th ed. (New York: Oxford University Press, 2005), 294–295; J. Rendel Harris, "New Points of View in Textual Criticism," *The Expositor* 8 (1914): 316–334.

3. Some of these, too, have been treated before. See especially the discussions of the variant in Luke 2:36, where we find that the Sinaitic Syriac manuscript claims Anna lived with her husband for seven days, not seven years (Metzger and Ehrman, *Text of the New Testament*, 295). The significant number of variants in 1 Corinthians 7 is worthy of a separate study in this regard—surely they demonstrate that the text the church fathers were working with was anything but fixed (cf. Clark, *Reading Renunciation*, 260).

4. For the Greek, see GCS 52, 197. The ANF edition, produced by Cleveland Coxe, rendered *Stromata* book 3 in Latin(!) rather than translate it into English, seeing Clement's arguments as too favorable to celibacy: "After much consideration, the Editors have deemed it best to give the whole of this Book in Latin. In the former Book, Clement has shown, not without a decided leaning to chaste celibacy, that marriage is a holy estate and consistent with the perfect man in Christ. He now enters upon the refutation of the false-Gnostics and their licentious tenets. Professing a stricter rule to begin with, and despising the ordinances of the Creator, their result was the grossest immorality in practice. The melancholy consequences of an enforced celibacy are, here, all foreseen and foreshown; and this Book, though necessarily offensive to our Christian tastes, is most useful as a commentary upon the history of monasticism, and the celibacy of priests, in the Western churches. The resolution of the Edinburgh editors to give this Book to scholars *only*, in the Latin, is probably wise" (p. 381, n. 1). Regarding such claims, see now Elizabeth A. Clark, *Founding the Fathers: Early Church History and Protestant Professors in Nineteenth-Century America* (Philadelphia: University of Pennsylvania Press, 2011).

5. There are excellent treatments of this subject: Averil Cameron, *Christianity and the Rhetoric of Empire: The Development of Christian Discourse*, Sather Classical Lectures 55 (Berkeley: University of California Press, 1991); Aline Rousselle, *Porneia: On Desire and the Body in Antiquity*, trans. Felicia Pheasant (Oxford: Blackwell, 1988); Margaret Miles, *Carnal Knowing: Female Nakedness and Religious Meaning in the Christian West* (Boston: Beacon, 1989), though not directly related to this subject, is important.

6. Clark, *Reading Renunciation*, esp. 80–81, 149–151, and 180–183.

7. For the diverse translations and interpretations, see especially Gordon D. Fee, *Paul's Letter to the Philippians*, The New International

Commentary on the New Testament (Grand Rapids, Mich.: Eerdmans, 1995), 392–396.

8. PL 23; English translation: NPNF s.s. 6; Jerome's reference to a textual variant here should be added to Bruce Metzger's collection: "St. Jerome's Explicit References to Variant Readings in Manuscripts of the New Testament," in his *New Testament Studies: Philological, Versional, and Patristic* (Leiden, the Netherlands: Brill, 1980), 199–210.

9. For English editions and introductions, see those of J. Keith Elliott, *The Apocryphal New Testament: A Collection of Apocryphal Christian Literature in an English Transition* (Oxford: Clarendon Press, 1993); Edgar Hennecke and Wilhelm Schneemelcher, eds., *The New Testament Apocrypha*, 2 vols. (Cambridge: James Clarke and Co., 1992); for the Greek I have relied especially on the edition by Richard A. Lipsius and M. Bonnet, *Acta Apostolorum Apocrypha* (Leipzig: Hermann Mendelssohn, 1891); for the Syriac, see William Wright, *Apocryphal Acts of the Apostles* (Hildesheim: Georg Olms Verlag, 1990; Piscataway, N.J.: Gorgias Press, 2005); for the Latin of the *AT*, see Klaus Zelzer, *Die Alten Lateinischen Thomasakten* (Berlin: Akademie Verlag, 1977).

10. From C. R. C. Allberry, *A Manichaean Psalm-Book*, pt. 2 (Stuttgart, Germany: W. Kohlhammer, 1938), 192–193; on Manichaean ideologies of the body, see especially Jason David BeDuhn, *The Manichaean Body: In Discipline and Ritual* (Baltimore, Md.: Johns Hopkins University Press, 2000); on Augustine and Manichaeism, see Peter Brown's foundational *Augustine of Hippo: A Biography* (Berkeley: University of California Press, 1967); and Brown, "The Diffusion of Manichaeism in the Roman Empire," *JRS* 59 (1969): 92–103.

11. Virginia Burrus, "Word and Flesh: The Bodies and Sexuality of Ascetic Women in Christian Antiquity," *JFSR* 10 (1994): 27–51; see also her article, "The Heretical Woman as Symbol in Alexander, Athanasius, Epiphanius, and Jerome," *HTR* 84 (1991): 229–248; for Brown's comments on Syria, see *Society and the Holy in Late Antiquity* (Berkeley: University of California Press, 1982), 114.

12. On the gaze, see especially Georgia Frank, *The Memory of the Eyes: Pilgrims to Living Saints in Christian Late Antiquity*, The Transformation of the Classical Heritage 30 (Berkeley: University of California Press, 2000).

13. William Wright, *Apocryphal Acts of the Apostles.*

14. Miles, *Carnal Knowing*, esp. 35–36.

15. Derek Krueger, "Between Monks: Tales of Monastic Companionship in Early Byzantium," *Journal of the History of Sexuality* 20 (2011): 28–61.

16. Krueger, "Between Monks," 29.

17. For chapters and the Greek text, I have relied on Jean-Marc Prieur, *Actes de l'apôtre André*, CCSA 5 and 6 (Turnhout, Belgium: Brepols, 1995), with comparison to Dennis R. MacDonald, *The Acts of Andrew and the Acts of Andrew and Matthias in the City of the Cannibals* (Atlanta: Scholars Press, 1990) and Maximilian Bonnet, *Acta Andreae cum laudatione contexta et Martyrium Andreae Graece: Passio Andreae Latine*, Supplementum codicis apocryphi 2 (Paris: C. Klincksieck, 1895). The three manuscripts are Jerusalem, Saint Saba 103 (thirteenth century?, H); Sinai gr. 526 (tenth century, S); and Vatican gr. 808 (eleventh century, V). The Bonnet edition forms the basis for Hennecke-Schneemelcher's edition, which does not put the three manuscripts together, but rather follows H and S, and translates V separately.

18. Translation in Elliott, *Apocryphal New Testament*, 232.

19. See Michael Philip Penn, *Kissing Christians: Ritual and Community in the Late Ancient Church* (Philadelphia: University of Pennsylvania Press, 2005).

20. See *Acts of John* 62, the arrival in Ephesus, where the kissing of John's hands is found only in ms. O and omitted in mss. M RZ. (See the edition by Eric Junod and Jean-Daniel Kaestli, *Acta Iohannis*, CCSA 1 and 2 [Turnhout, Belgium: Brepols, 1983], 251).

21. See Elizabeth A. Castelli, "'I Will Make Mary Male': Pieties of the Body and Gender Transformation of Christian Women in Late Antiquity," in *Body Guards: The Cultural Politics of Gender Ambiguity*, ed. Julia Epstein and Kristina Straub (New York: Routledge, 1991), 29–49; John Anson, "The Female Transvestite in Early Monasticism: The Origin and Development of a Motif," *Viator* 5 (1974): 1–32; for notions of manliness and martyrdom see L. Stephanie Cobb, *Dying to Be Men: Gender and Language in Early Christian Martyr Texts* (New York: Columbia University Press, 2008); Miles, *Carnal Knowing*, esp. 53–77; Kerstin Bjerre-Aspegren, *The Male Woman: A Feminine Ideal in the Early Church* (Stockholm: Almqvist and Wiksell, 1990).

22. I am relying here on *Cyril of Scythopolis: Lives of the Monks of Palestine*, trans. R. M. Price (Kalamazoo, Mich.: Cistercian Publications, 1991).

23. I am using the edition of George Nedungatt and Michael Featherstone, *The Council in Trullo Revisited* (Rome: Pontificio Istituto Orientale, 1995).

24. English and Latin: Herbert Musurillo, trans., *The Acts of the Christian Martyrs* (Oxford: Clarendon Press, 1972); for the critical edition, I have used C. Van Beek, *Passio Sanctarum Perpetuae et Felicitatis, latine et graece* (Bonn, Germany: Dekker, 1938). J. A. Robinson, *The Passion of S. Perpetua*, Texts and Studies, vols. 1, 2 (Cambridge: Cambridge University Press, 1891).

25. Benedicta Ward, *The Sayings of the Desert Fathers: The Alphabetical Collection* (Kalamazoo, Mich.: Cistercian Publications, 1975).

Conclusions

Chapter epigraphs. Quoted in Margaret R. Miles, *Carnal Knowing: Female Nakedness and Religious Meaning in the Christian West* (Boston: Beacon, 1989), 13.

Denise Riley, *"Am I That Name?": Feminism and the Category of "Women" in History* (Minneapolis: University of Minnesota, 1988), 5.

1. What follows is a revision of the introduction to my article "Engendering Palimpsests: Reading the Textual Tradition of the Acts of Paul and Thecla," in *The Early Christian Book*, ed. William E. Klingshirn and Linda Safran (Washington, D.C.: The Catholic University of American Press), 177–193. The story of this trip is told by A. Whigham Price, *The Ladies of Castlebrae: A Story of Nineteenth-Century Travel and Research* (Gloucester: Alan Sutton, 1985), 107ff; for later trips see also Agnes Smith Lewis, *In the Shadow of Sinai: A Story of Travel and Research from 1895 to 1897* (Cambridge: Macmillan & Bowes, 1898).

2. Price, *The Ladies of Castelbrae*, 125–126.

3. Janet Soskice, *Sisters of Sinai: How Two Lady Adventurers Found the Hidden Gospels* (London: Chatto and Windus, 2009), 295.

4. Agnes Smith Lewis, *Select Narratives of Holy Women from the Syro-Antiochene or Sinai Palimpsest as Written above the Old Syriac by John the Stylite of Beth-Mari Qanūn in AD 778* (London: C. J. Clay and Sons, 1900), vi.

5. I am grateful to Ross Kraemer who took my clunky "Engendering Palimpsests" and suggested the more elegant and simple *The Gendered Palimpsest*. On this Sinaitic Syriac palimpsest, see Bruce M. Metzger, *The Early Versions of the New Testament: Their Origin, Transmission and Limitations* (Oxford: Clarendon Press, 1977), 37–38; R. L. Bensly, J. Rendel Harris, and F. C. Burkitt, *The Four Gospels in Syriac Transcribed from the Sinaitic Palimpsest* (Cambridge: Cambridge University Press, 1894); and Agnes Lewis, *Some Pages of the Four Gospels Retranscribed from the Sinaitic Palimpsest with a Translation of the Full Text* (London: C. J. Clay, 1896); see also Agnes Lewis's standard edition of the manuscript: *The Old Syriac Gospels, or Evangleion da-Mepharreshe; Being the Text of the Sinai or Syro-Antiochian Palimpsest, Including the Latest Additions and Emendations, with the Variants of the Curetonian Text* (London: Williams and Norgate, 1910).

6. I am reminded of Wettstein's eighteenth-century acceptance of the attribution of the fifth-century Codex Alexandrinus to the hand of Thecla on the basis of its many mistakes with which I began (see also my *Guardians of Letters*, 51).

7. Lewis, *Select Narratives*, 206.

8. W. J. T. Mitchell, *Iconology: Image, Text, Ideology* (Chicago: University of Chicago Press, 1986), 38.

Works Cited

Aland, Kurt, and Barbara Aland. *The Text of the New Testament: An Introduction to the Critical Editions and to the Theory and Practice of Modern Textual Criticism*. Translated by Erroll F. Rhodes. Grand Rapids, Mich.: Eerdmans, 1987.

Albrecht, Ruth. *Das Leben der heiligen Makrina auf dem Hintergrund der Thekla-Traditionen: Studien zu den Ursprüngen des weiblichen Mönchtums im 4.Jahrhundert in Kleinasien*. Göttingen, Germany: Vandenhoeck and Ruprecht, 1986.

Allberry, C. R. C. *A Manichaean Psalm-Book*. Stuttgart, Germany: W. Kohlhammer, 1938.

Amidon, Philip R., trans. *The Panarion of St. Epiphanius, Bishop of Salamis: Selected Passages*. New York: Oxford University Press, 1990.

Anson, John. "The Female Transvestite in Early Monasticism: Origin and Development of a Motif." *Viator: Medieval and Renaissance Studies* 5 (1974): 1–32.

Apostolos-Cappadona, Diane. *In Search of Mary Magdalene: Images and Traditions*. New York: American Bible Society, 2002.

Arns, Paulo Evaristo. *La Technique du livre d'après Saint Jérôme*. Paris: E. De Boccard, 1953.

Azema, Yvan, ed. *Theodoret de Cyr: Correspondence*. SC 98. Paris: Éditions du Cerf, 1964.

Bagnall, Roger S. "An Owner of Literary Papyri." *Classical Philology* 87 (1992): 137–140.

Bagnall, Roger S., and Raffaella Cribiore. *Women's Letters from Ancient Egypt, 300 BC–AD 800*. Ann Arbor: University of Michigan Press, 2006.

Balough, J. "Voces Paginarum: Beiträge zur Geschichte des lauten Lesens und Schreibens." *Philologus* 82 (1927): 84–109, 202–240.

Barbet, Alix, and Claude Vibert-Guigue. *Les peintures des nécropoles romaines d'Abila et du Nord de la Jordanie*. 2 vols. Beirut, Lebanon: Institut français d'archéologie du Proche-Orient, 1988–1994.

Barrier, Jeremy W. *The Acts of Paul and Thecla: A Critical Introduction and Commentary*. Tübingen: Mohr Siebeck, 2009.

Barthes, Roland. *Image, Music, Text*. Trans. Stephen Heath. New York: Hill and Wang, 1977.

Barton, Carlin A. *The Sorrows of the Ancient Romans: The Gladiator and the Monster*. Princeton, N.J.: Princeton University Press, 1993.

Beach, Alison I. *Women as Scribes: Book Production and Monastic Reform in Twelfth-Century Bavaria*. Cambridge: Cambridge University Press, 2004.

Beaucamp, Joëlle. *Le Status de la Femme à Byzance (4ᵉ–7ᵉ siècle)*. 2 vols. Paris: De Boccard, 1990.

Beck, F. A. "The Schooling of Girls in Ancient Greece." *Classicum* 9 (1978): 1–9.

BeDuhn, Jason David. *The Manichaean Body: In Discipline and Ritual*. Baltimore, Md.: Johns Hopkins University Press, 2000.

Bell, Susan Groag. "Medieval Women Book Owners: Arbiters of Lay Piety and Ambassadors of Culture." *Signs: Journal of Women in Culture and Society* 7 (1982): 742–768.

Benjamin, Walter. *Illuminations*. Edited by Hannah Arendt. Translated by Harry Zohn. New York: Schocken Books, 1968.

Bensly, R. L., J. R. Harris, and F. C. Burkitt. *The Four Gospels in Syriac Transcribed from the Sinaitic Palimpsest*. Cambridge: Cambridge University Press, 1894.

Bergren, Ann. *Weaving Truth: Essays on Language and the Female in Greek Thought*. Cambridge, Mass.: Center for Hellenic Studies, 2008.

Bjerre-Aspegren, Kerstin. *The Male Woman: A Feminine Ideal in the Early Church*. Stockholm: Almqvist and Wiksell, 1990.

Bongie, Elizabeth Bryson, trans. *The Life of Blessed Syncletica by Pseudo-Athanasius*. Toronto: Peregrina Publishing Co., 1996.

Bonnet, M. *Acta Andreae cum laudatione context et Martyrium Andreae Graece: Passio Andreae Latine*. Supplementum codicis apocryphi 2. Paris: C. Klincksieck, 1895.

———. *Acta Philippi et Acta Thomae*. Leipzig, Germany: H. Mendelssohn, 1903.

————. *Acta Thomae*. Leipzig, Germany: H. Mendelssohn, 1883.

Bonwetsch, G. Nathanael. *Methodius*. GCS 27. Leipzig: J. C. Hinrichs, 1917.

Borges, Jorge Luis. Prologue to "Catalog of the Exhibition Books from Spain." In *Selected Non-Fictions*, edited by Eliot Weinberger. Translated by Esther Allen, Suzanne Jill Levine, and Eliot Weinberger. New York: Penguin Books, 1999.

Bowie, Ewen. "The Readership of Greek Novels in the Ancient World." In *The Search for the Ancient Novel*, edited by James Tatum, 435–459. Baltimore, Md.: Johns Hopkins University Press, 1994.

Brakke, David, trans. *Pseudo-Athanasius on Virginity*. CSCO 593. Leuven, Belgium: Peeters, 2002.

Bremmer, Jan N., ed. *The Apocryphal Acts of John*. Kampen, the Netherlands: Pharos, 1995.

————, ed. *The Apocryphal Acts of Paul and Thecla*. Kampen, the Netherlands: Pharos, 1996.

————, ed. *The Apocryphal Acts of Thomas*. Leuven, Belgium: Peters, 2001.

————. "The Novel and the Apocryphal Acts: Place, Time and Readership." In *Groningen Colloquia on the Novel* IX, edited by H. Hofmann and M. Zimmerman, 157–180. Groningen, the Netherlands: Egbert Forsten, 1998.

Bril, Alexander. "Plato and the Sympotic Form in the *Symposium* of St. Methodius of Olympus." *Zeitschrift für Antikes Christentum* 9 (2005): 279–302.

Brock, Ann Graham. *Mary Magdalene, the First Apostle: The Struggle for Authority*. Harvard Theological Studies 51. Cambridge, Mass.: Harvard Divinity School, 2003.

Brock, Sebastian P., and Susan Ashbrook Harvey, trans. *Holy Women of the Syrian Orient*. Berkeley: University of California Press, 1987.

Brooten, Bernadette. "'Junia . . . Outstanding among the Apostles' (Romans 16:7)." In *Women Priests: A Catholic Commentary on the Vatican Declaration*, edited by Leonard Swidler and Arlene Swidler, 141–144. New York: Paulist Press, 1977.

Brown, Peter. *Augustine of Hippo: A Biography*. Berkeley: University of California Press, 1967.

————. *The Body and Society: Men, Women, and Sexual Renunciation in Early Christianity*. New York: Columbia University Press, 1988.

————. "The Diffusion of Manichaeism in the Roman Empire." *JRS* 59 (1969): 92–103.

———. "The Patrons of Pelagius: The Roman Aristocracy between East and West." *JTS* n.s. 21 (1970): 56–72.

———. *Society and the Holy in Late Antiquity*. Berkeley: University of California Press, 1982.

Buchanan, E. S. *The Four Gospels from the Codex Veronensis (b). Being the First Complete Edition of the Evangeliarium Purpureum in the Cathedral Library at Verona. With an Introduction Descriptive of the MS and Two Facsimiles.* Oxford: Clarendon Press, 1911.

Burkitt, F. C. "Codex 'Alexandrinus.'" *JTS* 11 (1909–1910): 603–606.

Burrus, Virginia. *Chastity as Autonomy: Women in the Stories of Apocryphal Acts.* Studies in Women and Religion 23. Lewiston, N.Y.: Edwin Mellen Press, 1987.

———. "The Heretical Woman as Symbol in Alexander, Athanasius, Epiphanius, and Jerome." *HTR* 84 (1991): 229–248.

———. "Word and Flesh: The Bodies and Sexuality of Ascetic Women in Christian Antiquity." *JFSR* 10 (1994): 27–51.

Burton-Christie, Douglas. *The Word in the Desert: Scripture and the Quest for Holiness in Early Christian Monasticism.* New York: Oxford University Press, 1993.

Butler, Alban. *Lives of the Fathers, Martyrs, and Other Principle Saints.* Vol. 3. Dublin: James Duffy, 1866. Accessed October 2, 2010. http://www.bartleby.com/210/3/132.html.

Butler, Dom Cuthbert, ed. *The Lausiac History of Palladius.* 2 vols. Texts and Studies 6. Cambridge: Cambridge University Press, 1898–1904.

Byatt, A. S. *On Histories and Stories: Selected Essays.* Cambridge, Mass.: Harvard University Press, 2001.

Bynum, Caroline Walker. *Holy Feast and Holy Fast: The Religious Significance of Food to Medieval Women.* Berkeley: University of California Press, 1987.

Calderini, Rita. "Gli *agrammatoi* nell'Egitto Greco-romano." *Aegyptus* 30 (1950): 14–41.

Callahan, Virginia Woods, trans. *Saint Gregory of Nyssa: Ascetical Works.* Washington, D.C.: Catholic University of America, 1967.

Cameron, Averil. *Christianity and the Rhetoric of Empire: The Development of Christian Discourse.* Sather Classical Lectures 55. Berkeley: University of California Press, 1991.

Cameron, Averil, and Amélie Kuhrt, eds. *Images of Women in Antiquity.* Detroit: Wayne State University Press, 1983.

Cartlidge, David R., and J. Keith Elliott. *Art and the Christian Apocrypha.* London: Routledge, 2001.

Castelli, Elizabeth. "'I Will Make Mary Male': Pieties of the Body and Gender Transformation of Christian Women in Late Antiquity." In

Body Guards: The Cultural Politics of Gender Ambiguity, edited by
Julia Epstein and Kristina Straub, 29–49. New York: Routledge, 1991.

———. "Virginity and Its Meaning for Women's Sexuality in Early
Christianity." *JFSR* 2 (1986): 61–88.

Charlesworth, James H. *The Good and Evil Serpent: How a Universal
Symbol Became Christianized.* New Haven, Conn.: Yale University
Press, 2010.

Chartier, Roger. *Forms and Meanings: Texts, Performances, and Audiences
from Codex to Computer.* Philadelphia: University of Pennsylvania
Press, 1995.

———. *On the Edge of the Cliff: History, Languages, and Practices.*
Translated by Lydia Cochrane. Baltimore, Md.: Johns Hopkins Press,
1997.

———. *The Order of Books: Readers, Authors, and Libraries in Europe
between the Fourteenth and Eighteenth Centuries.* Translated by Lydia
G. Cochrane. Stanford, Calif.: Stanford University Press, 1994.

Churchill, Lauria J., Phyllis R. Brown, and Jane E. Jeffrey, eds. *Women
Writing Latin: From Roman Antiquity to Early Modern Europe.* 3 vols.
New York: Routledge, 2002.

Cixous, Hélène. *Three Steps on the Ladder of Writing.* Translated by Sarah
Cornell and Susan Sellers. New York: Columbia University Press, 1994.

Clark, Elizabeth A. *Founding the Fathers: Early Church History and
Protestant Professors in Nineteenth-Century America.* Philadelphia:
University of Pennsylvania Press, 2011.

———. *Jerome, Chrysostom, and Friends: Essays and Translations.* Studies
in Women and Religion 2. New York: Edwin Mellen Press, 1979.

———. *The Life of Melania the Younger: Introduction, Translation, and
Commentary.* New York: Edwin Mellen Press, 1984.

———. "Patrons, Not Priests: Gender and Power in Late Ancient
Christianity." *Gender and History* 2 (1990): 253–273.

———. *Reading Renunciation: Asceticism and Scripture in Early
Christianity.* Princeton, N.J.: Princeton University Press, 1999.

Clark, Elizabeth A., and Diane F. Hatch. *The Golden Bough, The Oaken
Cross: The Virgilian Cento of Faltonia Betitia Proba.* Chico, Calif.:
Scholars Press, 1981.

Cloke, Gillian. *This Female Man of God: Women and Spiritual Power in
the Patristic Age, AD 350–450.* London: Routledge, 1995.

Cobb, L. Stephanie. *Dying to Be Men: Gender and Language in Early
Christian Martyr Texts.* New York: Columbia University Press, 2008.

Cole, Susan G. "Could Greek Women Read and Write?" In *Reflections of
Women in Antiquity,* edited by Helene P. Foley, 219–245. New York:
Gordon and Breach Science Publishers, 1981.

Conybeare, Frederick Cornwallis, ed. *The Apology and Acts of Apollonius and Other Monuments of Early Christianity.* London: Swan Sonnenschein, 1894.

Coon, Linda L. *Sacred Fictions: Holy Women and Hagiography in Late Antiquity.* Philadelphia: University of Pennsylvania Press, 1997.

Cooper, Kate. "The Patristic Period." In *The Blackwell Companion to the Bible and Culture,* edited by John F. A. Sawyer, 28–38. Oxford: Wiley-Blackwell, 2006.

———. "A Saint in Exile: The Early Medieval Thecla at Rome and Meriamlik." *Hagiographica* 2 (1995): 1–23.

———. *The Virgin and the Bride: Idealized Womanhood in Late Antiquity.* Cambridge, Mass.: Harvard University Press, 1996.

Cowper, B. H., ed. *Codex Alexandrinus. He Kaine Diatheke. Novum Testamentum Graece: ex antiquissimo Codice Alexandrino a C.G. Woide olim descriptum.* London: Williams and Norgate, 1860.

Coyle, J. Kevin. "Mary Magdalene in Manichaeism?" *Le Muséon* 104 (1991): 39–55.

Cribiore, Raffaella. *Gymnastics of the Mind: Greek Education in Hellenistic and Roman Egypt.* Princeton, N.J.: Princeton University Press, 2001.

Crum, W. E., and H. G. Evelyn White. *The Monastery of Epiphanius at Thebes.* New York: Metropolitan Museum of Art, 1926.

Dagenais, John. The *Ethics of Reading in Manuscript Culture: Glossing the* Libro de Buen Amor. Princeton, N.J.: Princeton University Press, 1994.

Dagron, Gilbert, ed. and trans. *Vie et miracles de Sainte Thècle.* Brussels: Société des Bollandistes, 1978.

Dalton, O. M., trans. *The Letters of Sidonius.* 2 vols. Oxford: Clarendon Press, 1915.

D'Ambra, Eve. "Mourning and the Making of Ancestors in the Testamentum Relief." *AJA* 99 (1995): 667–681.

Danove, Paul L. *The End of Mark's Story: A Methodological Study.* Leiden, the Netherlands: E. J. Brill, 1993.

Davies, Stevan L. *The Revolt of the Widows: The Social World of the Apocryphal Acts.* Carbondale: Southern Illinois University Press, 1980.

Davis, Stephen J. "Crossed Texts, Crossed Sex: Intertextuality and Gender in Early Christian Legends of Holy Women Disguised as Men." *JECS* 10 (2002): 1–36.

———. *The Cult of Saint Thecla: A Tradition of Women's Piety in Late Antiquity.* Oxford Early Christian Studies. Oxford: Oxford University Press, 2001.

de Palol, Pedro, and Max Hirmer. *Early Medieval Art in Spain*. New York: H. N. Abrams, 1967.

de Strycker, Émile. *La forme la plus ancienne du Protévangile de Jacques. Recherches sur le Papyrus Bodmer 5 avec une édition critique du texte et une traduction annotée*. Brussels: Société des Bollandistes, 1961.

Dillon, Sarah. *The Palimpsest: Literature, Criticism, Theory*. London: Continuum, 2007.

Douglass, Laurie. "A New Look at the *Itinerarium Burdigalense*." *JECS* 4 (1999): 313–334.

Drijvers, Han J. W. "The Acts of Thomas." In *The New Testament Apocrypha*, edited by Edgar Hennecke and Wilhelm Schneemelcher, vol. 2, 322–411. Cambridge: James Clarke and Co. Ltd., 1992.

Dronke, Peter. *Women Writers of the Middle Ages: A Critical Study of Texts from Perpetua to Marguerite Porete*. Cambridge: Cambridge University Press, 1984.

Ehrman, Bart D., ed. and trans. *The Apostolic Fathers*. 2 vols. Loeb Classical Library. Cambridge, Mass.: Harvard University Press, 2003.

———. "The New Testament Canon of Didymus the Blind." *VC* 37 (1983): 1–21.

———. *The Orthodox Corruption of Scripture*. Oxford: Oxford University Press, 1993.

———. "The Text as Window: New Testament Manuscripts and the Social History of Early Christianity." In *The Text of the New Testament in Contemporary Research: Essays on the* Status Quaestionis, ed. Bart D. Ehrman and Michael W. Holmes, 361–379. Grand Rapids, Mich.: Eerdmans, 1995.

Elliott, J. Keith. *The Apocryphal New Testament: A Collection of Apocryphal Christian Literature in an English Translation*. Oxford: Clarendon Press, 1993.

———. *A Synopsis of the Apocryphal Nativity and Infancy Narratives*. Leiden, the Netherlands: Brill, 2006.

Eisen, Ute E. *Women Officeholders in Early Christianity: Epigraphical and Literary Sources*. Collegeville, Minn.: Order of St. Benedict, Inc., 2000; originally published as *Amtsträgerinnen im frühen Christentum: Epigraphische und literarische Studien*. Göttingen, Germany: Vandenhoeck and Ruprecht, 1996.

Elm, Susanna. "An Alleged Book-Theft in Fourth-Century Egypt: P. Lips. 43." *Studia Patristica* 18 (1989): 209–215.

———. *Virgins of God: The Making of Asceticism in Late Antiquity*. Oxford: Oxford University Press, 1994.

Elsner, Jas'. "The *Itinerarium Burdigalense:* Politics and Salvation in the Geography of Constantine's Empire." *JRS* 90 (2000): 181–195.

Epp, Eldon Jay. *Junia: The First Woman Apostle.* Minneapolis: Fortress Press, 2005.

———. "Minor Textual Variants in Romans 16:7." In *Transmission and Reception: New Testament Text-Critical and Exegetical Studies,* edited by J. W. Childers and D. C. Parker, 123–141. Piscataway, N.J.: Gorgias Press, 2006.

———. "Text-Critical, Exegetical, and Socio-Cultural Factors Affecting the Junia/Junias Variation in Romans 16,7." In *New Testament Textual Criticism and Exegesis: Festschrift J. Delobel,* edited by A. Denaux, 227–291. Leuven, Belgium: Leuven University Press/Peeters, 2002.

———. *The Theological Tendency of Codex Bezae Cantabrigiensis in Acts.* Cambridge: Cambridge University Press, 1966.

Fakhry, Ahmed. *The Necropolis of el-Bagawāt in Kharga Oasis.* Cairo: Government Press, 1951.

Fee, Gordon D. *Paul's Letter to the Philippians.* The New International Commentary on the New Testament. Grand Rapids, Mich.: Eerdmans, 1995.

Ferrante, Joan M. *To the Glory of Her Sex: Women's Roles in the Composition of Medieval Texts.* Bloomington: Indiana University Press, 1997.

Festugière, A.-J. *Collections grecque de Miracles: Sainte Thècle, Saints Côme et Damien, Saints Cyr et Jean (extraits), Saint Georges.* Paris: A. et J. Picard, 1971.

Flint, Kate. *The Woman Reader 1837–1914.* Oxford: Clarendon Press, 1993.

Foucault, Michel. *This Is Not a Pipe.* Translated and edited by James Harkness. Berkeley: University of California Press, 1983.

Frank, Georgia. *The Memory of the Eyes: Pilgrims to Living Saints in Christian Late Antiquity.* The Transformation of the Classical Heritage 30. Berkeley: University of California Press, 2000.

Frese, Dolore Warwick, and Katherine O'Brien O'Keeffe, eds. *The Book and the Body.* Notre Dame, Ind.: University of Notre Dame Press, 1997.

Geerard, Maurice. *Clavis Apocryphorum Novi Testamenti.* Turnhout, Belgium: Brepols, 1992.

Geertz, Clifford. *The Interpretation of Cultures: Selected Essays.* New York: Basic Books, 1973.

Gibson, Margaret D. *How the Codex Was Found: A Narrative of Two Visits to Sinai from Mrs. Lewis's Journals 1892–1893*. Piscataway, N.J.: Gorgias Press, 2001.

Gijsel, Jan, and Rita Beyers, eds. *Libri de Nativitate Mariae*. 2 vols. CCSA 9–10. Turnhout, Belgium: Brepols, 1997.

Gold, Barbara K. *Literary and Artistic Patronage in Ancient Rome*. Austin: University of Texas Press, 1982.

Goldhill, Simon. *Foucault's Virginity: Ancient Erotic Fiction and the History of Sexuality*. Cambridge: Cambridge University Press, 1995.

Good, Deirdre, ed. *Mariam, the Magdalen, and the Mother*. Bloomington: Indiana University Press, 2005.

Goodspeed, Edgar J. "The Book of Thekla." *American Journal of Semitic Languages and Literatures* 17 (1901): 65–95.

———. "The Acts of Paul and Thecla." *The Biblical World* 17 (1901): 185–190.

Gorce, Denys, ed. and trans. *Vie de Sainte Mélanie*. SC 90. Paris: Éditions du Cerf, 1962.

Graef, Hilda. *Mary: A History of Doctrine and Devotion*. Westminster, Md.: Christian Classics, 1985.

Green, D. H. *Women Readers in the Middle Ages*. Cambridge: Cambridge University Press, 2007.

Greg, W. R. "False Morality of Lady Novelists." *National Review* [London] 8 (1859): 144–167.

Gronewald, M. "Einige Fackelmann-Papyri." ZPE 28 (1978): 271–277.

Hägg, Thomas. *The Novel in Antiquity*. Berkeley: University of California Press, 1983.

Haines-Eitzen, Kim. "The Apocryphal Acts of the Apostles on Papyrus: Revisiting the Question of Readership and Audience." In *New Testament Manuscripts: Their Texts and Their World*, edited by Thomas J. Kraus and Tobias Nicklas, 293–304. Leiden, the Netherlands: E. J. Brill, 2006.

———. "Engendering Palimpsests: Reading the Textual Tradition of the Acts of Paul and Thecla." In *The Early Christian Book*, edited by William E. Klingshirn and Linda Safran, 177–193. Washington, D.C.: The Catholic University of America Press, 2007.

———. *Guardians of Letters: Literacy, Power, and the Transmitters of Early Christian Literature*. New York: Oxford University Press, 2000.

———. "Textual Communities in Late Antique Christianity." In *A Companion to Late Antiquity*, edited by Philip Rousseau, 246–257. Chichester, UK: Wiley-Blackwell, 2009.

Harpham, Geoffrey Galt. *The Ascetic Imperative in Culture and Criticism*. Chicago: University of Chicago Press, 1987.

Harris, J. Rendel. "Mary or Elisabeth." *Expository Times* 41 (1929/1930): 266–267; 42 (1930/1931): 188–190.

———. "New Points of View in Textual Criticism." *The Expositor* 8 (1914): 316–334.

———. *Side-Lights on New Testament Research.* London: Kingsgate Press, 1908.

Harris, William. *Ancient Literacy.* Cambridge, Mass.: Harvard University Press, 1989.

Harvey, Susan Ashbrook. "Women in Early Byzantine Hagiography: Reversing the Story." In *That Gentle Strength: Historical Perspectives on Women in Christianity,* edited by Lynda L. Coon, Katherine J. Haldane, and Elisabeth W. Sommer, 36–59. Richmond: University Press of Virginia, 1990.

Haskins, Susan. *Mary Magdalen: Myth and Metaphor.* New York: Riverhead Books, 1995.

Hayne, Léonie. "Thecla and the Church Fathers." *VC* 48 (1994): 209–218.

Heine, Ronald E., trans. *Gregory of Nyssa's Treatise on the Inscriptions of the Psalms.* Oxford: Oxford University Press, 1995.

———. *The Montanist Oracles and Testimonia.* Macon, Ga.: Mercer University Press, 1989.

Hemelrijk, Emily A. *Matrona Docta: Educated Women in the Roman Élite from Cornelia to Julia Domna.* London: Routledge, 1999.

Hennecke, Edgar, Wilhelm Schneemelcher, and R. McL. Wilson, eds., *New Testament Apocrypha.* 2 vols. Cambridge: James Clark and Co., 1992.; Louisville, Ky.: Westminster, 1992.

Hilberg, Isidorus, ed. *Sancti Eusebii Hieronymi Epistulae.* CSEL 54–56. 3 vols. Vienna, Austria: Verlag der Österreichischen Akademie der Wissenschaften, 1996.

Holmes, Michael W., ed. *The Apostolic Fathers.* 3rd ed. Grand Rapids, Mich.: Baker Academic, 2007.

Holzhey, Karl. *Die Thekla-Akten: Ihre Verbreitung und Beurteilung in der Kirche.* Munich: J. J. Lentner'schen Buchhandlung, 1905.

Hovhanessian, Vahan. *Third Corinthians: Reclaiming Paul for Christian Orthodoxy.* New York: Peter Lang, 2000.

Hulbert-Powell, C. L. *John James Wettstein, 1693–1754.* London: SPCK Publishing, 1938.

Humphrey, J. H., ed. *Literacy in the Roman World.* Journal of Roman Archaeology Supplementary Series 3. Ann Arbor, Mich.: Journal of Roman Archaeology, 1991.

Hunt, E. D. "The Date of *Itinerarium Egeriae.*" *Studia Patristica* 38 (2001): 401–416.

Hunter, David G. *Marriage, Celibacy, and Heresy in Ancient Christianity: The Jovinianist Controversy*. Oxford: Oxford University Press, 2007.

Huskinson, Janet. "Women and Learning: Gender and Identity in Scenes of Intellectual Life on Late Roman Sarcophagi." In *Constructing Identities in Late Antiquity*, edited by Richard Miles, 190–213. London: Routledge, 1999.

Ilan, Tal. *Mine and Yours Are Hers: Retrieving Women's History from Rabbinic Literature*. Leiden, the Netherlands: Brill, 1997.

Jensen, Anne. *Frauen im frühen Christentum*. Bern, Switzerland: Peter Lang, 2002.

Jensen, Robin Margaret. *Understanding Early Christian Art*. London: Routledge, 2000.

Johnson, Scott Fitzgerald. "Late Antique Narrative Fiction: Apocryphal Acta and the Greek Novel in the Fifth-Century *Life and Miracles of Thekla*." In *Greek Literature in Late Antiquity: Dynamism, Didacticism, Classicism*, edited by Scott Fitzgerald Johnson, 189–207. Aldershot, U.K.: Ashgate, 2006.

———. *The Life and Miracles of Thekla: A Literary Study*. Washington, D.C.: Center for Hellenic Studies, 2006.

Joshel, Sandra R. *Work, Identity, and Legal Status at Rome: A Study of the Occupational Inscriptions*. Norman: University of Oklahoma Press, 1992.

Judge, E. A. "The Magical Use of Scripture in the Papyri." In *Perspectives on Language and Text: Essays and Poems in Honor of Francis I. Andersen's Sixtieth Birthday, July 28, 1985*, edited by Edgar W. Conrad and Edward G. Newing, 339–350. Winona Lake, Ind.: Eisenbrauns, 1987.

Junod, Eric, and Jean-Daniel Kaestli. *Acta Iohannis*. CCSA 1 and 2. Turnhout, Belgium: Brepols, 1983.

Kampen, Natalie. *Image and Status: Roman Working Women in Ostia*. Berlin: Mann, 1981.

Kelhoffer, James A. *Miracle and Mission: The Authentication of Missionaries and Their Message in the Longer Ending of Mark*. Tübingen, Germany: Mohr Siebeck, 2000.

Kelly, J. N. D. *Jerome: His Life, Writings, and Controversies*. London: Duckworth, 1975.

Kenyon, Frederic G. *The Codex Alexandrinus in Reduced Photographic Facsimile: New Testament and Clementine Epistles*. London: British Museum, 1909.

King, Karen L. *The Gospel of Mary of Magdala: Jesus and the First Woman Apostle*. Santa Rosa, Calif.: Polebridge Press, 2003.

Klijn, A. F. J. *The Acts of Thomas: Introduction, Text and Commentary.* 2nd rev. ed. Leiden, the Netherlands: Brill, 2003.

———. "The Acts of Thomas Revisited." In *The Apocryphal Acts of Thomas,* edited by Jan N. Bremmer, 1–10. Leuven, Belgium: Peeters, 2001.

———. "The Apocryphal Correspondence between Paul and the Corinthians." *VC* 17 (1963): 2–23.

Knox, Bernard M. W. "Silent Reading in Antiquity." *GRBS* 9 (1968): 421–435.

Knust, Jennifer. "Early Christian Re-Writing and the History of the *Pericope Adulterae.*" *JECS* 14 (2006): 485–536.

———. "Jesus, an Adulteress, and the Development of a Christian Scripture." In *A Tall Order: Writing the Social History of the Ancient World. Essays in Honor of William V. Harris,* edited by Jean-Jacques Aubert and Zsuzsanna Várhelyi, 59–84. Munich: K. G. Saur, 2005.

Kraemer, Ross S. *Unreliable Witnesses: Religion, Gender, and History in the Greco-Roman Mediterranean.* New York: Oxford University Press, 2011.

———. *When Aseneth Met Joseph: A Late Antique Tale of the Biblical Patriarch and His Egyptian Wife, Reconsidered.* New York: Oxford University Press, 1998.

———. "Women's Authorship of Jewish and Christian Literature in the Greco-Roman Period." In Levine, *"Women Like This,"* 221–242.

———, ed. *Women's Religions in the Greco-Roman World: A Sourcebook.* Oxford: Oxford University Press, 2004.

Kraemer, Ross S., and Shira Lander. "Perpetua and Felicitas." In Philip F. Esler, ed., *The Early Christian World,* vol. 2, 1048–1068. London: Routledge, 2000.

Kraus, Thomas J. "Bücherleihe im 4. Jh. n. Chr. P.Oxy LXIII 4365—ein Brief auf Papyrus und die gegensetige Leihe von apokryph gewordener Literatur." *Biblos* 50 (2001): 285–296. Now translated as "The Lending of Books in the Fourth Century C.E., *P.Oxy.* LXIII 4365—A Letter on Papyrus and the Reciprocal Lending of Literature Having Become Apocryphal." In *Ad Fontes: Original Manuscripts and Their Significance for Studying Early Christianity—Selected Essays,* edited by Thomas J. Kraus, 185–206. Leiden, the Netherlands: Brill, 2007.

Kraus, Thomas J., and Tobias Nicklas, eds. *New Testament Manuscripts: Their Texts and Their World.* Leiden, the Netherlands: Brill, 2006.

Kreitzer, Larry J., and Deborah W. Rooke, eds. *Ciphers in the Sand: Interpretations of the Woman Taken in Adultery (John 7.53–8.11).* Sheffield, U.K.: Sheffield Academic Press, 2000.

Krueger, Derek. "Between Monks: Tales of Monastic Companionship in Early Byzantium." *Journal of the History of Sexuality* 20 (2011): 28–61.

———. "Hagiography as an Ascetic Practice in the Early Christian East." *Journal of Religion* 79 (1999): 216–232.

———. *Writing and Holiness: The Practice of Authorship in the Early Christian East.* Philadelphia: University of Pennsylvania Press, 2004.

———. "Writing as Devotion: Hagiographical Composition and the Cult of the Saints in Theodoret of Cyrrhus and Cyril of Scythopolis." *Church History* 66 (1997): 707–719.

Kuefler, Mathew. *The Manly Eunuch: Masculinity, Gender Ambiguity, and Christian Ideology in Late Antiquity.* Chicago: Chicago University Press, 2001.

Kuhn, Annette. *The Power of the Image: Essays on Representation and Sexuality.* London: Routledge, 1985.

Laurentin, R. "Traces d'allusions Etymologiques en Luc 1–2." *Biblica* 38 (1957): 1–23.

Lefkowitz, Mary R. "Did Ancient Women Write Novels?" In Levine, *"Women Like This,"* 199–219.

Lefkowitz, Mary R., and Maureen B. Fant. *Women's Life in Greece and Rome.* Baltimore, Md.: Johns Hopkins University Press, 1992.

Levine, Amy-Jill, ed. *"Women Like This": New Perspectives on Jewish Women in the Greco-Roman World.* Atlanta: Scholars Press, 1991.

Levinskaya, Irina. *The Book of Acts in its Diaspora Setting.* Grand Rapids, Mich.: Eerdmans, 1996.

Lewis, Agnes Smith. *In the Shadow of Sinai: A Story of Travel and Research from 1895 to 1897.* Cambridge: Macmillan and Bowes, 1898.

———. *The Old Syriac Gospels, or Evangelion da-Mepharreshe; Being the Text of the Sinai or Syro-Antiochian Palimpsest, Including the Latest Additions and Emendations, with the Variants of the Curetonian Text.* London: Williams and Norgate, 1910.

———. *Select Narratives of Holy Women from the Syro-Antiochene or Sinai Palimpsest as Written above the Old Syriac by John the Stylite of Beth-Mari Qanūn in AD 778.* London: C. J. Clay and Sons, 1900.

———. *Some Pages of the Four Gospels Re-transcribed from the Sinaitic Palimpsest with a Translation of the Full Text.* London: C. J. Clay, 1896.

Limberis, Vasiliki. *Divine Heiress: The Virgin Mary and the Creation of Christian Constantinople.* London: Routledge, 1994.

———. "Mary 1." In Meyers et al., *Women in Scripture*, 116–119.

Lindemann, Andreas. *Die Clemensbriefe.* Tübingen, Germany: Mohr-Siebeck, 1992.

Lipsett, B. Diane. *Desiring Conversion: Hermas, Thecla, Aseneth*. New York: Oxford University Press, 2011.

Lipsius, Richard A., Maximilian Bonnet, and Constantin von Tischendorf, eds. *Acta Apostolorum Apocrypha*. 2 vols. Leipzig, Germany: Hermann Mendelssohn, 1891–1903.

Lona, Horacio E. *Der erste Clemensbrief*. Göttingen, Germany: Vandenhoeck and Ruprecht, 1998.

Loyen, André, ed. and trans. *Sidoine Apolinaire, Poèmes et Lettres*. 3 vols. Paris: Budé, 1970.

MacDonald, Dennis R. *The Acts of Andrew and the Acts of Andrew and Matthias in the City of the Cannibals*. Atlanta: Scholars Press, 1990.

Madigan, Kevin, and Carolyn Osiek, eds. *Ordained Women in the Early Church: A Documentary History*. Baltimore, Md.: The Johns Hopkins University Press, 2005.

Maraval, Pierre. *Grégoire de Nysse Vie de Sainte Macrine*. SC 178. Paris: Éditions du Cerf, 1971.

Martimort, Aimé Georges. *Deaconesses: An Historical Study*. Translated by K. D. Whitehead. San Francisco: Ignatius Press, 1982.

McDonnell, Myles. "Writing, Copying, and Autograph Manuscripts in Ancient Rome." *CQ* 46 (1996): 469–491.

McDonough, Jacobus, and Paulus Alexander. *Gregorii Nysseni Opera 5*. Leiden, the Netherlands: Brill, 1962.

McKendrick, Scot. "The Codex Alexandrinus or the Dangers of Being a Named Manuscript." In *The Bible as Book: The Transmission of the Greek Text*, edited by Scot McKendrick and Orlaith A. O'Sullivan, 1–16 London: British Library, 2003.

McLaren, Margaret. *Feminism, Foucault, and Embodied Subjectivity*. Albany: State University of New York Press, 2002.

Metzger, Bruce M. *The Early Versions of the New Testament: Their Origin, Transmission and Limitations*. Oxford: Clarendon Press, 1977.

———. "Explicit References in the Works of Origen to Variant Readings in New Testament Manuscripts." In *Biblical and Patristic Studies in Memory of Robert Pierce Casey*, edited by J. Neville Birdsall and Robert W. Thomson, 78–95. Freiburg, Germany: Herder, 1963.

———. "St. Jerome's Explicit References to Variant Readings in Manuscripts of the New Testament." In *New Testament Studies: Philological, Versional, and Patristic*, edited by Bruce M. Metzger, 199–210. Leiden, the Netherlands: Brill, 1980.

————. *The Text of the New Testament: Its Transmission, Corruption, and Restoration.* 3rd ed. New York: Oxford University Press, 1992.

————. *A Textual Commentary on the Greek New Testament.* 2nd ed. London: United Bible Societies, 1995.

Metzger, Bruce M., and Bart D. Ehrman. *The Text of the New Testament: Its Transmission, Corruption, and Restoration.* 4th ed. New York: Oxford University Press, 2005.

Meyer, Robert T., trans. *Palladius: The Lausiac History.* New York: Paulist Press, 1964.

Meyers, Carol, Toni Craven, and Ross S. Kraemer, eds. *Women in Scripture: A Dictionary of Named and Unnamed Women in the Hebrew Bible, the Apocryphal/Deuterocanonical Books, and the New Testament.* Boston: Houghton Mifflin, 2000.

Miles, Margaret R. *Carnal Knowing: Female Nakedness and Religious Meaning in the Christian West.* Boston: Beacon, 1989.

Millard, Alan. *Reading and Writing in the Time of Jesus.* New York: New York University Press, 2000.

Miller, J. Hillis. "Narrative." In *Critical Terms for Literary Study*, 2nd ed., edited by Frank Lentricchia and Thomas McLaughlin, 66–79. Chicago: University of Chicago Press, 1995.

Miller, Patricia Cox. *The Corporeal Imagination: Signifying the Holy in Late Ancient Christianity.* Philadelphia: University of Pennsylvania Press, 2009.

————. "Is There a Harlot in This Text? Hagiography and the Grotesque." In *The Cultural Turn in Late Ancient Studies: Gender, Asceticism, and Historiography*, edited by Dale B. Martin and Patricia Cox Miller, 87–102. Durham, N.C.: Duke University Press, 2005.

————. *The Poetry of Thought in Late Antiquity: Essays in Imagination and Religion.* Aldershot, England: Ashgate, 2001.

Milne, H. J. M., and T. C. Skeat. *The Codex Sinaiticus and the Codex Alexandrinus.* 2nd ed. London: British Museum, 1955.

Mitchell, W. J. T. *Iconology: Image, Text, Ideology.* Chicago: University of Chicago Press, 1986.

————. *What Do Pictures Want? The Lives and Loves of Images.* Chicago: University of Chicago Press, 2005.

Moi, Toril. *Sexual/Textual Politics: Feminist Literary Theory.* London: Routledge, 1985.

Morales, Helen. *Vision and Narrative in Achilles Tatius' Leucippe and Clitophon.* Cambridge: Cambridge University Press, 2004.

Musurillo, Herbert, trans. *The Acts of the Christian Martyrs.* Oxford: Clarendon Press, 1972.

———, trans. *Méthode d'Olympe Le Banquet*. SC 95. Paris: Éditions du Cerf, 1963.

———, trans. *The Symposium, a Treatise on Chastity*. ACW 27. Westminster, Md.: Newman Press, 1958.

Natanson, Joseph. *Early Christian Ivories*. London: Alec Tiranti Ltd., 1953.

Nauerth, Claudia, and Rüdiger Warns. *Thekla: Ihre Bilder in der früchristlichen Kunst*. Wiesbaden, Germany: Otto Harrassowitz, 1981.

Nauta, Ruurd R. *Poetry for Patrons: Literary Communication in the Age of Domitian*. Leiden, the Netherlands: Brill, 2002.

Nedungatt, George, and Michael Featherstone, eds. *The Council in Trullo Revisited*. Rome: Pontifico Istituto Orientale, 1995.

Nicklas, Tobias and Tommy Wasserman. "Theologische Linien im *Codex Bodmer Miscellani?*" In *New Testament Manuscripts: Their Texts and Their World*, edited by Thomas J. Kraus and Tobias Nicklas, 161–188. Leiden, the Netherlands: Brill, 2006.

Norman, A. F. "The Book Trade in Fourth-Century Antioch." *Journal of Hellenic Studies* 80 (1960): 122–126.

Nussbaum, Martha C., and Juha Sihvola, eds. *The Sleep of Reason: Erotic Experience and Sexual Ethics in Ancient Greece and Rome*. Chicago: University of Chicago Press, 2002.

O'Donnell, James J. *Avatars of the Word: From Papyrus to Cyberspace*. Cambridge, Mass.: Harvard University Press, 1998.

Parker, D. C. *An Introduction to the New Testament Manuscripts and Their Texts*. Cambridge: Cambridge University Press, 2008.

———. *The Living Text of the Gospels*. Cambridge: Cambridge University Press, 1997.

Patlagean, Evelyne. "L'histoire de la femme déguisée en moine et l'évolution de la sainteté féminine à Byzance." *Studi Medievali* 3, no. 17 (1976): 597–623.

Payne, Philip B. "Fuldensis, Sigla for Variants in Vaticanus, and 1 Cor. 14.34–5." *NTS* 41 (1995): 240–262.

———. "Ms. 88 as Evidence for a Text without 1 Cor. 14.34-5." *NTS* 44 (1998): 152–158.

———. "The Text-Critical Function of the Umlauts in Vaticanus, with Special Attention to 1 Corinthians 14.34–35: A Response to J. Edward Miller." *JSNT* 27 (2004): 105–112.

Peltomaa, Leena Mari. *The Image of the Virgin Mary in the Akathistos Hymn*. Leiden, the Netherlands: Brill, 2001.

Penn, Michael Philip. *Kissing Christians: Ritual and Community in the Late Ancient Church*. Philadelphia: University of Pennsylvania Press, 2005.

Petzer, Jacobus Hendrik. "Reconsidering the Silent Women of Corinth: A Note on 1 Corinthians 14:34–35." *Theologia Evangelica* 26 (1993): 132–138.

Pick, Bernhard. *The Apocryphal Acts of Paul, Peter, John, Andrew and Thomas.* Chicago: Open Court Publishing, 1909.

Pollitt, Katha. *The Mind-Body Problem: Poems.* New York: Random House, 2009.

Pomeroy, Sarah B. "*Technikai kai Mousikai:* The Education of Women in the Fourth Century and in the Hellenistic Period." *American Journal of Ancient History* 2 (1977): 51–68.

Price, A. Whigham. *The Ladies of Castlebrae: A Story of Nineteenth-Century Travel and Research.* Gloucester, U.K.: Alan Sutton, 1985.

Price, R. M., trans. *Cyril of Scythopolis: The Lives of the Monks of Palestine.* Kalamazoo, Mich.: Cistercian, 1991.

Prieur, Jean-Marc. *Actes de l'apôtre André.* Turnhout, Belgium: Brepols, 1995.

Radway, Janice. *Reading the Romance: Women, Patriarchy, and Popular Literature.* Chapel Hill: University of North Carolina Press, 1984.

Rapp, Claudia. "Christians and Their Manuscripts in the Greek East in the Fourth Century." In *Scritture, libri e testi nelle aree provinciali di Bisanzio. Atti del seminario di Erice (18–25 settembre 1988),* edited by Guglielmo Cavallo, Giuseppe de Gregorio, and Marilena Maniaci, 127–148. Spoleto: Centro Italiano di Studi sull'Alto Medioevo, 1991.

———. "Figures of Female Sanctity: Byzantine Edifying Manuscripts and Their Audience." *Dumbarton Oaks Papers* 50 (1996): 313–343.

———. "Storytelling as Spiritual Communication in Early Greek Hagiography: The Use of Diegesis." *JECS* 6 (1988): 431–448.

Reichmann, Felix. "The Book Trade at the Time of the Roman Empire." *Library Quarterly* 8 (1938): 40–76.

Reimer, Ivoni Richter. *Women in the Acts of the Apostles: A Feminist Liberation Perspective.* Minneapolis: Fortress Press, 1995.

Reynolds, L. D., and N. G. Wilson. *Scribes and Scholars: A Guide to the Transmission of Greek and Latin Literature.* 2nd ed. Oxford: Clarendon Press, 1974.

Rich, Adrienne. *On Lies, Secrets, and Silence: Selected Prose 1966–1978.* New York: Norton, 1979.

Riley, Denise. *"Am I That Name?" Feminism and the Category of "Women" in History.* Minneapolis: University of Minnesota, 1988.

Roberts, Colin H., ed. *The Antinoopolis Papyri.* 3 vols. London: Egypt Exploration Society, 1950–1967.

———. *Manuscript, Society and Belief in Early Christian Egypt*. London: Oxford University Press, 1979.

Roberts, David. *Egypt and Nubia*. 3 vols. London: Moon, 1846–1849.

Robinson, J. A *The Passion of S. Perpetua*. Texts and Studies Vols. 1 and 2. Cambridge: Cambridge University Press, 1891.

Robinson, James M., ed. *The Nag Hammadi Library*. San Francisco: HarperSanFrancisco, 1990.

Robinson, James M. *The Pachomian Monastic Library at the Chester Beatty Library and the Bibliothèque Bodmer*. Institute for Antiquity and Christianity Occasional Papers 19. Claremont, Calif.: Institute for Antiquity and Christianity, 1990.

Roe, Thomas. *The Negotiations of Sir Thomas Roe, in his Embassy to Ottoman Porte, from the Year 1621–1628 inclusive*. London: Samual Richardson, 1740.

Rordorf, Willy. "Hérésie et Orthodoxie selon la Correspondance apocryphe entre les Corinthiens et l'Apôtre Paul." *Cahiers de la Revue de Théologie et de Philosophie* 17 (1993): 21–63.

Rosen, Tova. *Unveiling Eve: Reading Gender in Medieval Hebrew Literature*. Philadelphia: University of Pennsylvania Press, 2003.

Rousseau, Philip. "'Learned Women' and the Development of a Christian Culture in Late Antiquity." *Symbolae Osloenses* 70 (1995): 116–147.

Rousselle, Aline. "Images as Education in the Roman Empire (Second-Third Centuries AD)." In *Education in Greek and Roman Antiquity*, edited by Yun Lee Too, 373–403. Leiden, the Netherlands: Brill, 2001.

———. *Porneia: On Desire and the Body in Antiquity*. Translated by Felicia Pheasant. Oxford: Blackwell, 1988.

Rowlandson, Jane. "Gender and Cultural Identity in Roman Egypt." In *Women's Influence on Classical Civilization*, edited by Fiona McHardy and Eireann Marshall, 151–166. London: Routlege, 2004.

———, ed. *Women and Society in Greek and Roman Egypt*. Cambridge: Cambridge University Press, 1998.

Sanders, Henry A. *The New Testament Manuscripts in the Freer Collection. Part I. The Washington Manuscript of the Four Gospels*. New York: Macmillan Company, 1918.

Saxer, Victor. *Le Culte de Marie Madeleine en Occident des origenes à la fin du moyen âge*. Paris: Librarie Clavreueil, 1959.

Schaberg, Jane. "How Mary Magdalene Became a Whore." *Bible Review* 8 (1992): 30–37, 51–52.

———. *The Resurrection of Mary Magdalene: Legends, Apocrypha, and the Christian Testament*. New York: Continuum, 2002.

Schenkl, C., ed. *Poetae Christiani Minores*. CSEL 16. Vienna: Tempsky, 1888.

Schmidt, Carl. *Acta Pauli: Aus der Heidelberger Koptischedn Papyrushandschrift nr. 1*. Hildesheim, Germany: Georg Olms Verlagsbuchhandlung, 1965.

Schneemelcher, Wilhelm, ed. *New Testament Apocrypha: Revised Edition of the Collection Initiated by Edgar Hennecke*. English translation edited by R. McL. Wilson. 2 vols. Cambridge: James Clarke and Co. and Westminster/John Knox Press, 1992.

Schulenburg, Jane Tibbetts. *Forgetful of Their Sex: Female Sanctity and Society ca. 500–1100*. Chicago: University of Chicago Press, 1998.

Scott, Joan W. "The Evidence of Experience." *Critical Inquiry* 17 (1991): 773–797.

———. "Fantasy Echo: History and the Construction of Identity." *Critical Inquiry* 27 (2001): 284–304.

———. "Gender: A Useful Category of Historical Analysis." *American Historical Review* 91 (1986): 1053–1075.

Shanzer, Danuta R. "The Anonymous *Carmen contra paganos* and the Date and Identity of the Centonist Proba." *Revue des Études Augustiniennes* 32 (1986): 232–248.

———. "The Date and Identity of the Centonist Proba." *Recherches Augustiniennes* 27 (1994): 75–96.

Shaw, Teresa M. *The Burden of the Flesh: Fasting and Sexuality in Early Christianity*. Minneapolis: Fortress Press, 1998.

Shoemaker, Stephen J. *Ancient Traditions of the Virgin Mary's Dormition and Assumption*. Oxford Early Christian Studies. New York: Oxford University Press, 2002.

———. "A Case of Mistaken Identity? Naming the Gnostic Mary." In *Which Mary? The Marys of Early Christian Tradition*, edited by F. Stanley Jones, 5–30. SBL Symposium Series 19. Atlanta: Society of Biblical Literature, 2002.

———. "Jesus' Gnostic Mom: Mary of Nazareth and the 'Gnostic Mary' Traditions." In Good, *Mariam, the Magdalen, and the Mother*, 153–182.

———. "Rethinking the 'Gnostic Mary': Mary of Nazareth and Mary of Magdala in Early Christian Tradition." *JECS* 9 (2001): 555–595.

Silvas, Anna M. *Macrina the Younger, Philosopher of God*. Turnhout, Belgium: Brepols, 2008.

Sivan, Hagith. "Who Was Egeria? Piety and Pilgrimage in the Age of Gratian." *HTR* 81 (1988): 59–72.

Smith, Lesley, and Jane H. M. Taylor. *Women and the Book: Assessing the Visual Evidence*. Toronto: University of Toronto; London: British Library, 1997.

Snyder, Jane McIntosh. *The Woman and the Lyre: Women Writers in Classical Greece and Rome*. Carbondale: Southern Illinois University Press, 1989.

Soskice, Janet. *Sisters of Sinai: How Two Lady Adventurers Found the Hidden Gospels*. London: Chatto and Windus, 2009.

Späth, Thomas, and Beate Wagner-Hasel, eds. *Frauenwelten in der Antike: Geschlechterordnung und weibliche Lebenspraxis*. Stuttgart, Germany: J. B. Metzler, 2000.

Spitzer, Leo. "The Epic Style of the Pilgrim Aetheria." *Comparative Literature* 1 (1949): 225–258.

Stählin, Otto, and Ludwig Früchtel, eds. *Clemens Alexandrinus*. 2 vols. Berlin: Akademie Verlag, 1960.

Stallybrass, Peter, and Allon White. *The Politics and Poetics of Transgression*. Ithaca, N.Y.: Cornell University Press, 1986.

Starr, Raymond J. "The Circulation of Literary Texts in the Roman World." *CQ* 37 (1987): 213–223.

Stephens, Susan A. "Who Read Ancient Novels?" In *The Search for the Ancient Novel*, edited by James Tatum, 405–418. Baltimore, Md.: Johns Hopkins University Press, 1994.

Stephens, Susan A., and John J. Winkler, eds. *Ancient Greek Novels: The Fragments: Introduction, Text, Translation, and Commentary*. Princeton, N.J.: Princeton University Press, 1995.

Stevenson, Jane. *Women Latin Poets: Language, Gender, and Authority, from Antiquity to the Eighteenth Century*. Oxford: Oxford University Press, 2005.

Stock, Brian. *Augustine the Reader: Meditation, Self-Knowledge, and the Ethics of Interpretation*. Cambridge, Mass.: Harvard University Press, 1996.

———. *Listening for the Text: On the Uses of the Past*. Baltimore, Md.: Johns Hopkins University Press, 1990.

Talbot, Mary-Alice., ed. *Holy Women of Byzantium: Ten Saints' Lives in English Translation*. Washington, D.C.: Dumbarton Oaks, 1996.

Tatum, James, ed. *The Search for the Ancient Novel*. Baltimore, Md.: Johns Hopkins University Press, 1994.

Testuz, Michel. *Papyrus Bodmer VII–IX*. Cologny-Genève, Switzerland: Bibliothèque Bodmer, 1959.

———. *Papyrus Bodmer X–XII*. Cologny-Genève, Switzerland: Bibliothèque Bodmer, 1959.

Thomas, Christine M. *The Acts of Peter, Gospel Literature, and the Ancient Novel.* Oxford: Oxford University Press, 2003.

Thomas, Rosalind. *Literacy and Orality in Ancient Greece.* Cambridge: Cambridge University Press, 1992.

Thompson, Edward Maunde, ed. *Facsimile of the Codex Alexandrinus.* 4 vols. London: Trustees of the British Museum, 1879–1883.

Thorley, John. "Junia, a Woman Apostle." *NovT* 38 (1996): 18–29.

Tischendorf, Constantinus. *Acta Apostolorum Apocrypha.* Leipzig, Germany: Avenarius et Mendelssohn, 1851.

Tilley, Maureen A. *The Bible in Christian North Africa: the Donatist World.* Minneapolis: Fortress Press, 1997.

Tuck, Anthony. "Stories at the Loom: Patterned Textiles and the Recitation of Myth in Euripides." *Arethusa* 42 (2009): 151–159.

Tuckett, Christopher. *The Gospel of Mary.* Oxford: Oxford University Press, 2007.

Turner, Eric. *Greek Manuscripts of the Ancient World.* Princeton, N.J.: Princeton University Press, 1971.

———. *Greek Papyri: An Introduction.* Oxford: Clarendon Press, 1968.

———. "Scribes and Scholars of Oxyrhynchus." *MPER* 5 (1955): 141–149.

———. *Typology of the Early Codex.* Philadelphia: University of Pennsylvania Press, 1977.

Vassilaki, Maria. *Mother of God: Representation of the Virgin in Byzantine Art.* Athens: Benaki Museum, 2000.

van Beek, C. *Passio Sanctarum Perpetuae et Felicitatis, latine et graece.* Bonn, Germany: Dekker, 1938.

van Bremen, Riet. *The Limits of Participation: Women and Civic Life in the Greek East in the Hellenistic and Roman Periods.* Amsterdam: J. C. Gieben, 1996.

von Gebhardt, Oscar. *Passio S. Theclae virginis: die lateinischen Übersetzungen der Acta Pauli et Theclae nebst Fragmenten, Auszügen und Beilagen.* Leipzig, Germany: J. C. Hinrichs, 1902.

Wagner, Richard. *My Life.* Authorized translation from the German. 1939; repr., New York: Dodd, Mean & Co., 1911.

Walker, Alice. *In Search of Our Mothers' Gardens: Womanist Prose.* San Diego: Harcourt Brace, 1983.

Ward, Benedicta. *The Desert Fathers: Sayings of the Early Christian Monks.* London: Penguin Books, 2003.

———. *Harlots of the Desert: A Study of Repentance in Early Monastic Sources.* Kalamazoo, Mich.: Cistercian Publications, 1987.

———. *The Sayings of the Desert Fathers: The Alphabetical Collection.* Kalamazoo, Mich.: Cistercian Publications, 1975.

Wasserman, Tommy. *The Epistle of Jude: Its Text and Transmission.* Stockholm: Almqvist and Wiksell International, 2006.

———."Papyrus 72 and the *Bodmer Miscellaneous Codex.*" *NTS* 51 (2005): 137–154.

Watson, Janet, ed. *Speaking Volumes: Orality and Literacy in the Greek and Roman World.* Leiden, the Netherlands: Brill, 2001.

Wegner, Judith Romney. *Chattel or Person? The Status of Women in the Mishnah.* New York: Oxford University Press, 1988.

Weitzmann, Kurt. *Age of Spirituality: Late Antique and Early Christian Art, Third to Seventh Century.* New York: Metropolitan Museum, 1979.

Wettstein, J. J. *Prolegomena ad Novi Testamenti.* Amsterdam: R. and J. Wetstenios and G. Smith, 1730.

White, H. G. Evelyn. *The Monasteries of the Wadi 'N Natrun.* New York: Metropolitan Museum of Art, 1926.

White, Robert J., trans. *The Interpretation of Dreams (Oneirocritica) by Artemidorus.* Park Ridge, N.J.: Noyes Press, 1975.

Wicker, Kathleen O'Brien. *Porphyry the Philosopher to Marcella.* Atlanta: Scholars Press, 1987.

Wilfong, Terry G. *Women of Jeme: Lives in a Coptic Town in Late Antique Egypt.* Ann Arbor: University of Michigan Press, 2002.

Wilkinson, C. K. "Early Christian Paintings in the Oasis of Khargeh." *The Metropolitan Museum of Art Bulletin* 23 (1928): 29–36.

Wilkinson, John. *Egeria's Travels to the Holy Land: Newly Translated with Supporting Documents and Notes.* Rev. ed. Jerusalem: Ariel Publishing House, 1981.

Wimsatt, Jr., W. K., and M. C. Beardsley. "The Intentional Fallacy." *The Sewanee Review* 54 (1946): 468–488.

Winlock, H. E., W. E. Crum, and H. G. Evelyn White. *The Monastery of Epiphanius at Thebes.* 2 vols. New York: Metropolitan Museum of Art, 1926.

Wire, Antoinette Clark. *The Corinthian Women Prophets: A Reconstruction through Paul's Rhetoric.* Minneapolis: Fortress Press, 1990.

Witherington, Ben. "The Anti-Feminist Tendencies of the 'Western' Text in Acts." *JBL* 103 (1984): 82–84.

Wollstonecraft, Mary. *A Vindication of the Rights of Woman,* edited by Deidre Shauna Lynch. New York: W. W. Norton, 2009.

Woolf, Virginia. *A Room of One's Own.* New York: Harcourt Brace Jovanovich, Inc., 1929.

Wright, F. A. *Select Letters of St. Jerome.* London: W. Heinemann Ltd., 1933.

Wright, William. *Apocryphal Acts of the Apostles*, I/II. Hildesheim, Germany: Georg Olms, 1990; repr. Piscataway, N.J.: Gorgias Press, 2005.

———. *Catalogue of the Syriac Manuscripts in the British Museum Acquired since the Year 1838*. 3 vols. London: Trustees of the British Museum, 1870–1872.

Youtie, Herbert C. "Agrammatos: An Aspect of Greek Society in Egypt." In *Scriptiunculae* II, 611–627. Amsterdam: Adolf M. Hakkert, 1973.

———. "Because They Do Not Know Letters." *ZPE* 19 (1975): 101–108.

———. "ΥΠΟΓΡΑΦΕΥΣ: The Social Impact of Illiteracy in Graeco-Roman Egypt." *ZPE* 17 (1975): 201–221.

Zelzer, Klaus. *Die Alten Lateinischen Thomasakten*. Berlin: Akademie Verlag, 1977.

Zetzel, James E. G. *Latin Textual Criticism in Antiquity*. New York: Arno Press, 1981.

Zorzi, M. Benedetta. "The Use of the Terms ἀγνεία, παρθενία, σωφροσύνη, and ἐγκράτεια in the *Symposium* of Methodius of Olympus." *VC* 63 (2009): 138–168.

Citation Index

General Index